Politics and
Policy in
Australia

Politics and Policy in Australia

Geoffrey Hawker,
R. F. I. Smith, and
Patrick Weller

University of
Queensland Press

©University of Queensland Press, St. Lucia, Queensland, 1979

Typeset by Press Etching Pty. Ltd., Brisbane
Printed and bound by Silex Enterprise & Co. Hong Kong

Distributed in the United Kingdom, Europe, the Middle East, Africa,
and the Caribbean by Prentice-Hall International, International Book
Distributors Ltd., 66 Wood Lane End, Hemel Hempstead, Herts.,
England.

National Library of Australia
Cataloguing-in-Publication data

Hawker, Geoffrey Nelson, 1941.
    Politics and policy in Australia.

    Index.
    Bibliography.
    ISBN 0 7022 1306 3
    ISBN 0 7022 1307 1 Paperback

    1. Australia — Politics and government. I. Smith, Robert Frederick
    Ingram, 1941-, joint author. II. Weller, Patrick Moray, 1941-, joint
    author. III. Title.

320.9'94

The best lack all conviction, and the worst are full of passionate intensity.

Yeats, The Second Coming

... whoever has many to please or to govern, must use the ministry of many agents, some of whom will be wicked, and some ignorant; by some he will be misled, and by others betrayed. If he gratifies one he will offend another: those that are not favoured will think themselves injured; and, since favours can be conferred but upon few, the greater number will be always discontented.

Samuel Johnson, Rasselas

Contents

Acknowledgments

This book was substantially written while the authors were research fellows in the Department of Political Science, Research School of Social Sciences, Australian National University, between 1974 and 1977.

We were fortunate in the timing of our research. The advent of the Whitlam government in 1972 led to increased interest in the machinery and processes of Australian government and to more access to outsiders than had previously existed. The Royal Commission on Australian Government Administration, appointed in June 1974, provided us with valuable experience. Hawker was director of research for the commission, while Smith and Weller acted as consultants.

These opportunities affected the direction and style of our research. We hope that they have given our analysis a freshness and authenticity that would otherwise have been difficult to achieve. But the approach has also led to problems of citation. Wherever possible we have given detailed references, but where this would identify sources and breach confidences we have preferred to present some material unreferenced rather than leave it out.

This book has been a cooperative effort, and it would be impossible to distinguish the authorship of much of it. However, chapters 7 and 8 are primarily the work of Hawker, chapter 6 of Smith, and chapters 5 and 9 of Weller.

Our thanks are widespread, not least to those public servants, politicians, and other practitioners who provided us with insights about their work. David Butler, Peter Self, and Bernard Schaffer all helped us at various stages. For comments on earlier drafts we are grateful to Robert Parker, J. R. Mallory, John Ballard, and David Adams. Gillian O'Loghlin, Gillian Evans, and Liz Cham helped to find much of the information. Kath Bourke, Mary Pearson, Celia Westwood, Margrit Sedlacek, and Karen Votto typed numerous drafts.

Two people deserve particular thanks. Jane North edited the manuscript, compiled the bibliography and shamed the authors into finishing it. Peter Loveday acted throughout as colleague, critic, editor, and friend. Above all, he had the uncanny ability to know when we needed advice, criticism—or a drink.

G. N. H.
R. F. I. S.
P. M. W.

May 1978

List of Abbreviations

ACER	Australian Council for Educational Research
ADAA	Australian Development Assistance Agency
ADP	Automatic Data Processing
AEC	Australian Education Council
ALP	Australian Labor Party
ANZUS	Australia, New Zealand, United States Treaty
APS	Australian Public Service
ASRRC	Australian State Regional Relations Committee
AUC	Australian Universities Commission
AWF	Australian Wheatgrowers' Federation
CCAE	Canberra College of Advanced Education
CCPSO	Council of Commonwealth Public Service Organizations
COE	Commonwealth Office of Education
CPD, H of R	*Commonwealth Parliamentary Debates,* House of Representatives
CPRS	Central Policy Review Staff (Britain)
CSD	Civil Service Department (Britain)
DLP	Democratic Labor Party
DURD	Department of Urban and Regional Development (now Environment, Housing and Community Development)
EEC	European Economic Community
ERC	Expenditure Review Committee
FAO	Foreign Affairs Officer
GPS	Great Public School
IAC	Industries Assistance Commission
IDC	Interdepartmental Committee
ISRD	Information and State Relations Division

LAA	Libraries Association of Australia
L-CP	Liberal-Country Party coalition
OECD	Organization for Economic Cooperation and Development
OPB	Overseas Property Bureau
PAR	Programme Analysis and Review (Britain)
PCO	Privy Council Office (Canada)
PCU	Policy Coordination Unit
PESC	Public Expenditure Survey Committee (Britain)
PJT	Prices Justification Tribunal
PMC	Department of the Prime Minister and Cabinet
PMO	Prime Minister's Office (Canada)
PPB	Planning Programme Budgeting
PRS	Priorities Review Staff
PSB	Public Service Board
RCAGA	Royal Commission on Australian Government Administration
REDS	Regional Employment Development Scheme Committee
RIPA	Royal Institute of Public Administration
RSL	Returned Services League
RSPacS	Research School of Pacific Studies
RSSS	Research School of Social Sciences
SANMA	Special Assistance to Non-Metropolitan Areas Committee
SEATO	South East Asia Treaty Organization
SMOS	Department of the Special Minister of State
SSLC	Secondary Schools Library Committee
UFG	United Farmers and Graziers
UFWA	United Farmers and Woolgrowers' Association
VFU	Victorian Farmers' Union

Introduction

Australia is a stable society. It has known no revolutions and few permanently unsettling discontents. Its polity has a mature and firmly established shape: the major parties were formed early and have maintained their shares of votes with great consistency; the machinery of government has undergone only gradual change; and even the issues of Australian politics have a long history for such a young country. The stability of Australian government dominates both the perceptions and expectations of those it engages. The same is true of the way policy is shaped; policy making in Australia is usually an incremental, piecemeal, and pragmatic activity. An expectation of stability is unsurprising, and it is a potent conditioner of the making of public policy. This is so even when expectations are disappointed, when stability begins to disappear and the unexpected starts to happen. We suggest in a moment that policy making in Australia may indeed be taking place within an increasingly unstable environment.

Stability does not imply an absence of political change. Fifty years ago, perhaps even thirty, it might have been sensible to begin the study of public policy in Australia with a study of the state governments. This is still needed, but an examination of policy making at the federal level now seems likely to generate more initial light. The formal and informal powers of the commonwealth government have grown immensely, especially since the Second World War, and national politics now dominates the federation. In 1906–7, for example, the six state governments spent more than six times as much as the commonwealth; seventy years later, they were dependent for most of their funds on federal beneficence.

Political change has been obvious. Barely a decade after the event, it is already clear that the retirement in 1966 of Sir Robert

Menzies, after sixteen years as prime minister, marked a watershed in Australian post-war politics. The stability of the Liberal–Country Party coalition government was rapidly eroded as a succession of Liberal prime ministers followed Menzies — Holt 1966 – 67, Gorton 1967 – 71, and McMahon 1971 – 72. The internecine feuds within the Liberal Party and between it and its coalition partner, the Country Party, helped the prospects of a Labor Party which had recovered from the split of 1955 and, under the leadership of Gough Whitlam, took office in 1972. The reforming intentions of the new government survived one general election in 1974 but came increasingly under threat from an ailing economy and internal dissension; and the government fell to the Senate and the governor-general in November 1975. The subsequent election returned a Liberal–Country Party government with a record majority, and now Australian politics is perhaps more uncertain and difficult to predict than ever before.

We have not tried to set any precise chronological limits upon our analysis, because explanation can demand reference to quite distant events. Many of the problems of the Whitlam Labor government of 1972 – 75, for example, can be usefully illuminated by reference to the experience of the Curtin and Chifley Labor governments. Our main concern, however, is with the last decade or so and especially with the 1970s, about which most information is available.

One change that has occurred is that many of the recognized "rules of the game" that help to direct political activity have been called into question. Many of the assumptions held over the last fifty years about the way the Constitution should be interpreted have been swept away. A government now requires a majority in both houses before it can be certain of a three-year term. If it lacks a majority in the Senate, its political horizons can never stretch further than six months ahead, or beyond the next occasion when the Senate must pass supply. Temporary unpopularity, a standard mid-term problem for most governments, can lead now to a summary ejection from office. Nor, at present, can the behaviour of any governor-general be forecast with certainty in time of crisis. The Liberal–Country Party opposition set a precedent by breaking what were thought to be established conventions. Now no one can be sure which convention might be broken next or by whom; political and constitutional uncertainty has never been so great.

The constitutional crisis has had social implications too. After 11

November 1975, the uproar from and alienation of some sections of the community was intense. The cynicism and opportunism of politics was plain. Gradually the waves of indignation have subsided, but it is still too early to see if that uproar was merely a temporary phenomenon or whether it has left more deep-seated wounds that have the potential to cause further divisions (Evans 1977).

Yet in a deeper sense nothing has changed. Australia remains what it has always been: a small, becoming medium-sized capitalist society with fortunate historical tenure and, perhaps, fortunate geographical location. The parties in Australia accept as they always have done the existence of a parliamentary system; the minor parties do not matter much. Australia is a comfortable middle-class Western democracy; it is governed by the elected representatives of the majority party. The power of the governing party is everything that legitimacy can make it within the constraints of the federal Constitution; government is limited by its capacity and by its ability to command popular support. The institutions of Australian society are free; the system is open; anyone can get into parliament and hope to help in changing the laws. These propositions are offered not as an elementary lesson in civics but because they summarize the perceptions that permeate the Australian polity and generate strong expectations of stability in the formulation, execution, and study of policy making. These rules of the game, this is simply to say, have barely changed and rarely been questioned. Australia is not fertile ground for proposals of major political or constitutional change, let alone any ideas of broader revolution (Aitkin 1977; Connell 1977).

All the same, public policy within that comfortable framework has become, over the last ten years or so, increasingly a matter of contention and doubt. Two points are involved. The first is simply that new issues and new leaders have been emerging for some time, new questions about policy are being asked, and the institutions of government are coming under new pressures. It is hard to stand close to contemporary events and not see in them many swirls and eddies which time will obliterate; but it is clear that many new and major questions of public policy have been raised in the past decade. The second point, however, is that these very developments have been regarded with unease by the policy participants themselves, who worry increasingly about the grasp upon policy that they and other actors have. In a very broad sense, the volatility of Australian political life over the last decade has simply reflected the uncertainties of Australia's place in the world. The relative tranquillity of the Menzies years, though easy to overestimate, rested on the foundation of reforms laid by Labor governments in the 1940s, on the post-war economic boom in the West, and on the protection of an isolated country by powerful allies. The time was right for conservatism, especially when the Australian conservative parties were able skilfully to exploit the internal divisions of the Labor Party which they portrayed as a radical and unsafe alternative. At the same time, Menzies both divided and then isolated his more strident right-wing supporters and governed with a coalition based on the satisfied centre.

The price exacted was high for the Australian polity, primarily because stability led to political and institutional rigidity and to a lowered capacity to respond to changed circumstances. The anxiety that greeted British withdrawal from east of Suez showed how deeply dependent materially and psychologically Australia was on its allies. More recently, the coincidence of international financial dislocation and the energy crisis in the early 1970s, together with the withdrawal of the United States from Vietnam, affected Australian assumptions profoundly. Australia is not, of course, in a peculiar position. Nations have events thrust upon them, and so do governments; even the attempt to maintain an existing state of affairs requires new thoughts and new activity. New individuals arise with more appealing solutions to old problems. Since Menzies, Australian government has not had the luxury of attempting to stand still.

This can best be illustrated by reference to the growing uncertainty in the management of the economy. In the 1960s unemployment and inflation were important, although less so than they were to become in the 1970s; disputes over the proper tools of economic management were few. On one or two occasions, as in 1961 when credit was cut, there was real debate; more often, disputes were part of the political rhetoric. The country was prosperous. But now the situation has changed. World-wide recession has led to both inflation and unemployment. Governments may be able to minimize or exacerbate their effects (although no one is certain how it is actually done), but they cannot remove them. Australia is part of the international economic system. It cannot isolate itself. As a result, the management of the economy has become the most crucial and intractable problem to face any government.

Changes to the institutions of government have also occurred. In part this is because the broad changes have led to a feeling of uncertainty. New institutional procedures and structures have been created to allow the government to puzzle (to use Heclo's term) over new problems (Heclo 1974), which too often appear insoluble. As a result, the question of how problems should be approached has, to an increasing degree, been intermingled with the debate about the content of policy itself. Changes to political and bureaucratic personnel, to party programmes, and to the machinery of central government are symptomatic of the new concern. It is not always at all clear that the changes mean anything, or at any rate that they have their intended outcomes. Rather there are a good many officials engaged in reforming the structures and procedures of policy making, and they often feel that they are acting in the dark. In recent years, institutional structures have changed rapidly. The changes have included the formation and dismantling of departments; the splitting of the Treasury and the burgeoning of the Department of the Prime Minister and Cabinet; the use of advisory commissions for a whole range of purposes; reviews of administrative discretions, of parliamentary machinery for administrative supervision, and of the public bureaucracy generally; the establishment of new units for policy planning and review; and the sharpening of questions about the effectiveness of governments in formulating and applying policy. An understanding of the basic stability of Australian politics and of the types and range of changes that are taking place within that framework is necessary to appreciate the context within which the policy processes work. These processes, and the changes that have occurred to them, are the subject of this book.

1

Public Policy and Policy Processes

Governments make policy — or least they like to think they do. That is what politics is meant to be about. Politicians get into positions of power in order to make decisions that convert policy into action. It sounds simple.

But it is not so straightforward. Power is not concentrated but dispersed unevenly within the institutions of government, and it is not easily applied in support of policies. The policies that politicians believe they will apply when they win office are soon fragmented or diverted and do not have their desired effects. Besides, people are often not sure which policy should be adopted and which results should be sought even though they agree that something should be done. Even if they agree on the ends to be attained they may well argue about the measures to be taken.

Given the simplicity of many conventional notions about government, it is to be expected that frustration, irritation, annoyance, anxiety, and other feelings of discontent will arise — and if suitably orchestrated may become politically effective — when the confusions and complexity of policy-making processes are daily brought home to the public. In the late twentieth century, partly because of both the growth of state welfare services and the general increase in the level of governmental activity and partly as a result of growing and intractable economic difficulties in advanced capitalist societies, dissatisfaction with the performance, flexibility, and responsiveness of government has increased, and large injections of money do not reduce it. For instance, in Australia massive funds are directed towards urban renewal — but how many people notice a difference? Education spending is trebled, and then doubled again — but does education actually improve? More and more people are questioning the governability of our societies, with comments that range from fears that government has become "overloaded" to despair that it can no longer adequately meet the demands of the community.

One result of the disparagement of governmental performance has been the encouragement of attempts to explain, and sometimes even improve, its policies and policy-making machinery. The more conscious study of public policy has emerged in the last decade or so from dissatisfaction with the limits of traditional institutional studies and with the modern trend of behaviourism. The disquiet of the 1970s has strengthened that trend.

The growing popularity of policy studies has not been accompanied by agreement about what should be studied and how these studies should be carried out. Indeed, the opposite has occurred. Recent work has varied widely in form, method, and theoretical predisposition, as the many commentaries and review articles now published make plain (Heclo 1972, 1974; Dearlove 1973; Elkin 1974; Rose 1973, 1976; Simeon 1976; Schaffer 1977). Themes that are common to some studies do not appear at all in others; terms are used differently; the field of study itself does not have an agreed name, nor is there agreement on whether there is one field or several; categories used to characterize trends in study are different. There is more advice available about what to do than there is time in which to explore it or to experiment with more than selected parts of it. Even definitions of policy are numerous. In his review article, Heclo (1972) mentions some eight of them. Brian Smith (1976) notes a different five. The one common factor, Heclo contends, is that policy is "usually considered to apply to something bigger than particular decisions, but smaller than general social movements" (Heclo 1972, p. 84).

Anyone who wants to make further contributions to existing work needs to say what stance he is taking and why he is taking it. The necessity for a clear stance can be shown by identifying six different strands in recent studies of public policy.

1. The first consists of structural and administrative studies of policy-making institutions, often developed from the perspectives of sociology or public administration. These are designed to show how institutions work and may also examine the effects of structures on the content of policy. For example, John Dearlove's work on local government in Britain (Dearlove 1973) shows the way that rules and perceptions shape activity.

2. Process studies, usually the work of political scientists, may be case-studies of particular events or longitudinal studies of different policy areas. Hugh Heclo's skilful analysis of the development of social policy in Britain and Sweden (Heclo 1974) exemplifies the best of recent process studies; he examines the influence of the various institutions of government on social policy in the two countries.

3. Output studies examine variations in expenditure across a number of political systems and policy fields and generally argue that particular decisions are less important than general economic and social conditions as an explanatory factor for change. The writing of Thomas Dye (1976) is characteristic of works in this field, often described as the "demographic approach".

4. Economists are also usually concerned with studies of output, rather than processes leading to it. Using technical methods, such as cost-benefit analysis and systems analysis, they attempt to test the effectiveness of policies by reference to achieved output, to improve management in the implementation phase, or to ensure precision or comprehensiveness in the policy design phase.

5. Economic reasoning may also be applied to the analysis of political and bureaucratic behaviour. Writers like Gordon Tullock (1965), J. M. Buchanan (Buchanan and Tullock, 1962), W. A. Niskanen (1971), Anthony Downs (1967), A. O. Hirschman (1970) and Mancur Olsen (1965) have developed theories intended to predict the likely behaviour of participants or to describe the basic modes of behaviour in terms of postulates and models analogous to those developed in economic literature.

6. In hortatory studies, writers are concerned explicitly to encourage the making of "better" policy. Blending material from various sources, including the studies listed above, they try to turn their insights into direct advice to governments. Yehezkel Dror's detailed proposals (Dror 1968) are the most striking example of this genre. Edward Heath's attempted reforms of British central government in 1970 show such a plan in action (Dillon 1976).

These strands are not all mutually exclusive; indeed, if they appear as separate strands, it is sometimes because the writers are so concerned to prove that their way of studying public policy is the most fruitful that they tend to ignore the perspectives of others. The development of policy studies has thus gone in several different directions and has too often failed to build on available theoretical advances.

In the 1970s it is no longer possible to assume that when policies fail it is because they are badly designed or because implementation has been inadequate. It is not simply that we need new or better-administered policies. Often the reasons for failure are inherent in the institutions themselves. The institutional machinery itself must therefore be subjected to much closer and much less formalistic study than in the past. It must be studied in action, in the making and implementation of public policy. We aim to combine the institutional and process approaches, which we find most illuminating in understanding how policy is made. We divide our empirical material into two main parts: a survey of the structures of central government — parties, departments, cabinet, and the central agencies — and a set of five case-studies, including ones that display a variety of forces contributing to the formation, maintenance, and change of policies as well as ones focused on distinct episodes of activity.

The study of policy processes will reveal how institutions work to shape and direct ideas and political pressures. Public policies do not spring fully formed from environmental conditions, however important these may be. We wish to see how issues — that is, questions for public dispute and decisions — generate policies and how policies are placed on, removed from, or excluded from political agendas; how institutions deal with issues once they are raised; how differences in outcomes are produced by different institutional arrangements; and how institutions differ in the contributions they make to policy outcomes both in particular episodes and over longer periods.

These are middle-range questions. Our interest is in what C. E. Lindblom (1965) has called the proximate policy makers, those who are closest to the actual making of decisions. This must be emphasized because some of the more ambitious strands of policy studies are quickly lost in searches for general theories not only of policy making but of societies. At the same time we are aware that by examining proximate policy makers we are leaving untreated important questions about the social and economic environments in which they work. These include, for example, the distribution of wealth and resources in the Australian community, the inequalities and unevenness in this distribution which commentators have often described, and the implications these issues have for the shape of public policy. These questions could validly be made the focus of study, but in our discussion they enter only at the margin.

Since we are concerned with institutional and process studies, it is worth reviewing the kinds of factors that affect the shape of public policy. The list could extend indefinitely, but the main items are of five general kinds: social and economic conditions; prevailing ideas; institutions and individuals; technical and analytical procedures; and general theories of the ways in which policy is made. All five are interrelated, although the analysis of particular cases may not give equal emphasis to each. Social and economic conditions form the raw material of policy processes. They set the limits on the supply of physical resources. Ideas and values form the basis on which assumptions about policy are made. Individuals, acting either alone or collectively, informally or officially, understand and interpret their environment in a way that must be structured by the institutions in which they operate. Technical methods may or may not assist their outputs. General processes of analysis and policy making in a polity reflect particular political and administrative arrangements.

SOCIAL AND ECONOMIC CONDITIONS

The impact of social and economic conditions on public policy has been vigorously debated. Proponents of output studies or the "demographic approach" have sought to demonstrate that levels of social and economic development are more important in shaping public policy than are political and administrative arrangements. The sophistication of their analytical techniques has been impressive, but as their work has proceeded they have been forced to accept that political factors independently shape policy and outcomes. As Cameron and Hofferbert commented at the conclusion of a study of education finance in federal systems: "Research such as reported here can form an essential back-drop and focusing function in policy analysis. It must be filled out, however, with direction and observation" (Cameron and Hofferbert 1976, p. 155). The political factors, in other words, must be readmitted.

Generally, the explanatory power of this approach is limited. It can offer descriptions of differences in certain policy outcomes and correlate these with social and economic conditions, but it cannot go much further. Dearlove states the shortcoming in these terms: "We are not really offered hypotheses which suggest *why* we can expect these associations and neither are we told just *how* it is that certain socio-economic conditions are translated into public policies by the structures of government" (Dearlove 1973, p. 69). The approach has also been limited by a concentration on variables which are readily specified, such as the broad character of a system of government, by restricted attention to factors that can be seen and compared as operating at a number of governmental levels, and by a concentration on outputs conceived as levels of expenditure but with little regard to questions of efficiency, effectiveness, and equity (Elkin 1974, p. 401).

As discussion has proceeded, some critics have suggested that dispute between advocates of economic and of political variables is unnecessary. Heclo suggests that the two are in fact complementary; he argues:

> The fact of economic development is little help in accounting for policy leads and lags, for substantive policy contents, and for ever emerging policy problems with indeterminate outcomes. In short there is no valid either/or choice — political versus socio-economic variables. . . . The grand choice between economic and political explanation turns out to be little more than a difference in analytic levels, a difference between the socio-economic preconditions and the political creation and adjustment of concrete policies. [Heclo 1974, p. 288]

Heclo's attempt at reconciliation is persuasive. It allows both for studies of a statistical nature dealing with background factors and for the activities of individuals and institutions a they try to give meaning to such factors and make judgments about them. From this perspective, processes of policy making are open but choices are not unlimited or cost free.

IDEAS

Just as there has been debate about the degree to which economic and social conditions determine public policy, there has been disagreement about the role of ideas and values and how their influence can best be estimated. There is a danger that if discussion of these factors is broadened into the notion of political culture then it explains too much. However, Anthony King has persuasively argued that differences between the scope of government activity in the United States and in other industrialized countries are related fundamentally to differences in ideas. He examines the influence of elites, demands, interest groups, and institutions and concludes that no single one provides a sufficient explanation for the policy patterns that are discernible in America. He concludes: "Ideas, we contend, constitute both a necessary condition and a sufficient one" (King 1973, p. 423).

While he is sympathetic to King's argument, Richard Simeon has suggested caution. He stresses the need for analysis to combine ideas with other factors: "Ideas do not provide complete explanations. They tend to be general and thus to account for broad orientations rather than the specific details of policy; in this sense they are especially important in providing the assumptions which define the problems and limit the range of policy alternatives considered at any point" (Simeon 1976, p. 573). Simeon also distinguishes between procedural and substantive ideas, and suggests three fields for particular investigation: the prevailing theories held by proximate policy makers about the nature of problems and their solutions; the nature of elite and mass values and the location and significance of differences between them; and the extent of ideological homogeneity and heterogeneity in systems under study. One contemporary example may illustrate the utility of his suggestions. In Australia, as in other Western capitalist economies, the economic problems of the 1970s have provoked political dissension and intense debate. That economic forces are substituting constraints for opportunities in the determination of policy is clear. But equally the alternative solutions proposed by Friedmanite and neo-Keynesian schools of thought present policy makers with a choice of appreciations of the economic situation. Which ones they choose make all the difference to the distribution in the community of the costs and benefits of government responses to the changed economic environment.

A discussion of the influence of ideas on policy is not the same as trying to explain how ideas become influential. Why do some ideas become accepted as popular currency while others are rejected? Why do some prevail? In a study of policy processes with a fairly short time-span, the interest is not in the emergence or origin of ideas as much as in their influence on policy after they have become established as patterns of thought in individuals and institutions.

INDIVIDUALS AND INSTITUTIONS

Public policy is shaped by individuals with ideas in action within institutions. Interaction between them is bounded by the consequences of past actions and by perceived opportunities presented by the environment. The problems of relating individual activity to the activity of institutions and then to patterns of policy have led to the emergence of many theoretical ideas and analytic devices which are often not easy to apply.

In relating individuals to organizations, C. I. Barnard's view is central: "The individual is always the basic strategic factor in organization. Regardless of his history or his obligations he must be induced to cooperate or there can be no cooperation" (Barnard 1938, p. 139). Stated simply and baldly, this seems self-evident. But concentration on the organizational goals or the systematic basis of organizations — two of the most prominent trends in organizational analysis — can be carried so far that the individual is neglected altogether. Developing Barnard's approach, J. Q. Wilson (1973) emphasizes in particular the importance of different incentive systems in shaping the activity of organizations. The character of the incentives that bring together individuals in particular kinds of coalitions markedly affects the ability and willingness of such coalitions to participate in policy making.

Social anthropology provides a useful supplement to organizational analysis. In their study of financial control by the British Treasury, Heclo and Wildavsky (1974) brilliantly portray Whitehall as a village society where norms of "community" are used by Treasury officers to maintain their hegemony. Dearlove's use of role theory to show how senior councillors in Kensington and Chelsea exacted the compliance of their more junior colleagues (Dearlove 1973) is a related approach founded in sociological literature.

In the literature of bureaucratic politics, other writers also emphasize the importance of coalitions of individuals and focus attention on individual motivation in coalition formation. To take just three examples: Downs bases his study of bureaucracy on the view that "every official is significantly motivated by his own self-interest, even when acting in a purely official capacity" (Downs 1967, p. 2). He then develops such categories of officials as zealots, climbers, and conservers to help explain how bureaucracies work. In another book, based more on personal experience than on theoretical assumptions, Douglas Hartle (1976) has listed a set of "rules of the game" for Canadian bureaucrats involved in the expenditure process. Patterns of self-interest and power are the underlying theme. Graham Allison (1971) has gone further. In his important work *Essence of Decision*, he argues that the reactions and behaviour of individual bureaucrats are directed both by organizational constraints and the need to participate in the game of bureaucratic policies. Downs and Allison thus relate the self-interests of bureaucrats to outcomes in public policy. They derive from their studies a set of maxims. Bureaus tend to maximize their budgets, expand their programmes, reward their staffs, and defend their own turf. Bureaucratic advice is not disinterested; bureaucratic battles are a vital contribution to the mix of factors giving shape to policy. Hartle also suggests that for central agencies the accretion of power, rather than funds or staff, is the main objective. In these discussions it is possible to emphasize calculating tough-mindedness, as in Allison and Downs, or gentlemanly, if somewhat feline, methods of control and accommodation, as in Heclo and Wildavsky.

While no student of public policy can afford to ignore the role of bureaucratic politics, the critics of that genre question whether it alone is sufficient to explain outcomes. R. J. Art (1973) has suggested that Allison's maxims have only limited explanatory value for particular cases. Lawrence Freedman (1976) goes further and argues that when Allison sets up a dichotomy between his "rational actor" model and his "bureaucratic politics" model, it is essentially a false division. Bureaucrats have much in common — shared images, assumptions and beliefs, and an acceptance of some "rules of the game". Conceptions of the national interest and policy substance may well be intermingled with bureaucratic infighting, but, Freedman argues, this is not to say that they cease to matter once the infighting begins. In addition, the self-interest of bureaucrats is not necessarily contradictory to or destructive of the development of a policy based on other considerations. Observers may tend to find what they seek, to the exclusion of equally important factors, and if they look for the bureaucratic infighting they will find it; but that will not necessarily explain by itself how policy processes work. Freedman suggests that other forces must be reintegrated into the study.

These other forces may be less abstract than the national interest. The interaction of individuals both internally within particular departments and between departments may well depend on the style of the organization itself. In a classic study, Burns and Stalker (1961) distinguish between the mechanistic and organic forms of organization and argue that the latter is more likely to encourage innovation. Mechanistic organizations emphasize routines and fixed roles; organic ones allow tasks and roles to be redefined at short notice and provide an environment in which creativity can flourish. This distinction is a useful underpinning for Bernard Schaffer's characterization of the "institutional maintenance man" who "defended his setting by ensuring as far as possible that troublesome occurrences in routine would come to notice and at the same time the potentially crucial would be reduced to the merely critical" (Schaffer 1977, p. 148). The existence of hierarchical and mechanistic organizations often allows such an official to prevent change; a different type of body might make such evasion difficult. The point is that different tasks require different types of institution and officials within them.

Whatever the style of an institution, it has to exist within an environment that is not static. Changing pressure and demands will require new reactions and perhaps even new policies. Dearlove has noted that organizations are often assumed to be passive recipients of environmental pressures. He suggests that it is useful also to identify strong organizations in passive environments. Special attention needs to be given "to the way in which governmental structures select and search and exclude certain environmental factors from impinging on their decisional activity, while giving sympathetic consideration to others" (Dearlove 1973, p. 76). This is especially important "where the organisational situation of a government is secure so that there is no real possibility of its being replaced. In these circumstances, environmental influences can only effect public policy if they penetrate the perceptual screen of those in power" (Dearlove 1973 p. 81). Dearlove's emphasis on the importance of what governments or departments choose to notice reinforces the need to study carefully the distribution of resources and orientations within official institutions.

Each of these ways of thinking about individuals and institutions is hostile to the recurring attractions of rationalistic and managerial models often presented, especially in the name of administrative reform. Coalitions intent on changes in government normally use models like this as assets in their internal politics, but the more precise setting of objectives, allocation of functions, and monitoring of outputs that they promise rarely follow. Styles change, but confusion and cloudiness in government remain.

A desire to understand the prevailing messiness of organizational life is the starting point of March and Olsen's elaboration of the "garbage can" model of organizational choice (March and Olsen 1976). This model is explicitly concerned with the internal processes of organizations. Although March and Olsen are aware of the need to make connections between such processes and wider social, economic, and political forces, they have not tried to do it themselves. The garbage can model suggests that proposed policy solutions are not always directly related to the problems they are said to be solving. For instance, an official in a department may have a scheme he wants to introduce. When a problem in a related field develops, he puts forward his scheme as a means of solving that problem. The solution, in other words, is not a response to an emerging need, but an independent proposal "looking for" a problem to which it can be attached.

March and Olsen suggest that "organizations are sets of procedures for argumentation and interpretation as well as for solving problems and making decisions. A choice situation is a meeting place for issues and feelings looking for decision situations in which they may be aired, solutions looking for issues to which they may be an answer, and participants looking for problems and pleasure" (March and Olsen 1976, p. 25). They emphasize that problems and choices are often "decoupled". Decision making is not simply solving problems; choices are made only when "shifting combinations of problems, solutions and decision makers happen to make action possible". The accidental coincidence of ideas, individuals, and opportunities means that the result of the conjunction of these forces can seldom be anticipated.

The garbage can model deals with particular cases, and is difficult to use to account for patterns of activity; nevertheless it may readily be linked with the approaches to organizational analysis mentioned above. One may proceed from a discussion of the coalitions operating within and between institutions to a focus on their impact in specific situations of choice. Because the garbage can model is designed to accommodate ambiguity, it is unnecessary to impose a tidiness which would be spurious on the activities of cooperating and competing groups.

ANALYTICAL METHODS

Some writers are concerned not so much to explain policy outcomes as with how those results are affected by techniques of analysis and, thereafter, how techniques can be used to improve the content of policy. Economists in particular favour such an approach. They have advocated new procedures such as planning programme budgeting (PPB), management by objectives, and cost-benefit analysis. In the search for accuracy and some synoptic vision, they often try to develop a "rational" analysis of policy where objectives are clearly stated, choices are explicit, and consequences known, and they argue that a clearer statement of objectives, a more careful analysis of data, and a more systematic evaluation of alternatives and effects would reduce some of the problems of modern government.

Most of these advocates accept that there are limitations to its use. Charles Schultze (1968), for example, acknowledges the necessity for techniques to be adjusted to political reality. Nevertheless, as Heclo comments, this approach "resembles an analytic framework in search of realism" (Heclo 1972, p. 104). It is no more value free than other methods of analysis, because the values are often hidden behind complex techniques and protestations of objectivity, as Peter Self (1975) persuasively argues in his critique of the "econocrats". Thomas Balogh, who is an economist and has been an adviser to government, has discussed the limitations of economists in government:

> The difficulties now manifest in the task of giving economic advice are not mainly the consequence of lack of data or of the sophistication of statistical method and manipulations — although both play an important part in misdiagnoses. It is the dauntingly complex character of economic problems, the rapidity and continuousness of change in the economy, the paucity of observations in sufficiently similar circumstances, the operation of a multitude of factors, indeed, which render *relevant* model building impossible. [*Times Literary Supplement,* 9 July 1976]

It is the ambiguity and uncertainty of the political scene that makes managerial models difficult to develop. Some economists want a clear statement of objectives, when there seldom is one; they look for direction in policy analysis and complain when they do not find it. One side-effect of such an approach is that some policy analysts or economists decide to impute objectives to government (because they can find none), and then test the effectiveness of policies on the basis of those objectives. Since their assumptions are often half-truths at best, it is inevitable that they should impute failure to governments. The point is not that managerial models or approaches have no validity. Schultze's careful work shows that they can provide the capacity for a better analysis of policy problems if they can accept the need for political realism; but too often their advocates are evangelists for new methods.

GENERAL APPROACHES TO POLICY MAKING

So far we have been looking at factors discussed in the literature which may be influential in determining the processes of policy making. But we must also examine, more broadly, analyses which attempt to characterise the policy processes themselves. We concentrate here on three of them: the sequential model of phases of decision making; disjointed incrementalism and partisan mutual adjustment; and the social learning model developed by Heclo.

The most familiar statement on the phases of the sequential model has been H. D. Lasswell's seven stages of decision making (Lasswell 1963): intelligence, recommendation, prescription, invocation, application, appraisal, and termination. Many others have proposed similar taxonomies, and some have extended the list drastically (Dror 1968). It is possible to make such taxonomies the basic ordering device in quite extensive studies; for example, Richard Rose (1969, 1976) has made this approach the foundation much of his writing on public policy. Especially when diagrammed in circular form with the possibility of multiple relations between phases (Lasswell 1975), this approach can be instructive. However, it has distinct limitations. It provides a "verbal accounting system" (Heclo 1972, p. 105) rather than a means of examining relationships. Even if it is accepted, say, that the stage of intelligence gathering may take place simultaneously with the stage of application, the approach is still difficult to apply without losing much of the richness of policy processes. Reference to the insights provided by the garbage can model makes this plain. In all but the most simple of decisions, the approach is a means of filleting policy processes and not of representing reality. If it is to be used, it needs to be in conjunction with analytically richer perspectives. For example, the intelligence phase can be subdivided into three: identification, definition, and analysis of problems. The analysis can be further complicated by the use of Rittel and Webber's notion of "wicked problems" (Rittel and Webber 1973) — that is, problems that defy satisfactory definition, let alone solution — or Sir Geoffrey Vickers's discussion of the process of combining reality judgments and value judgments in the making of appreciations (Vickers 1965). Pressman and Wildavsky in *Implementation* (1973) have, for instance, shown the consequences for programmes of poor policy formulation.

Lindblom's work on disjointed incrementalism and partisan mutual adjustment (Lindblom 1965) occupies a central place in debates about policy processes. It can be used not only for the simpler decision making of individuals but for more complex decisions involving several institutional participants. It emphasizes the influence of patterns of past policy, and it is immediately relevant to attempts to describe and understand actual cases. When managerial reformers characteristically try to get beyond Lindblom's approach by advancing the claims of new techniques, they usually fail. The main criticisms of Lindblom's work are that it may encourage policy makers not to try hard enough and that as a strategy for making policy it is contingent. It depends on the acceptability of existing patterns of policy to policy makers and their supporters, continuity in the nature and definition of problems, and continuity in the resources available for dealing with them (Dror 1969; Schaffer 1977). As long as this is kept in mind, the general perspective is useful for our purposes, especially as the government in Canberra has not been quick to explore new methods of decision making.

Heclo's social learning model is anticipated in his well-known review article (Heclo 1972, p. 107) and developed in his book on social politics (Heclo 1974). It shares some of the assumptions of Lindblom's work, including the tendency to encourage complacency. Heclo seems confident that processes of learning, adaptation, and integration are continuous and cumulative. By contrast, March and Olsen (1976) draw attention to cases where organizational learning is sharply discontinuous, and Arnold Meltsner (1976) points out in his study of policy analysts that one of their jobs may be to rediscover for organizations what once they knew but have forgotten in recent years. Yet Heclo's emphasis directs attention to ways of understanding "the extent to which governments have always been learning mechanisms and the fact that complexity has been endemically beyond the capacity of synoptic central direction" (Heclo 1972, p. 107). He shows how to unite an interest in power with an understanding of social adaptation. He says:

> Politics finds its sources not only in power, but also in uncertainty — men collectively wondering what to do. Finding feasible courses of action includes, but is more than, locating which way the vectors of political pressure are pushing. Governments not only "power" (or whatever the verb form of that approach might be); they also puzzle. Policy-making is a form of collective puzzlement on society's behalf; it entails both deciding and knowing. [Heclo 1974, p. 305]

Like Lindblom's work, this directs attention to the importance of existing policy patterns and to the activites of a variety of institutional and individual actors in policy processes, particularly their appreciative systems. Further, Heclo issues a telling caution about trying to reduce institutional activity to patterns similar to that of individuals:

> A better image for social learning than the individual is a maze where the outlet is shifting and the walls are being constantly repatterned; where the subject is not one individual but a group bound together; where this group disagrees not only on how to get out but on whether getting out constitutes a satisfactory solution; where, finally, there is not one but a large number of such groups which keep getting in each other's way. [Heclo 1974, p. 308]

Heclo is concerned to see how this can lead to social learning and non-learning rather than simply to "random bumping" (Heclo 1974, p. 308). Provided one keeps in mind the possibility of random bumping and persistent and uninstructive quarrelling, this perspective assists the understanding of complex patterns of activity.

THE RANGE OF POLICY PROCESSES

It is easy to talk about public policy as if it were made in the same way as a craftsman makes shoes or other products. Indeed, proximate policy "makers" characteristically try to shape policies to their design and thereby to achieve particular ends. But patterns of policy contain unintended as well as intended effects, and interaction between policy makers is usually complex. There is no single craftsman and nothing as unambiguous as a pair of shoes. As Heclo has put it:

> Policy does not seem to be a self-defining phenomenon; it is an analytic category, the contents of which are identified by the analyst rather than by the policy-maker or pieces of legislation or administration. There is no unambiguous datum constituting policy and waiting to be discovered in the world. A policy may usefully be considered as a course of action or inaction rather than specific decisions or actions, and such a course has to be perceived and identified by the analyst in question. Policy exists by interrogating rather than intuiting political phenomena. [Heclo 1972, p. 85]

Schaffer has made a complementary comment: he sees —

> Policy as a committed structure of important resources. The public policy process is then a multi-person drama going on in several arenas, some of them likely to be complex large-scale organizational situations. Decisions are the outcome of the drama, not a voluntary, willed, individual instial action. "Drama is continuous. Decisions are convenient labels given *post hoc* to the mythical precedents of the apparent outcomes of uncertain conflicts." [Schaffer 1977, p. 148]

These writers both emphasize complexity, contingency, uncertainty, and muddle. If men make their own policy, they do not make it entirely as they choose. The analysis of policy processes requires a readiness to define patterns of activity and resources, and to identify and assess the significance of a variety of actors and forces. The term *policy making* implies action. It is therefore important to note that activity is not to be confused with change. The prevention of change may require considerable attention. Actors may commit resources to maintain policy rather than to change it. Patterns of policy maintenance (Dearlove 1973) may be worth as much attention as the making of new policy.

THE APPROACH OF THIS BOOK

Our discussion is guided by this broad-ranging overseas literature. As we have already stated, our approach brings together institutional and process perspectives. To ensure that our position is clear, we now explain our assumptions and show how they fit within the context of the policy studies we have discussed.

Policy is not simply "made"; policy processes are pluralist; they do not follow any neat rational model. Single individuals and single institutions seldom dominate them or impose on them a consistent logic or direction. Every individual may be rational according to his own lights, whether his perspective is political, bureaucratic or ideological; but there can be no unified perspective and no one over-riding scheme for rational interpretation and explanation. One person's solution may be for another the means to an end. Ministers, parties, and departments all may have a role to play, but individuals seldom operate in isolation. Even a prime minister's edict usually has to be filtered through advisers and departments. Observers may sometimes see simple, even neat, policies that have an illusion of rationality; their view may occasionally be correct. But too often this illusion is created by a hindsight that is dazzled by success (or failure); the more details that emerge, the more complex this decision becomes.

There is no simple or single process by which policy is made. The "black box" of systems analysts does not exist. Some institutions may shut out all kinds of influences. Others are porous. They not only react to direct influences; they also soak up ideas from the cultural environment and the normative assumptions of the society in which they operate. The latter influence may be, at least implicitly, as important in directing action as the more obvious political factors. But it cannot be easily identified, even though it may be longer lived than more obvious pressures. The institutional ideologies of departments, the incentive systems of parties and bureaucracies, the perceptual screens which keep some issues permanently off the agenda — these are important influences that can help to explain the policy processes.

Public policy consists of continuing patterns of political and administrative activity that are shaped both by deliberate decisions and by the interplay of political and environmental forces. The sources of policy include strategic individuals in powerful organizations who attempt to shape policy to their own design, past patterns of policy, the political processes and structures through which policy proposals pass, and the political and social environment in which relevant activity takes place. Public policy is not simply an aggregation of decisions and programmes; it is wider than the results of discrete decisions and it does not necessarily have the coherence and definition of a programme. It includes non-purposive as well as purposive elements and unintended as well as intended consequences. We want to take issue with the notion that policy is something distinct, something that can be identified apart from the processes themselves. It is not. Policy serves a wide variety of purposes; political actors may use it as a means or an end, and they may not even give it a high priority. The processes of government are not simply about the creation of policy; nor is policy necessarily the outcome of activity.

We thus accept the view that emphasizes the uncertainty, complexity, and intermittent activity of policy making, the diversity of influences making it and the fragmentation of institutions. At one level the policy processes under consideration may be the activity in a particular sector, such as health or welfare; at another they may be the general and broad activity of government, that is, its political or economic management. But the two levels normally influence each other; how policy is made in one sector will be shaped by the government's general approach. To discuss either in isolation from the other is essentially artificial. Therefore, because of its complexity we talk of policy-making "processes", and not simply the policy-making process. There is no one process in Australia — or anywhere else. But this pluralist view of the processes of government does not in fact commit us to a world of complete disorder and confusion. Far from it. To assume that no individual or institution is omnipotent is not to say that the processes are random. Governments and departments may be able to achieve some ends by purposive action, but influence is unevenly distributed. Some departments or groups are more powerful than others. The power of some is intense, but of limited and intermittent scope; of others, weak but of frequent application; of yet others, weak and infrequent in its effect.

Broad patterns of activity and influence do exist, but often they are not consciously imposed by individuals or deliberately chosen by them. While it may not be possible to predict the outcome of particular events, in a stable situation those patterns of influence tend to change slowly. Government institutions have enduring strengths and inbuilt weaknesses. But their relationships do change, and this process of change — in influence, in procedure, in capacity — is one of the themes of this book. We want to show how the balance between institutions has shifted, what elements of continuity and stability have been changed, and how activity (or lack of it) has affected the way policy emerges.

Such a view of policy does not make institutions or their processes easy to study. If the question How powerful is a particular institution? is asked, we can only conclude that some institutions have some influence some of the time over some policies. That is not a very useful answer, even if it is an accurate one. But then, it is not a useful question either. It is the mix or pattern of institutional influences that is important. If institutions only have intermittent influence and unequal resources, we can never talk in terms of absolutes, but only in terms of interactions and interrelationships.

Little of the secondary literature about Australian politics and administration has approached the problem in this manner. What is written can be loosely placed into three categories — general reviews, institutional studies, and policy and case-studies. In the general reviews of Australian politics, institutions are usually considered one after another, separately; first the parties, then parliament, and then, if at all, the bureaucracy.[1] The links between these institutions are often not studied in any consistent way, nor is policy making a central theme.

Institutional studies have usually been written from a formal public administration viewpoint. G. E. Caiden's study of the commonwealth bureaucracy (Caiden 1967) and R. N. Spann's massive *Public Administration in Australia* (1973) are immensely useful, if traditional, studies of the bureaucracy. David Butler has raised interesting questions about the relationship of ministers and the bureaucracy in *The Canberra Model* (1973), which can usefully guide inquiry. But, regrettably, practitioners have seldom explained how they operated. With the exception of Paul Hasluck (1976), no

---

1. See Crisp 1973, Emy 1974, Miller and Jinks 1971, and, in a less coherent way, Mayer and Nelson 1976. The one general book that emphasizes the Australian talent for bureaucracy is Davies 1964.

minister has written usefully about his experiences, while few public servants have written in an illuminating way about their roles. What there is tends to be bland and formal. Nor are most biographies of politicians helpful.[2]

There are a few recent exceptions. Studies of bodies like the Prices Justification Tribunal (Nieuwenhuysen and Daly 1977) and the Industries Assistance Commission (Nieuwenhuysen and Norman 1976) have been published and usefully describe the roles of these bodies; they have been written mainly by economists and, although they indicate the confusion of administration, they do not directly illuminate the tensions and dynamics of the policy processes within these organizations. In a similar way, an earlier monograph on the formation of the department of trade illustrates the non-rationality of administrative arrangements (Deane 1963).

The most useful work for our purposes is that of L. F. Crisp. His articles on the central departments of government illustrate the intricate institutional influences at work in them, although the subtleties in his analysis are often disguised by the robust language characteristic of his work (Crisp 1961, 1967, 1972). Further, his chapter on public servants in *Ben Chifley* (Crisp 1961 *a*) remains the best available account of the informal networks of bureaucratic influence.

The third category, of policy and case-studies, is scarcely more useful. It is not that policy areas are not discussed. Far from it. There is now a considerable literature on such policy areas as education, medical services, agricultural economics, defence, and foreign affairs.[3] The Centre for Research on Federal Financial Relations has also produced a number of studies, many of which were written by economists (see Mathews 1974, 1976). But most are concerned with

---

2. See Dunk 1961, Cooley 1974, and Bland 1975 for the writings of public servants. Crawford 1960 is the most useful such article. Most political biographies like Menzies 1967, Edwards 1977, Oakes 1973, Daly 1977, Freudenberg 1977 or instant histories like Reid 1969, Oakes and Solomon 1973, 1974, Oakes 1976, Lloyd and Clark 1976, and Kelly 1976 pay little attention to routine policy and administration. The one exception — and the best study of the Whitlam years — is Lloyd and Reid 1974.

3. See, for example, D'Cruz and Sheehan 1975, Allwood 1975, Jecks 1974, Bessant and Spaull 1976, Harman and Selby-Smith 1976, Smart 1975 and Birch and Smart 1977 for studies of education; Brown and Whyte 1970, Sax 1972 and Scotton 1974 for medical policy. For foreign affairs see Millar 1968, 1972, Altman 1973, Watt 1968, and Albinski 1977. Forward 1974 provides a useful range of case-studies.

policies and not with the processes that shape those policies. Institutions are usually incidental to the process. There are a few exceptions, such as R. L. Wettenhall's study of the bushfire disaster in Tasmania (Wettenhall 1975) and work in progress by D. M. Adams and Desmond Ball. It is noticeable that in Australia there are no Marxist studies that explain policy processes from that more general viewpoint, although the work of R. W. Connell (1977) at least tries to open up some of these perspectives. We must therefore rely heavily on our own research to produce this work, for existing Australian literature is of little help to anyone approaching policy processes from our perspective.

Our analysis is at two levels. The case-studies in chapters 5-9 examine how particular decisions or policies are dealt with by existing policy processes; they show how institutions cope with specific problems and can thus be used to exemplify more general propositions. But neither the broad generalizations in the introduction that map the contours of policy and politics in Australia nor the case-studies can tell us much about the regular patterns of relationships between institutions, or, to put it another way, about the enduring strengths and weaknesses of institutions in different situations. A case-study may show (as one of ours in fact does) how a public service department with privileged access to information can perform less well than its "natural" advantages might lead us to expect it would. But this reveals little about its more typical encounters. We need, in short, to explain policy not only from the perspective of the process as a whole, and from the viewpoint of how particular problems work out; we need to see how relationships work out from the vantage point of institutions. Then we can link the general with the specific.

Therefore, in "Institutions and Policy Processes" we are concerned with organizational strength, with the capacity of organizations to influence agendas and make decisions; we are concerned generally to see how changes may occur in the distribution of influence. In the case-studies we deliberately reverse the approach and concentrate on particular decisions or policies and ask how their progress is affected by the strength of participating organizations. These cross-cutting approaches are designed to ensure that the emphasis remains on the central topic — the policy processes in Australia.

Institutions and Policy Processes

2
Policy, Parties, and the Public Service

Australian government is a variant of the Westminster model. According to this model the origins of policy are clear. Political parties, with some help from pressure groups, formulate alternative platforms of policies and then present them to the electors who choose between them. The successful party then forms a government and proceeds to put its promised policies into effect, again with more or less help and stimulation from pressure groups. It acts through an obedient, neutral, career public service.

The Westminster model makes several normative assumptions about how policy is made. First, policy is formulated by political parties, while the bureaucracy is the neutral instrument of implementation: there is meant to be a dichotomy between politicians who make policy and public servants who implement it. Second, policy is made on a sequential basis. Demands emerge from the community or the electorate and are articulated through pressure groups or the media; they are then aggregated by parties and translated into policies; the elected politicians make the choice between proposals; parliament authorizes and legitimizes them and then the public service implements them. Third, the process is regarded as a rational one, at least as far as the choice of ends and means. The legislation, incorporating cabinet decisions, represents the ends; the allocation of resources and the choice of methods are the means; and both are influenced by parliamentary debates (see, for instance, Fraser 1977).

In reality the whole process is far more complicated and muddled. The distinction between policy and administration has long since been discredited (Parker 1960), but criticism of the other assumptions about the way policy is developed in Westminster systems is less-well known. Politicians are often undecided about what policy they want, and they may be more interested in power and office than in policy. Public servants are often not pliable or neutral. They are often involved in initiating policy, aggregating demands, and settling means, while politicians are concerned with the details of administration. Pressure groups often bypass parties and parliament altogether and deal directly with the administration in formulating policy or in reformulating it when it is implemented.

In Australia it is not surprising to note that the Westminster model is inappropriate. Many parts of the policy processes are constrained by factors that are outside the direct influence of the government. Some of these constraints are created by the federal Constitution under which parliament must operate, a Constitution that can only be changed by a referendum procedure or by the interpretations of an autonomous high court. Other constraints have been created by the tendency for Australian parliaments to delegate important powers to independent statutory bodies; for instance, the control of wage policy has been ceded to the Conciliation and Arbitration Commission and is out of the direct control of the parliament. We are not concerned here with these relatively well-known influences on the policy processes but with the other inadequacies of the Westminster model at its central point — the special relationships and roles assigned to the parties, parliament, the executive, and the bureaucracy.

One political scientist, R. S. Parker, has tried to make the original model more realistic by revising it and calling it the "Westminster syndrome" (Parker 1978). He argues that the difference between politicians and public servants is one of status, not function. The former are elected and responsible to parliament; the latter are appointed and secure. Parker suggests that both ministers and public servants are concerned with proposing, choosing, and implementing policies; they fulfil similar and overlapping roles. The one major difference is that if they differ over the most desirable action, it is the politicians, who can be held publicly responsible for their choices, who must be allowed the last word and whose decision must be accepted by the public servants. In this reformulation, the Westminster syndrome is able to account far more accurately for the role of the public service in the policy processes than can the highly abstract ideal of the Westminster model.

To develop an understanding of these relationships and hence an understanding of the concepts of the Westminster syndrome, what is required is an examination of the capacity of the various institutions of government to make or influence policy within the constitutional constraints that exist. Since the final result must inevitably spring from a variety of inputs, it is the mix that is important. This study thus begins with a brief consideration of the two traditionally important institutions: the political parties and the departments. We are concerned here only with their capacity to shape and influence policy, not with their other functions.

THE POLICY CAPACITY OF POLITICAL PARTIES

The capacity of political parties to be effective in the policy-making and implementation processes depends on two factors. First, they must formulate their own views of what the policies of a government should be; second, they must be able to ensure that their views about desirable policy are accepted as authoritative and final and are later implemented. To do the latter, they must be able to win office and control the machinery of government; there is little that a party in opposition can do to influence policy through parliament. At most it can use public opinion; if it has the capacity, it can introduce new issues or make old ones more salient. In both stages, people must gain access to the processes — whether in the party machinery or in office itself — and must have appropriate resources (see Rose 1969; Weller and Smith 1975).

Parties have a wide variety of other functions which cut across the process of forming and promoting policies. Parties must win elections. Without electoral success, a party's skill in making policy is sterile. To win office, parties seem to accept that policies are necessary, but necessarily vague and ambiguous, so that they will appeal to competing interests in the community. A variety of supporting groups, some stronger and more important to the party than others, will want to have their say in the councils of the party about policy, leadership, and candidates; no party can afford to offend these groups. Even when specific promises are made, they are likely to suggest that some action will be taken rather than spell out in detail when or how it will occur. More often, electoral promises simply suggest that the party concerned will, for instance, reduce inflation and unemployment. But electoral ambiguity also entails little in the way of commitment by the party; when it comes to power there are few ideas that a party may be insistent on introducing and that it wants to force on to the public service.

Parties are also concerned with internal struggles for power and with the jockeying for position to determine which faction — or leader — will be dominant for the time being. Ideological purity is only one weapon in this struggle and is often considered to be unimportant. Policy may not be the outcome of careful deliberation about the question at issue but the side product of factional struggles in which the alignments of members are determined by considerations of power as much as by the merits of the question. This is especially true of the policy of the Liberal Party, which is often marked by an ideological fuzziness, but it is also true of Labor where a person's factional standing may determine what view he or she takes on an issue of current dispute.

Further, parliamentary parties provide the pool of talent from which ministers are drawn, whether they are chosen by a Liberal prime minister or a Labor caucus. In the search for ministerial office, skilful development and exploitation of policy is often not a major criterion in the choice of a minister. A good performance on the floor of the House, the correct factional alignment, or careful nurturing of support in the state branches may be as important; these responsibilities compete for time and the limited resources available to parliamentarians. All of these activities influence policy formation, some because they distract attention from it and channel activities in different directions; others by giving parties information and support they need in the promotion of policy. Whether they are dysfunctional for policy formulation or not, all are indispensable activities for parties.

When the parties are concerned to formulate policy, they suffer from severe limitations (Walker 1975). First, they suffer from a lack of resources. Expertise and information e limited, especially when the party is in opposition and does not have access to the resources of the public service. Shadow ministers often have limited knowledge of their policy areas; they have to rely heavily on other contracts — friends, journalists, sympathetic academics, and party members. Time, too, is limited. Politicians have many competing demands on their time; they must be electoral ombudsmen, party members, and parliamentarians. Thinking about policy is not only a low priority; it has no immediate return.

Further, there are organizational limitations that militate against the effective formulation of policy. In the Labor Party the machinery is far more elaborate than that in the Liberal Party, but it is still inadequate for the task. Labor's official federal platform is drafted by a federal conference of forty-nine delegates. They are the four leaders of the federal parliamentary party, the state parliamentary leader and six delegates from each state, and one delegate each from the Northern Territory, the ACT, and Young Labor. The conference meets every second year for five days. It spends most of its time considering the reports of committees which, having worked more or less energetically for some weeks beforehand, propose changes to the platform. In effect, the reports act as the base from which changes, usually small, in the policies are made by conference. The coherence of the platform depends on the work of the committees. The final result is a document that covers some sixty to seventy pages, some sections proposing in minute detail what any incoming Labor government should do, others presenting in broad terms the general direction a government should take. Yet other parts of the platform simply express the party's confusion about an issue and its inability or lack of desire to formulate any policy on it.

The whole party, including cabinet and MPs, is bound by this platform, at least formally (Crisp 1955; Weller 1975). The Labor Party believes in democratic procedures, even if it does not always adopt them. Decisions are taken by majority vote, after what is meant to be a free and full discussion. All those eligible to vote are thereafter bound by that decision, and this applies to MPs as much as to other members of the party. The leader is meant to be no more than *primus inter pares*. Yet when Labor is in government, the platform is little more than a broad constraint upon the leaders, indicating some things they might do and other things they cannot do. Planks on a few politically sensitive subjects, like uranium, may have an enduring impact, but conference does not, indeed cannot, determine priorities for an incoming government, and no other party body is allowed to do so. Conference meets too infrequently, is too inexpert, and, consisting of forty-nine members, is far too large and unwieldy. Finally, it cannot forecast the political or economic climate in which a Labor government has to work.

For the Liberals, policy is much less tangible. The Liberals argue that MPs are representatives of their electors and of the community as a whole, not delegates of the "movement" or the party and therefore that the extra-parliamentary party has no right to bind them on matters of policy. The Liberal platform, which was revised in 1975 for the first time since 1949, is full of rhetorical phrases and serves even less than Labor's as any guide to detailed action. The electoral policy speech is determined by the leader, perhaps after consultation with the leader of the Country Party or advice from central office or PR consultants. Party committees to consider policy are either non-existent or weak and advisory only. A Liberal leader is given considerable freedom of action; he is trusted and supported so long as the party is electorally successful. If he falters, he may be ruthlessly rejected. For the Liberals there is a lesser commitment to particular policies, more belief in the necessity of holding power to ensure the "safe management" of the country.

For both parties, the extra-parliamentary parties have a tenuous relationship with the institutions of government, explicitly so in the case of the Liberals, practically so for Labor. They may be influential in setting the agendas for ministers, but considerations of electoral and organizational maintenance remove them from day-to-day involvement with policy. The national secretariats of both parties have played an increasingly influential role in recent years in advising the prime minister on the potential electoral impact of proposed policies, but this influence depends, in both cases, on personal relationships between the party leader and extra-parliamentary officials. Influence is not a matter of right.

The relationships of pressure groups with representative institutions are more tenuous. As cabinet and the bureaucracy have become more important, and as the power of parliament has been seen to decline, so the strategy of groups is directed far more at the former. It is always difficult to generalize about the influence of groups on policy, at either the planning phases or in implementation; some are influential and covert; others are open and unimportant. Their strategies differ. Some, like the education lobby, try to mobilize public opinion by flooding MPs with telegrams. Others, like trade unions, have a direct input into the Labor Party's policy-making machinery. Their influence on policy may nowadays be more marked at the administrative than at the party stage (Matthews 1976*a*, Loveday 1970).

Parties may be important in broad terms in deciding what will be debated, what will be fought over, and what will be ignored. They do not have a monopoly of control over the agenda. The activities of pressure groups or changed political circumstances may lead to the emergence of new issues on which parties may be forced to take a stand, as for example with Aboriginal education and social welfare in the late 1960s. But generally the political agenda is composed of those issues to which parties choose to pay attention. This is an important power.

But different considerations affect the party when it has gained power and has to promote and formulate policy as a government. If the party, in contrast to the executive (that is, cabinet), is to control the execution of its policies, then ministers must to some extent be answerable to the party and must also be able to control the bureaucracy through which they work. Parliament as a whole is not an effective institution for the making of policy, the Westminster model notwithstanding (but see Solomon 1978). Debates may be serious discussions of way and means, of ends and objectives, but votes determine the outcomes and the votes are determined by party discipline.

The parliamentary parties from which ministers and would-be ministers are drawn experience great difficulty in maintaining an active involvement in policy making. Parliament in general has few formal links with the bureaucracy, for Australian governments have traditionally been reluctant to encourage the extension of parliamentary supervision of administrative activity through, say, backbench investigatory committees. Even such innovations as the House of Representatives Expenditure Committee have yet to prove their long-term worth. The government parties do not fare well: government backbenchers are seldom directly involved with the public service, and the party policy committees to which they belong are usually a way to soak up the surplus energy of those who cannot be promoted to the ministry for one reason or another. But opposition members are in an even more distant position. Shadow ministers, for example, have only recently been guaranteed access to the public service in the period before a general election in order to discuss the implementation of their policies in the event of electoral victory (Hawker and Weller 1974). Ministers and public servants have a common interest in maintaining the exclusion of parliamentary outsiders, whether they are politically friendly or not (Reid 1966).

At other times, ministers and public servants both may need to seek allies in the party room. This was especially true of the Labor caucus during the period of Whitlam government. In theory, caucus had the right to decide both what issues were reviewed and what action was to be taken by the Labor Party. Its decision on what should be done in parliament was binding on ministers. In fact, during sessions its members could scarcely keep up with the rush of initiatives by ministers. Under Whitlam, caucus committees reviewed the legislation that was to be introduced and also reviewed a wide variety of administrative decisions, but not all of these. The caucus rules allowed ministers to introduce directly to the House any matters considered confidential; at other times caucus was simply not given time. In 1974 a mini-budget was presented to caucus a mere half-hour before it was to be presented to the House. Some ministers appealed to caucus to overturn a decision after they had been defeated in cabinet; on other occasions caucus was briefed by pressure groups that hoped to overturn or influence government policy. But caucus was essentially reactive and not constructive. Occasionally its members were able to ensure that the bills they saw in advance were amended, that administrative insensitivities were corrected, or even that cabinet decisions were reversed. But they could seldom instruct cabinet to act, and they did not meet during the parliamentary recess to review the overall government strategy. The capacity of caucus to intervene meant that wise ministers kept one eye on its possible reactions, but its intervention was erratic, and skilled ministers were not closely constrained by it. Despite the occasional press headlines, the Labor caucus was neither overweening nor overinterfering between 1972 and 1975 (Weller 1974; Lloyd and Reid 1974; Smith and Weller 1977).

The Liberal parliamentary party plays an even smaller role. Occasionally antagonism in the party room can lead to a decision to delay or drop a government measure. The removal of the funeral benefits scheme (which was destroyed by defections in the Senate) and the dilution of the proposals to change the Broadcasting Control Board were two examples in 1976 of changes in Liberal cabinet policy. They illustrate the kind of activity that can be undertaken; but they are reactive and rare. It is more difficult, especially in the light of the long period of Liberal dominance and the party attitudes to leadership, for any more constructive roles to be played (Weller 1976).

But ministers, too, face difficult problems. The strongest control the ministers have over the machinery of government is collective control through cabinet. But collective backing from cabinet for a minister's control is not available in many aspects of his or her relations with the department. When a minister is acting on his or her own, the ability to direct and influence the actions of the department, especially in areas of policy formation, is always restricted by limitations of time, inexperience, and personal ability. This is not simply because time is always too short for ministers to do everything they want to do, or because there are too many public servants doing too much for any group of ministers to know about, or because ministers do not want to know everything — although all these are limiting factors. It is also because departments have a large and continuing fund of experience in policy in their field and intimate knowledge of the public service which few, if any, ministers can equal. The relationship between the minister and the permanent head of a department is essentially unequal. Permanent heads have usually been promoted through the public service because of their administrative ability. They can be expected to understand the working of departments, to be able to control the access of others to the minister, to have allies in the bureaucracy, and, above all, to have experience of policy issues in the area of their department. The minister, on the other hand, may not be an expert in the field for which he or she is responsible; he or she may have no administrative experience or ability and may be intellectually the inferior of the permanent head. The qualities that take politicians to the top are not necessarily those that make a good minister. Above all, ministers are isolated in office from those supporters or interest groups who were involved in formulating policy but are subsequently distanced from its implementation.

A determined or lucky minister can still play a decisive role in the development of policy. He or she can create a mood or sense of direction, even if unable to control the actual details or initiation of programmes. The early weeks of the Whitlam government in 1972–73 were such a period. Departments were ready with ways to implement by administrative action many of the simple, if symbolic, wishes of the incoming government; the optimism of the government and probably of the bulk of the public service was at its height (Lloyd and Reid 1974).

Even when the government was in rapid decline three years later and none of these conditions prevailed, some ministers were obviously faring better than others. They were not always the ministers who had been around longest and who had had time to learn how best to make use of the public service. Some of the longest-serving ministers had surrendered their early intentions and found others that fitted more comfortably the institutions of the public service. Ministers sometimes played a necessary and constructive role under Labor, but it would be incorrect to suggest that they were uniformly or consistently influential, on behalf of the party, in pressing policies on the administration. Any minister can bring resources to bear on particular problems and ensure that he or she is successful. But the range and capacity is limited. Usually he or she has to rely exclusively on advice and information from official advisers.

Parties are aware of these limitations and wish to change them, especially by trying to develop alternative, and perhaps more politically sensitive, sources of advice. This is one way to see Labor's experiments with ministerial advisers during 1972–75. Some ministers felt the need for politically acute advisers who would maintain a link between themselves and their constituents, especially with Labor Party members. They saw ministerial advisers as a counterweight to the policy advice which came to them from their departments and which, in the absence of alternatives, they felt all too weak to resist. Labor did not invent this system. It merely expanded the existing machinery, and the Liberal-Country Party government elected in 1975 has retained reduced elements of it. It would, however, be difficult to judge the Labor experiment a success, because of the wide variations that existed. Not all ministers wanted policy advisers on their private staffs; some advisers proved incompetent for the job; and a larger number acted as bridges between minister and department and not as critics of departmental advice. This is to deny neither the usefulness of that role nor the potency of some advisers as policy actors. Their influence could at times be crucial, as our study of the establishment of the RCAGA illustrates. But on those occasions they were not simply extensions of their minister. They were an addition to the policy mix, not merely agents for one of its existing elements (Hawker 1975; Anthony 1975; Smith 1977).

The same could be said of the committees of inquiry favoured by all governments but especially utilized by the Whitlam government. It was the intention of Whitlam to add to the policy capacities of existing departments and to make good their deficiencies by appointing expert inquisitorial and appreciative committees across a broad range of policy areas. There were over a hundred committees in all with a total membership approaching five hundred. Whitlam also created or expanded the functions of a number of advisory commissions (for example, the IAC) to give policy advice. But these inquiries became part of the institutional structure we are considering and struck up their own relationships with other institutions.

The impact of parties on policy is often limited; they seem comparatively impotent in many policy areas. They may, by direct action or by reaction to events, be capable of setting or changing the political agenda, both electorally and while in office. But their resources for formulating policy are so limited and their activity for devising it so complicated by other activities that their policies are too vague or incoherent, too systematically ambiguous, to be effective as a means of directing the activities of a government once it is elected. Richard Crossman once remarked: "The point of a manifesto is not to persuade the voters. The point of a manifesto is to give yourself an anchor when the civil service tries to go back on your word" (quoted in Rose 1974, p. 387). But if the party itself is not precisely certain how it wants to act, if its own policy views are general or incoherent, then it becomes difficult to see how it can direct the public service in anything but the most general of ways.

THE ROLE OF DEPARTMENTS

Just as sections of the party have variable degrees of influence, so it is with bureaucratic institutions. They do not have equal capacities: some departments, like the Treasury and Foreign Affairs, have a historic ability to attract able staff which gives them enduring strength, a tradition of being headed by the most senior and better ministers, and an ability to surround themselves with client institutions. These attributes certainly add to their strength even if they do not guarantee organizational success. The strongest departments, like the Treasury, may be temporarily overwhelmed by events, as one of our case-studies shows. But this does not mean that it and similar institutions are not relatively strong and enduring; they are. Their existence is built upon the continuity of their tasks.

Most of what government departments do they did last year and they expect to do next year; and they are most confident doing what they know best. Defence, Foreign Affairs, and the Treasury, for example, are essential to any government. Rules, procedures, and the motivation of individuals are directed toward the handling of main tasks. The predominance of routine means that it may be difficult for bureaucrats to perceive new challenges. Yet government departments are incessantly active if only in order to select from their environment what it is they wish to know. They can never be completely successful in doing this. Whether demands are generated by politicians fresh from electoral victory or by clients at the counter dissatisfied with what they are getting and how they are getting it, they are the raw material which departments have to cope with, and usually they cannot all be met at once, let alone be permanently reconciled.

For instance, in the 1970s departments had to meet a new challenge when advisers and committees of inquiry were, as they saw it, foisted on them. They found some of these difficult to deal with; others they managed to ignore or submerge. A few were useful, either as bridges to those with whom departments wanted to have dealings or for assistance in the exposition of their own interests. At times, advisers and committees served as the focal point for disagreements between departments. This was not always what was intended. Departments sought to use new policy participants for their own benefit. Sometimes they were of temporary use, as in the resolution of particular disputes with ministers or with other public servants. At other times, departments incorporated the new players and made them part of their permanent equipment, as in the case of committees of inquiry into education, recreation and the environment (Hawker 1977).

In doing this, departments were changing their normal approach to the development of policy. Though organizational maintenance requires a capacity to respond to problems presented in an unexpected way, it also requires a capacity to reduce the likelihood of the unexpected. This may be done, for example, by the use of advisory boards, which have long enabled departments to bring into their permanent orbits those individuals and representatives of interests with whom they feel most comfortable. The importunings of clients whom departments see as less legitimate are offset by the support from those felt to be more legitimate. The established leaders of business and the unions are more likely to secure representation than are dissatisfied migrants and Aborigines. But the new initiatives in health and welfare associated with the Whitlam government created new expectations which departments were sometimes unable either to meet or to ignore (Matthews 1976a). Departments cannot always determine the shape of the environment in which they must operate.

Indeed, the relationship between departments and the pressure groups in the community is always complex. It is not simply that the groups try to influence the direction of policy or the details of regulations introduced under delegated legislation, although some, like the RSL, clearly do this (Kristianson 1966). Often the minister or the department may use or manipulate the groups, as one of our case-studies (chapter 6) shows. The groups can be used to provide information, to act as a sieve for grievances, to help in the smooth administration of a scheme, or actually to run it. The consent of groups is often useful before a new proposal is implemented (Matthews 1976b, pp. 232-33). Departments do not act in isolation; they are in constant contact with client groups, both responding to and manipulating them as circumstances demand. Negotiations are not always successful, but are a necessary part of policy processes.

The size, importance, and durability of departments vary. In the early 1970s there were thirty-six; under the Labor government the number was first increased and then reduced to twenty-seven. Several departments, like Tourism and Recreation or Services and Property, were created in order to find some formal responsibilities for the less important ministers; they had formal status but little real responsibility, which did not prevent them from trying to develop a field of influence. Other departments, like Treasury, Overseas Trade, Manufacturing Industry, and Labour, whatever their various names and reincarnations, are always likely to be influential because they must deal with recognizably important problems or sectors in Australian society. Departments like Social Security will always be there too, even if they are not always influential. A third group can also be identified; it includes those departments like the Department of Urban and Regional Development (DURD, now Environment, Housing, and Community Development) which grow in influence in given circumstances and then decline when their initial advantages are removed.

Departments — and the individuals within them — are

competitive. They struggle for power and influence. Policy processes are adversarial, made competitive by the struggle for limited resources and by disagreements about policy objectives. Bureaucratic imperialism is common and can be explained by several factors. Sometimes a minister may try to expand his influence by increasing the capacity of his department, as Sir John McEwen tried to develop the Department of Trade as a counterbalance to the Treasury. At other times the public servants in a department, and especially the department heads, take opportunities to extend their influence. Alan Carmody, the late head of PMC, was one notable example. Sometimes, as with R. F. X. Connor and Sir Lenox Hewitt, an imperialistic minister and an expansionist bureaucrat combine.

The structure and patterns of bureaucratic power vary. In some cases changes are dramatic. DURD rose rapidly under Labor because it had a politically acute minister and was involved in a wide range of functions; it declined (under a different name) almost as rapidly when it was headed by a junior minister and faced the direct enmity of the prime minister and of some of the central bureaucratic agencies which objected to its earlier expansionist attitudes. Partly as a result, it lost many of its more able officers. Other variations of influence are less dramatic; the Treasury temporarily lost influence during 1974, while Overseas Trade has been trying to regain the earlier influence that it once enjoyed under McEwen. Bureaucratic influence is never static.

Competition within a bureaucracy generates a range of bureaucratic ideologies. These may indicate what a department will draw on in justifying its advice or activities. Often these are publicly identified as "departmental lines". The Department of Overseas Trade, for instance, has long waged a war with Treasury over the degree of intervention that should be permitted in the economy. It supports the recent IMPACT programme, under which various departments, headed by the IAC, are trying to forecast the future demographic and industrial structure of Australia. It also challenges the way Australia's trade should be represented overseas. Foreign Affairs argues that all overseas representation should be controlled by their department (as is shown in chapter 7); Overseas Trade wants control of its own representation. One former officer of the Overseas Trade Department remembers being asked to write a paper on whether Australia should enter the OECD. After two drafts supporting entry had been rejected, he realized that senior members of the department opposed it because they saw immediate advantage to the Treasury in such a move but none for Overseas Trade.

Another example can be seen in the clash between DURD and the departments of Education, Health, and Tourism and Recreation. DURD wanted to develop an integrated regional policy, bringing together the different services that the Commonwealth offered in each region. And DURD wanted to be the coordinator and overseer. The other departments objected because they saw themselves becoming subordinate to DURD in some of their activities and thus opposed such a situation.

Departmental loyalty is considered an important quality which, coupled with bureaucratic imperialism, leads to the practice of departmentalism, described by one British observer in these terms:

> Within departments, it is associated with a strong and sometimes uncritical adherence to particular lines of policy, and attitudes of mind, which have become established as traditional . . . The prestige of a department as a whole, and of its minister in particular, depends on the success with which its predetermined policies are defended and upheld in interdepartmental disputes. Between departments, it is associated with a disposition to regard issues of policy as being normally if not necessarily decided by a somewhat stylized process of quasi-diplomatic bargaining between ministries, in which the arguments presented are in no way impartial or disinterested . . . There is danger that the economic considerations which are relevant to particular policy decisions, in so far as they are presented at all, will be treated as merely *ex parte* statements by the department from which they originate. [Quoted in Hayward and Watson 1975, p. 7]

These comments were made about the British civil service, but they are as applicable to Australia. Australian departments are notoriously aggressive. One senior officer, returning from a posting in Washington, commented that he had forgotten the extent to which Australian departments competed rather than cooperated with each other (Visbord 1976, p. 10). Public servants are regarded as hired guns, responsible to their present department even at the risk of appearing personally inconsistent. Thus one officer who as a Treasury man on a Friday was rejecting the concept of forward estimates put forward by an officer of another department was on the Monday telephoning the same officer to find out how they could most persuasively be compiled. He had changed his job (and his department) over the weekend.

Institutional ideology may therefore relate to policy views — as it does or did with Overseas Trade, Treasury, and DURD; or to procedural norms about how activity should be carried on. Departmental perspectives will always differ. Some departments are concerned with a narrow range of special problems and view all items from the one angle. For example, a Department of Labour may regard economic policy primarily in terms of employment prospects, for this is its function. The Treasury, on the other hand, is concerned primarily with the costs, not the effects, of programmes and with their impact on overall spending. As a result, just as resources are varied and shared unequally between departments, so are the institutional ideologies. The Australian public service has grown rapidly and has been subject to little scrutiny. The historically created environment encourages departmentalism, a monopolization of information, unwillingness to change existing programmes, and secretiveness towards other departments. This is not to suggest that coordination never takes place, that no one trusts anyone else, that integrity is necessarily missing, or that empires are always at risk. Rather, it is to suggest that the internal procedures require that policy or resource allocation is settled through an adversarial process and that views and interests are usually narrowly restricted. Such a process is characteristic of Canada and Britain, but in Australia it has been so exacerbated by the bitter rhetoric of the political culture that it has had a pervasive influence on the way that line departments develop policy proposals, advise ministers and evaluate or implement programmes.

Up to this point we have been speaking as though each department is united in the way it approaches other actors in the policy process. But nothing of the sort is or could be the case. All public service departments have a great deal in common just because they are similar bureaucratic organizations. Despite its rapid expansion in size (roughly trebling between the Second World War and now), the Australian public service is cohesive at its top levels. Its senior officials have worked together for years. Their careers have overlapped as they have progressed. The 1960s, moreover, saw the creation of a general administrative division (the second division) which has within it the deliberate seeds of an administrative elite. The numbers involved are small — a few hundred persons shared among the central departments in Canberra — and the sense of style and community is strong. Recruitment practices which once varied greatly between departments are now standardized, and as a result people with similar skills are selected for most departments. Service-wide training and development programmes promote a further integration of expectation and outlook throughout the public service. Senior officers usually have similar experiences whatever their departments (Encel 1970, pp. 278-84).

But the corollary of the emergence of an administrative elite in Canberra has been the corresponding emergence elsewhere in Australia of groups of public servants who are less privileged as regards salary, status, and expectation of power. This observation applies beyond the Australian public service. The concentration of commonwealth power is symbolized in the capacity of the Canberra bureaucracy to attract able people who might once perhaps have entered the state administrations. There are, however, disparities of influence within the commonwealth public service itself. The disparity of rewards available to different levels of the service is acute, and this helps to create feelings at both the centre and the periphery that each knows best how the bureaucracy should operate, greatly complicating normal problems of internal management. It means also that the relatively distant parts of the bureaucracy are more receptive to the demands of their clients than are their head offices.

Disputes between departments over the distribution of work and functions are an inevitable part of bureaucratic life. Disputes can arise wherever there are no clear principles to set the boundaries of work or authority; organizations and individuals assert their opposing interests and try their strength. Moreover, any division of functional responsibilities, whether between organizations or individuals, is arbitrary in the sense that other taxonomies can and always will be envisaged. Of course, some are more sensible than others, but none can maintain unanimous support. This is another source of political activity within the bureaucracy.

Departments, and more particularly ambitious individuals within them, wish to expand their empires, responsibilities, and power. At the margins of any department's official work will lie tasks that could equally well be carried out elsewhere. Even the most "rational" attempt to divide at the grossest level — where work is distributed among the agencies of government — must be arbitrary. Between the elements of any division are gaps; some things end up on one side when they could well be on another. Federalism adds another division — of authority — to the division of tasks inherent in the bureaucracy, adding to the arbitrariness of arrangements at the margins. Hierarchical relationships exist between the agencies of different levels, as for example, between federal grant-giving agencies and the implementing agencies at local government level. Some activities are exclusive to a particular level of government, but overlapping is growing more common; education and agriculture policies, as our case-studies show, provide good examples of conflict where overlapping and duplication occur at the boundary.

The imperatives of division, hierarchy, and distance are clear enough: the functions of government are diverse and they must be allocated before activity can proceed. At once the need for co-ordination enters. Work that has been allocated for ease of execution and shared out among different agencies must also be co-ordinated if it is to accomplish general policy objectives. As with work, so with the authority shared out in the federal system; agreed policies may be more — or less — effectively implemented depending on the degree of cooperation and coordination between governments at different levels and the agencies they depend on to do the work. The effectiveness and easy of coordination are, however, reduced by the interdepartmental conflicts arising at the boundaries or margins of authority and work.

Divisions of responsibility and interest in policy activities there-fore create problems for many parts of the policy processes. The division of functions between departments, and the historical devel-opment of those functions and their division, create a diversity of opinions about the nature and resolution of current policy problems. Responsibility for a particular policy or programme may be obscure and contested; no one may want responsibility for exploring the dimensions of a new problem and for proposing ways of handling it.

Policy is not simply about the conflict of ideas, however. It is also about the maintenance of the organizational resources that allow this conflict to be sustained. In a narrow sense, for example, promotional opportunities for individuals are often dependent upon a particular department maintaining its capacity to act in old fields and to extend its capacity into new ones. In a broader sense, organ-izations, whether parties or bureaucracies, can prove themselves right in what they do only by continuing to exist and by continuing to get their way on a reasonable number of occasions. But when in-novations must be made, especially if they have extensive effects, they will usually entail some degree of institutional reconstruction and damage to the career prospects of individuals. So the struggle for organizational maintenance, personal advancement, and policy effectiveness in a highly competitive but departmental structure results in great rigidities and a system that is resistant to innovation.

Further, many technical innovations that are proposed as a means of producing "better" policy soon become weapons for use in the contest for organizational maintenance. The scheme of forward estimates, tentatively introduced in 1970 and since then supported by the RCAGA report as a suitable method of forcing cabinet to set priorities, has now degenerated into a means of allowing the cabinet an early look at the budget bids (Weller 1978; Self 1978). The new demands for efficiency or evaluation audits are similarly not neutral techniques. Evaluation reports will be used by departments to justify increases, by central agencies to demand cuts. Technical procedures do not exist independently of their environment. Whether they are part of a general plea for planning or for greater rationality in government (Wildavsky 1973) or limited to specific policy areas in their approach, they are soon absorbed into the environment. The impediments to a general view of "rationality" — the difficulty in specifying objectives, in retaining consistency, in looking ahead — cannot be removed by a new technique (Schaffer 1977; Self 1975). They are an inevitable part of the political and bureaucratic environment.

Similar factors can help explain the distribution of the government's functions. Large-scale alterations in institutional arrangements often accompany the development of new policies. These too are essentially political responses to stress, as prime ministers try to overcome administrative problems which prevent the effective solving of policy problems. This has been the experience in Australia since the retirement of Menzies. The departments of the public service were not much altered during his tenure, and innovations in policy were seen as matters to be approached cautiously. The Department of Trade was created in 1956 to bring into the one institution a number of the concerns of the Country Party (Deane 1963), and the creation of the Department of Health in 1958 gave substance to some elderly electoral promises. Under Gorton's prime ministership the Prime Minister's Department was broken in two in order to set up a separate cabinet office and to nurture the development of sections within it concerned with the environment, Aborigines and the arts. Further changes were contemplated by the McMahon government.

A flurry of administrative changes began when the Whitlam government came to office. The Department of Urban and Regional Development, for example, was founded to initiate the government's innovative policies in the area. The creation of a separate Education Department was another indication of policy priorities. The old protectionist empire built up by the Department of Trade was dismantled. The three armed service departments and the Department of Supply were all merged into the enlarged Department of Defence. The new administrative arrangements were a public statement of Australia's new directions. The Fraser government too has sought to demonstrate its intentions by rearranging the machinery. One new creation has been a department for negotiations with the EEC.

Ostensibly such changes are made for reasons of "better policy". New policies seem to call for new institutions. But this is not the only reason for institutional rearrangements which may occur without a change in policies when it becomes necessary to shift a minister, to change the size of the ministry or to reduce the power of a difficult department head. The creation and destruction of departments and the rearrangement of their constituent parts are now prominent in the policy processes.

INTEGRATION AND COORDINATION

All governments need procedures for coordinating functions and pulling together the threads of policy. One way of providing that integration is to produce a plan that gives guidance for the major proposals of government. But plans have been thought to be politically and bureaucratically unacceptable in Australia. Integration can also be achieved, without a plan, by special coordinating departments and, at the political level, by cabinet. This has been the traditional way of the Westminster system. What is important, then, is not to understand in isolation the capacity of parties or departments to make policy, as that capacity is always changing, but to understand the links that unite the component parts of the government's activities. To fail to understand how the system of coordination and integration operates is to misinterpret the essence of government in Australia.

For that reason the next two chapters examine the problems of coordination. Chapter 3 looks at the development and activity of cabinet; chapter 4 examines the changes and activities in the coordinating authorities. In a sense, then, cabinet pulls together the threads of political activity, and the coordinating authorities act similarly for those of bureaucratic activity. But this distinction is purely one for convenience. There is no clear distinction between policy and administration, between the political and the bureaucratic; there is no "proper" distribution of power or authority. Rather, cabinet and the central departments, often rather haphazardly, interlock with one another and provide the arena within which policy is, or is not, brought together.

3
Cabinet

Cabinet is the most important focal point of all the institutions of government; the point where political, legislative, and administrative forces intersect. In both conventional and less conventional accounts of policy making it is allocated a heroic role. Whether these accounts are traced back to Bagehot, to contemporary political considerations, or to theories of organization and management, cabinet is seen as the central source of authoritative decisions and pronouncements. It coordinates, directs, and arbitrates; it resolves, disposes, and legitimizes. Its members stand high in political prestige; their activities are protected by elaborate webs of custom, mystique, and secrecy.

In his evocative and pragmatic discussion of the Britsh cabinet of the 1860s, Bagehot noted that no description, "at once graphic and authentic", of cabinet's workings had been given. His tone hints that he would have welcomed a chance to write such an account, and Richard Crossman might now have satisfied that need. But there is no equivalent account in Australia; nor is one likely to appear. We cannot describe the process of actual cabinet meetings; that is obvious. No academic has been able to attend and then write about them afterwards. The most we can do is to gather and make something of the fragmentary information that does become available.

But we can describe the environment in which cabinet operates, the role of the prime minister and his colleagues, the responsibility of officials and the structure and procedures of cabinet itself. The last category includes cabinet's size and composition, its internal arrangements and committee systems, and its relations with various public service agencies and with its supporters in the ruling party. From this description much can be deduced about the capacity of the cabinet to make policy.

As processes of government have become more complex, the stresses on cabinet have grown more obvious and intense. Its ability to assimilate and integrate the demands thrust before it by ministers, their departments, and the coalitions of interests that surround them has been thrown into doubt. The style and ability of ministers, and in particular the capacity of the prime minister to draw together the various threads of government, assume strategic importance. The question of how cabinet should be organized has become a matter for dispute and debate, while the decisions that emerge from it are often considered inadequate, hasty or ill informed. Cabinet is a victim of overloaded government.

Cabinet is usually discussed in formal terms. Conventionally the work of academics and journalists has concentrated on arguments about the collective responsibility of ministers, individual ministerial responsibility for the work of departments, the need for confidentiality, and the extent to which cabinet arrangements have deviated from accepted standards on these matters. Although important, these themes are essentially formalistic, even legalistic, and they appear to assume that as long as certain conditions are adhered to cabinet is working well. But debate about them does not take very far any discussion of cabinet's capacity to shape or review public policy.

The tradition of secrecy makes such a discussion difficult. It may be reasonable to maintain that what ministers discuss in cabinet should remain secret, but there is also a widely accepted view that cabinet's procedures and working habits should also be kept from public view. This argument suggests that those who gain cabinet office or work in supporting bureaucratic agencies understand the range of roles that can be played; that those who have to make the arrangements work know what to do; and that those without this responsibility do not need to know. But the performance of recent cabinets suggests that the operations of cabinet would benefit from increased public information about them and from public analysis of the context in which they take place.

In this chapter we will concentrate on two sets of themes. The first concerns cabinet arrangements. As this chapter will illustrate, cabinet arrangements need a lot of attention; they will not automatically work. Therefore the organization of cabinet, the type of questions that may or may not be settled by cabinet, and its appreciative system (that is, its ability to keep in touch with the changing political climate and adapt its policies to suit) will be considered. The second theme concerns the role that particular people play — with the way that officials who serve cabinet are influential in shaping its procedures, with the capacity of ministers to learn how cabinet works and how their own resources can be put to best use in it and with the centrality of the prime minister.

The performance of cabinets from Chifley onwards provides useful evidence, but for topicality and because more material is available about it, the Whitlam cabinet receives most attention. Inevitably, given the available evidence, our emphasis is structural and procedural, but from it some conclusions about the capacity of cabinet to shape policy processes can be deduced and the frailty of cabinet's grasp on policy exposed.

PERSPECTIVES FROM BRITAIN AND CANADA

Since little has been written about the Australian cabinet, some of the main problems of a study such as this can be illuminated by a review of recent discussions of cabinet in Britain and Canada. In Britain the image of cabinet as an effective instrument for making authoritative decisions has been the subject of a notable challenge by Richard Crossman. Crossman first put forward his arguments about the replacement of cabinet government by prime ministerial government in a much-noticed introduction to Bagehot's *The English Constitution* (Crossman 1963). Later, after experience as a cabinet minister in the Wilson Labour governments of 1964-70, he elaborated his theme in *The Diaries of a Cabinet Minister* (Crossman 1975, 1976, 1977). He deplored the failure of cabinet to formulate political and governmental strategy, the isolation of senior ministers from each other and from the prime minister, the ways in which important business eluded systematic cabinet attention, and the shifting alliances of ministers and civil servants who came together to deal with particular items and then dispersed. Further, he recorded with disappointment Harold Wilson's private and evasive style of leadership. In Crossman's view, Wilson handled issues as they came, trying, now confidently, now pessimistically, only to ensure political survival. Crises were to be endured rather than circumvented by forward thinking. Achievements happened rather than came from conscious and coordinated striving. Too much depended on how the prime minister defined issues and on what he chose to ignore or follow through. This part of Crossman's argument ran parallel to some extent with arguments by others about the "presidentialization" of prime ministerial roles. Crossman also outspokenly criticized civil servants' responses to ministerial wishes. He was especially concerned with dangers for cabinet of civil service committees having too much influence over the flow of cabinet business. The volume and complexity of government business made it difficult for cabinet to deal with more than a fraction of it, while the predigestion of cabinet material in official committees, he argued, pre-empted much of cabinet's ability to debate alternatives and to choose between them.

Crossman's critical and angry views have been given much sympathetic attention. But views like his have been rebutted energetically by one careful scholar, George Jones. Jones has provided a thorough analysis of the structure, composition, and working methods of recent British cabinets, including a discussion of the means and problems of providing cabinet members with timely and effective policy advice. While defending conventional notions and doctrines about cabinet, he makes illuminating use of such empirical material as has come to public knowledge. "What emerges", he argues, "is that the cabinet is alive and doing well" (Jones 1975, p. 31). He accepts that many items of public policy never reach cabinet but contends that on vital issues cabinet remains the effective decision-making body. Indeed, he argues that the pre-cabinet transaction of important business is what has allowed the cabinet to maintain its grasp of affairs. He says: "What has enabled the Cabinet to survive into the 1970s as the central decision-making institution, while government business increased in amount and complexity, is the elaborate network of arrangements through which government business is transacted before the meetings of the Cabinet" (Jones 1975, p. 31). He continues: "The Cabinet remains the prize of the political battle. Politics in Britain involves the struggle between parties to win a majority at an election so as to be able to form a Cabinet, and once formed it is the central driving force in government, arbitrating as the final tribunal of policy and issuing authoritative directions, like the medieval monarchs whose governmental powers it has inherited" (Jones 1975, p. 32).

Jones argues that the existence of partial cabinets and circles of prime ministerial confidants and even the acceptance of the utility of ministerially inspired leaks do not alter this conclusion. Similarly, he accepts the substantial influence of the prime minister while emphatically rejecting the notion that prime ministers can do as they will with cabinet. He says: "The Prime Minister's role is to advise, encourage and warn his colleagues: not to do their jobs for them. He may involve himself in one or two areas of policy, which seem most important at the time or with which he is publicly associated, but he lacks the administrative resources and the knowledge to make a significant impact on a wide range of governmental responsibilities." Finally, he develops the analogy of cabinet as a chamber orchestra: "The Prime Minister is conductor, but from time to time he feels like reverting to his old position as leader of one of the principal sections; yet he also knows perfectly well that a chamber orchestra has to be led, and directed, in a style which recognizes that this is a group of highly-skilled, hand-picked players some of whom may feel confident that they too could direct" (Jones 1975, p. 57). Jones's analysis is perceptive and persuasive. His strength is that while adopting a conventional argument to order his material he does actually confront many of the points made by critics of that argument.

The discussions by Crossman and Jones by no means exhaust the range of argument about cabinet's place in contemporary British government. But they do focus attention on cabinet's ability to make decisions and exert influence on policy. So far we have discussed their disagreements. It is therefore important to note that while their views diverge on how cabinet operates, they have much more in common when it comes to how cabinet *ought* to operate. Implicitly both share a rationalistic model in which policy should be produced by specific decisions after a systematic examination of the issues involved. While Jones believes that the bureaucracy can adequately canvass and transmit items for decision to cabinet, Crossman believes that both the prime minister and senior civil servants hinder cabinet from assuming its proper responsibilities. However, as has already been suggested, public policy is more than the product of discrete decisions. Institutions trying to shape policy have difficulty in matching up streams of actors, problems, and opportunities for choice. Definitions of both problems and solutions are likely to be disputed. From this perspective, both Crossman's expectations (he might be less angry if he expected less) and Jones's conclusions (he is too sanguine by half) are called into question. It may be more appropriate to see cabinet as an institution with a range of abilities (and disabilities) depending both on the broad social context in which it operates and on the specific institutional arrangements that surround it.

Recent Canadian experience illustrates the value of such a perspective. Since the middle 1960s a number of significant adjustments have been made to Canadian arrangements. The amount of published comment on these developments gives a reasonably clear view of what was intended and what has happened. The main body of changes has consisted of structural and procedural innovations to improve the flow of business through cabinet and the ability of the government to coordinate and review policy. To a considerable extent, adjustments were formulated according to systems analysis and management theory. They were put forward against a background that included a history of formal cabinet predominance over other central institutions, extensive practical devolution of influence to senior bureaucrats, and a prevailing atmosphere of incrementalism, confusion, and inefficiency. The main changes included the creation of a more elaborate set of cabinet committees, a reshuffle and upgrading of the central departments and agencies in the civil service and increased institutional support for the prime minister. The new system of cabinet committees was especially important because of the size of cabinet — usually rather larger than in either Britain or Australia. The committee system promised a means of meeting the continuing need for a large "representative" cabinet while allowing smaller groups to give detailed attention to particular business. Second, in the bureaucracy the upgrading of the Privy Council Office, the separation of the Treasury Board secretariat from the Department of Finance, and the introduction of new techniques of policy analysis gave the government more impressive sources of bureaucratic advice. Third, the expansion of the Prime Minister's Office provided the prime minister with a versatile group of politically recruited staff, although it is selective in its intervention in policy matters. These developments began before Prime Minister Trudeau took office, but they were accelerated by and became identified with him (see Matheson 1976; Hockin 1971; Robertson 1971).

The changes have not led to dramatic leaps in governmental performance. Indeed, the elegant, rational, and managerial style in which they were proposed provides a measure of the shortfall between aspirations and results. But on the whole the position of the prime minister has been further enhanced. Canadian cabinets have often been ruled by imperious and energetic prime ministers with a proprietorial approach to official business. The present arrangements increase the resources available to incumbents taking this approach. The growth of the PMO has been criticized as has the tendency for elements of the PCO to acquire obvious political tinges. While the intellectual and bureaucratic prowess of the Ministry of Finance and the Treasury Board secretariat is respected, they have not had spectacular success in managing the economy and regulating public expenditure. Further, the cabinet committee system, although widely admired, has worked unevenly. In particular, the Priorities and Planning Committee, often regarded as a *de facto* inner cabinet, has not established itself as a consistent source of strategic guidance. Shifting informal groupings around the prime minister remain important. What emerges is that particular institutions and officers, especially the prime minister, have gained increased resources with which to tackle policy problems but that this has not increased their ability to exert consistent control over problems of public policy.

Isolation at the Centre

This discussion of British and Canadian experience suggests that cabinet arrangements and influence are much more fragile than is often proposed. This is not surprising. Cabinet is, after all, a committee, and committees in their various forms are noted for the frustrations that they engender. Cabinet is unusual not in its abilities but in the forces operating on it and on the expectations that its mystique arouses. Cabinet is involved in continuous struggles to manage the unmanageable, routinize the extraordinary, systematize the disorderly, and coordinate the incoherent. Cabinet's position as a source of authority attracts not only matters of moment but matters of detail which are nevertheless too gritty to be dealt with elsewhere. How it deals with business is always contingent because it is also the meeting place of a variety of incentive systems. Ministers come to the cabinet room with antagonisms as well as points of agreement. Further, despite cabinet's central position it does not automatically get its way. Its attention even to important matters is intermittent, and it can easily let them slip by. While from cabinet's perspective everything comes, or ought to come, to it, from other perspectives its intervention in affairs is much less substantial. Its attention is restricted to summaries and abstracts of policy issues which often come to it after long processes of consideration elsewhere. Similar processes are likely to continue, whatever is decided. From this point of view, cabinet's intervention may appear to consist of fleeting and even arbitrary acts in long and complex processes with lives of their own. This is not to say that cabinet's position of authority is inconsiderable or that the effect of its concentrated attention on an issue may not be decisive. But cabinet's resources can easily be spread too thinly or marshalled too erratically. In order to maximize its influence cabinet needs constant care and attention and persistent organization and reorganization. This constant care is not secured automatically.

In this process, as recent Canadian experience has made plain, the role of the prime minister has assumed increasing importance. His position gives him more resources than other ministers, and it has been strengthened further by tendencies to institutionalize the provision of support and service for him. The pre-eminence of the position has been developed by the increasing use incumbents have made of the resources they have found to hand. Relations between prime ministers and their cabinets can still vary widely, but prime ministerial preferences are crucial. However, it is easier for a prime minister, by wilfulness or omission, to disrupt the working of cabinet than it is to ensure that it operates smoothly. George Jones has correctly emphasized that prime ministers cannot always get their own way; but, pursuing his comparison between cabinet and various kinds of orchestra, it is necessary to remember that orchestras can easily become discordant. Further, tendencies for prime ministers to gather informal groups about them, forming and re-forming such groups as they choose, can take important business out of cabinet.

These points indicate that cabinet can work in many different ways. There is no one best way to organize it. Some institutional arrangements are, however, stoutly and eloquently defended as essential. These include the collective responsibility of ministers for cabinet decisions, the confidentiality of cabinet proceedings, and, to a lesser extent, the exclusion of officials from taking part in proceedings. As presented, these requirements usually have strong normative aspects. But their strongest foundations are pragmatic.

The main political functions of collective responsibility, confidentiality and exclusiveness are to ensure that the cabinet appears to maintain coherence and unity, since this is generally regarded as a necessary condition if the government is to be re-elected. Arguments and disputes between its members may be conducted in private. But privacy is not all or nothing; cabinets, like other bodies, can choose to have more or less of it. Cabinet members may find it convenient to agree to disagree in public on some issues, to allow more open access to information about how they work, and to involve officials in some of their deliberations. Such choices may be made because the benefits of collective responsibility, for example, may be outweighed on a range of matters by costs in terms of tension, gossip about internal divisions, and inspired leaks. As Crossman has pointed out, collective responsibility can be used as a weapon against ministers as well as in their collective interest. Where issues are handled primarily in committees it can mean simply that ministers not directly involved can have no say, publicly or privately, on what should be done. This can lead to demands for adjustments in procedures. Such adjustments may change the way in which politics proceeds but do not mean the abrogation of all rules. Similar points apply to other aspects of cabinet structure and procedures.

Different institutional arrangements may be made to emphasize particular aspects of cabinet's work. But while procedural changes can help cabinet members transact business, they cannot force good choices, or indeed any choices. Procedures cannot bring items to effective notice if ministers do not wish to recognize them, although to ignore items may have costs too. Similarly, they cannot move business at a pace faster than ministers' other obligations allow. Procedures can provide check-lists and check-points but not formulas for defining and dealing with policy problems. Further, the refinement of procedures in line with managerial principles cannot provide benefits without limit. Procedural sophistication is no proof against the forces generated by the incentive systems of politicians. Better procedures can still lead to worse results if in the meantime policy problems have become less tractable.

CABINET UNDER CHIFLEY

Although our main focus in examining the role of cabinet in

Australia is on developments since 1972, an adequate foundation for the discussion requires some consideration of events in the 1940s. The rapid growth of the scope of federal government activity during the 1939-45 war contributed to the construction of more elaborate cabinet arrangements than had hitherto existed. The effectiveness of cabinet came to depend on more than simply the wit and skill of the prime minister and his colleagues.

Under Chifley the full ministry of nineteen sat in cabinet. During the war much business had been transacted in cabinet committees (including the war cabinet), and Chifley's arrangements included a set of committees which had evolved from the wartime system. These were the Defence Council and four economic committees — Trade and Employment, Industry and Employment, Secondary Industries, and Dollar Budget. Other *ad hoc* committees were appointed from time to time. Although it is not clear to what extent committees took final decisions, it seems that some of them did.

Full cabinet received comparatively little bureaucratic support. The secretary to cabinet, who had begun to attend cabinet meetings during the war, saw his responsibility as the collection and circulation of submissions and the recording of decisions. He believed that the support of cabinet committees should be the function of the department of the minister chairing the committee and did not try to build up a major coordinating role for PMC (Crisp 1967, pp. 31-32).

As a result, cabinet committees were served in more depth than was full cabinet. The Chifley government was fortunate in that it was served by a conspicuously able group of public servants who contributed enthusiastically to thinking about how a confident and ambitious government could fulfil some of its bold declarations of social and economic policy. Much of their confidence sprang from the belief, engendered by the promise of Keynesian economics, that the national economy could now be managed.

The working of the cabinet committee system depended as much on the way ministers and officials approached their tasks as on formal structures. The committees' secretarial services were provided by the department of the convening minister (for the economic committees, usually Treasury or Post-War Reconstruction). More importantly, commitees were supported by parallel committees of senior officials and, below them, by groups of "offsiders", often the proteges of senior officials. At many committee meetings ministers were accompanied not only by senior officials but by "offsiders" as well, and some of these meetings took on the character of "mass seminars" (Crisp 1967, p. 49). Relations between ministers and the public servants most involved with cabinet business were close. The whole group has been described as Chifley's "official family". Ministers accepted the need for expert advice and obtained it from public servants more than from any other single source. Within the "official family" full use was made of the abilities of people at different levels, as ideas were tossed around between ministers and their "offsiders" (RIPA 1955, p. 199).

A notable illustration of how formal and informal roles merged in the provision of guidance and advice for the prime minister is provided by the career of F. H. Wheeler. In the early 1940s he was a personal assistant to the secretary of the Treasury and one of the original group of "offsiders". By the late 1940s his more senior position in the public service, combined with continuing prominence among the "offsiders", put him at the centre of —

> a small group from within and a little outside the "official family" which met from time to time to look over the field of economic problems. Wheeler also usually attended the meetings of the Bank Advisory Committee, which had replaced the Bank Board in 1945, and from that time was on all the main economic officers' committees at official level or closely in touch with them. He very frequently sat beside Chifley at Cabinet Committees and the Treasurer ordinarily had written Wheeler comments on papers before him at those meetings and at full cabinet. Wheeler, of course, drew on the knowledge of other men in the Treasury team and acted in consultation with, and with the endorsement of, the Secretary of the Treasury. [RIPA 1955, p. 203]

Wheeler did not necessarily agree all the time with his public service colleagues or with Chifley, but his activities showed how one person could bring together the different and often conflicting strands of advice available within the "official family". However, the group did not depend solely on his efforts. The particular strength of Chifley's system was that "the matter of consultation had become an ingrained habit; the particular status of people to be consulted had become, up to a point, of secondary importance; and formality was usually kept to a minimum" (RIPA 1955, p. 203). Hierarchy and formality were not absent from or unimportant in these relations. But the substantial organic component in the organization of the "official family" was striking.

The success of these arrangements depended heavily on Chifley's own role in integrating the various elements of government. As prime minister and treasurer he carried a large work-load but in consequence also gained an excellent view of political and bureaucratic proceedings. He handled cabinet and caucus with sensitivity, distributing small favours to prepare the way for when he wanted to ask for big ones, and was able to maintain the personal loyalty of those around him.

The Chifley cabinet's procedures succeeded for four reasons: Chifley's leadership; a pool of talented and probing public servants; a common set of activist ideas, especially about economic management; and the broadening scope of government activity, a legacy of wartime events. Although the lack of success of some of Chifley's policies and the 1949 defeat warn against exaggerating the success of such a system, the combination of these factors meant that cabinet, more than its predecessors, had the capacity to draw together the various threads of policy.

But these factors also meant that there was "nothing perfect or inevitably right about the 1945-49 pattern . . . In large measure it was fortuitous" (RIPA 1955, p. 203). There was no assurance that they could be transferred to different circumstances. The Chifley government's cooperative consultative style of decision making can be seen in retrospect as a delicate if not exceptional growth. Nevertheless, it did provide some structural and procedural answers to the pressing problems of cabinet and policy management which were to be an irritant to its next Labor successor twenty-three years later. That much of the experience of this period was filtered into obscurity is a measure of the ease with which collectivities "forget". A period of rapid learning about political and bureaucratic relationships was followed by a period of leisurely and, some would say, debilitating amnesia.

CABINET UNDER MENZIES

Menzies was unenthusiastic about officials attending any formally constituted ministerial meetings, and although the network of officials established under Labor did not immediately disappear, the distinctive mixing of formal and informal relationships of the Chifley period soon vanished. Moreover, although Menzies set up initially no less than nineteen cabinet committees, this profuse growth soon withered. Attention shifted back to full cabinet — Crisp has noted the major role of Liberal cabinets in the actual discussion of contentious issues (Crisp 1967).

This situation was emphasized by two other steps in the evolution of cabinet. First, Menzies divided the ministry into a inner cabinet and an outer ministry in 1955, when the size of the ministry rose to twenty-two. Cabinet itself was reduced to twelve and remained at that number even when the rest of the ministry increased. Non-cabinet ministers attended cabinet meetings only by invitation, usually to participate in discussion of items of business concerning their departments. The system tried to balance the advantages of a small, powerful cabinet against the disadvantages of non-cabinet ministers not fully appreciating the context in which discussion on their items took place and thus proceeding with departmental work in isolation. Menzies' personal ascendancy in the government ensured that the system worked well enough for him.

The introduction of the system reduced the importance of cabinet committees. Menzies continued to operate both standing and *ad hoc* committees, but as Crisp has pointed out, the list was "rather thin", "thin more especially in the economic policy and co-ordination field where the Chifley picture was strong" (Crisp 1967, p. 49). Crisp has listed five committees known to exist in the mid-1960s: Defence and Foreign Affairs; Legislation; General Administrative; Economic Policy; and Ex-Servicemen's. Of these the General Administrative Committee was the most interesting. Crisp has described it as "a large busy committee made up of some cabinet and most or all non-Cabinet Ministers. It [met] weekly during Parliamentary Sessions to despatch very usefully a great deal of 'second order' business" (Crisp 1967, p. 49). Its task was to relieve cabinet of business that required the authority of a cabinet decision but did not have a substantial policy content or need sustained attention. No firm estimate is available of what proportion of cabinet business fell into this category, but it appears that it was reasonably large. The Defence and Foreign Affairs Committee was also noticeable because of its composition (prime minister, deputy prime minister, treasurer, ministers for external affairs and defence, and one or two others) and because, exceptionally in Menzies' arrangements, it had a parallel committee of officials. The Legislation committee had the important but mainly procedural task of examining drafts of proposed legislation, while Crisp suggests that the roles of the

Economic Policy and Ex-Servicemen's committees had more to do with public relations than with substantive policy. The reduction in cabinet size combined with the creation of the General Administrative Committee allowed Menzies to do without an elaborate structure of committees.

Second, Menzies enhanced cabinet's capacity by widening the context in which cabinet considered the annual budget. During the 1950s, cabinet received more and different information than previously as the budget's role as an instrument of national economic policy, evident under Chifley, was consolidated under the Liberals. Whereas Chifley had made one main submission on the budget, under Menzies the number and range of submissions increased dramatically, including the introduction of a statement of total cash prospects for the federal government. This presented a wider analysis than the statement of consolidated revenue which hitherto had been cabinet's main starting point. Cabinet also regularly received papers on the state of the economy and reviewed economic prospects before making actual budget allocations. Managing the economy became recognized as a year-round occupation. The fullness of cabinet's consideration of the budget contrasted with the much smaller role given to British cabinets and was regarded with great satisfaction by senior Treasury officers (see R. J. Randall, quoted in Crisp 1961, p. 325).

At the same time, Menzies developed the cabinet secretariat on lines earlier proposed by Labor to fill the gap left by the minimal role of the cabinet secretary up to that time. Following the appointment of Allen Brown as secretary of the department in 1949, "the Secretariat [had] for the first time serviced all Cabinet Committees as well as Cabinet meetings proper. Practices associated with the receipt, processing and circulation of Cabinet and Cabinet Committee submissions and with the processing and circulation of decisions or reports were centralized, regularized and generally tightened up" (Crisp 1967, p. 48). Menzies approved these arrangements, and under him Brown and his successor, Sir John Bunting, developed the position of secretary of the Prime Minister's Department into one of the most prestigious in the public service. For the first time the prime minister had in his own department officers able to brief him on all streams of cabinet and cabinet committee business. The nature of such briefing and the deficiencies later identified in it by some of Menzies' successors are considered in another chapter. The establishment of a systematically organized and prestigious cabinet secretariat was nevertheless in itself an important institutional development.

The main burden of communicating information about cabinet proceedings, both formally and informally, rested with the secretary to cabinet. His central role has been described in the following terms: "The Secretary, alone of public servants, will be privy at first hand to the full range of the top layer of Government business as it unfolds in and around Cabinet documents and discussions. Indeed, he works with the Prime Minister and Cabinet very much as 'one of the team' " (Crisp 1967, p. 50).

While departmental heads might receive either copious or parsimonious reports from their ministers, the most authoritative source of information would remain the cabinet secretary. He could write some of the flavour of discussion into the formal record; where this was inappropriate he could supply confidential briefings to departmental heads; he could mediate between competing interests; and he could offer informed advice to the prime minister about tactics and procedures for handling particular issues (Crisp 1967, p. 51). Under Menzies, Bunting developed the office of secretary with skill and diplomacy, assisted by his deputy when a second recording officer was admitted to cabinet. But their methods of working emphasized the particularity and privileged nature of the information they passed on to departments. The main linking point between cabinet and the public service remained extremely narrow. Although Menzies' term in office saw the institutionalization in the Prime Minister's Department of a cabinet secretariat, this did not counteract the tendency through.out the period for effective contacts between cabinet and public servants to contract.

Under Menzies, personal rather than institutional bonds and points of contact were important, but compared with the Chifley period these moved upwards to become the preserve of senior ministers and public servants. Many of the problems of policy development and coordination addressed by Chifley's arrangements were not even clearly identified under Menzies. Despite the evolution of the Prime Minister's Department, the creation of an inner cabinet, and the increased flow of information to budget cabinet, relations at the centre were not systematically worked out. The sense of calm, routine, and propriety characterizing relations within the government disguised the tendencies towards institutional fragmentation and decay at the centre. So long as the flow of government activity did not grow too drastically in volume, while the bureaucracy remained insulated from the impact of political battles, and political strife did not extend into the political elite of the governing parties itself, these tendencies were not vital. But after Menzies was gone they emerged disconcertingly into the open.

AFTER MENZIES

Following Menzies' retirement, problems at the centre did not take long to emerge. None of Menzies' immediate Liberal successors found workable roles as prime minister or found effective means of organizing cabinet's work. Between 1965 and 1972 the Liberal Party endured three successions, two of them bitter and intense, instead of the expected one. Menzies' chosen successor, Harold Holt, disappeared while swimming in heavy surf late in 1967. Although his administration had been returned overwhelmingly at the 1966 elections, by the time he disappeared his grasp on the government's affairs had clearly slipped. John Gorton, who followed him, did no better and was in turn replaced by William McMahon in 1971. McMahon continued the government's downhill run to defeat in 1972. Under the pressure of such events, the personal and institutional arrangements that Menzies had maintained were soon in trouble. But the government's problems from the mid-1960s did not depend solely on Menzies' departure. The kind of politics on which Menzies had thrived gave way to more turbulent times. His successors were faced with shifting and less congenial circumstances both at home and abroad and with a reviving opposition. Not only had Menzies gone, but many of his methods could no longer be applied. The central political and bureaucratic arrangements he had used with such effect gave little useful guidance to those who followed him.

Gorton came to the prime ministership by an unorthodox route from the Senate, where as leader of the government he had gained a reputation for decisive and effective leadership. However, as prime minister his individualistic and erratic performance dashed the high expectations of his supporters which had won him the position. On a number of occasions he made enemies by taking uncompromising positions and then made more by precipitately backing down. While he made some important decisions quickly and on the run, on other matters he exhibited a disconcerting indecisiveness. These contradictory aspects of his approach to office upset cabinet, which soon came to regard him with scant respect.

Similarly, within the bureaucracy his efforts to shape the Prime Minister's Department to his own design and to choose departmental heads compatible with his aspirations produced few positive effects. The removal of Bunting to a specially created cabinet office and his replacement as head of the Prime Minister's Department by C. L. S. Hewitt seriously disturbed senior public servants. Regardless of the merits of such appointments, they stimulated talk of a "Gorton-Hewitt complex, people who are on side" (Jonathan Gaul, *Canberra Times*, 25 March 1969). Gorton also upset and disconcerted many people within the non-parliamentary Liberal Party. Even party officials who valued his early popularity with the electorate acknowledged the difficulties his changing stances posed for party members who were used to the set-piece views of the Menzies period. In early 1969, for example, the state president of the New South Wales division of the Liberal Party, F. M. Osborne, told a group of endorsed candidates: "You may at times find it difficult to follow the Prime Minister's approach, but you must do your best" (Maximilian Walsh, *Financial Review*, 14 February 1969).

Gorton soon used up most of the political credit with which he began. He neither delivered rewards that satisfied his party and government nor, for long, could hold out compelling hopes that such rewards would be forthcoming. He became isolated and frustrated. As the *Financial Review* commented, he was a prime minister "marooned at the centre of Government" (7 November 1969). Further, the criticism stimulated by his attempts to move chosen politicians and public servants into positions of influence showed how easily a deliberate attempt to construct a reliable prime ministerial network could fail. Whereas Chifley's arrangements were characterized as an "official family", Gorton received relentless criticism for advancing his "cronies". The difference between the labels is revealing.

Within the Liberal Party McMahon had a reputation as an able administrator. He was respected rather than liked, but his commitment to the style and values of the Menzies period promised those who had been confused by Gorton's activities a return to things they knew. Further, he emphasized his own commitment to working through cabinet and in this respect seemed to have identified some of the points where Gorton had erred. But as with Gorton, these expectations were unfulfilled. Within a short time McMahon was as isolated and frustrated as Gorton had been. He declared that he was prepared to override the wishes of cabinet and like Gorton made a number of well-publicized decisions unilaterally. During the 1972 election campaign he even accused some of his colleagues of incompetence, suggesting they lacked political sensitivity. Throughout his term as prime minister, cabinet leaks were a source of friction within the government, and sections of the press assiduously canvassed the possibility that McMahon himself was the source of much leaked information. He was unwilling to delegate responsibility to ministers and did not take them into his confidence. Only a narrow circle of ministers had regular access to him. He tried to refurbish government policy through committees of backbenchers, but despite the assistance of a firm of management consultants, the attempt did not produce conspicuous results. Although his relations with senior public servants were better than Gorton's had been, his principal contacts were still confined to a few men. Neither Gorton nor McMahon had the skill possessed by both Chifley and Menzies of developing and maintaining a wide range of personal contacts among senior public servants, and McMahon's performance emphasized the gap between the effective discharge of even senior ministerial posts and the prime ministership. As prime minister he did not have the support of a department with a well-defined set of interests and responsibilities and able to supply him with a single, if complex, brief. Partly this was a matter of departmental organization. The Prime Minister's Department, as he had reconstituted it after amalgamating the separate departments created by Gorton, was unable to provide him with the authoritative briefs he was used to. But more significantly his problems lay in the more diffuse nature of the prime ministerial role. The task of reviewing the whole range of government activity exposed his limited ability to move out from the experience of his earlier, more easily defined responsibilities.

The troubles of the Liberal prime ministers succeeding Menzies also included more difficult relations with the Country Party. Both Holt and Gorton had to contend with the ageing but still ambitious Sir John McEwen, whose political toughness and skill far outstripped their own. The agreement between the parliamentary leaders of the Liberal and Country parties on the basis of the coalition was the subject of a written but private memorandum. When Holt succeeded Menzies the terms of the agreement remained unchanged as they did when Gorton in turn succeeded Holt. However, after the 1969 election McEwen insisted that Gorton's individualistic handling of government business be curbed by including in the agreement the stipulation that all significant government decisions must be made in cabinet (*Age*, 5 April 1971). The baldness of the stipulation indicated the extent to which Gorton had tried to bypass cabinet. When McMahon became prime minister, J. D. Anthony, who in the meantime had succeeded McEwen, took the opportunity to insert a section reminding the Liberals of the impact on country dwellers of the rural recession then current (*Age*, 5 April 1971).

Despite the long record of cooperation between the two parties, in opposition as well as in government, the activities in cabinet of Country Party ministers could also still cause irritation. Just as organizationally the Country Party resisted absorption by the Liberals, so Country Party ministers preserved their ability to caucus together and to act as a group. While they did not always exercise this ability, and on occasion took pains to emphasize the absence of partisan differences within cabinet, their capacity to act together when they saw the strategic interests of the party at stake was undoubted. They were not always quick to formulate group demands but were unrelenting once they had done so. They had the reputation of an unrivalled ability to pursue demands single-mindedly. In effect, Country Party ministers in cabinet had it both ways. They could play as part of the team and even, as with Gorton, complain that they were not offered full cooperation in return. But they could also choose to remember their own separate identity. As one participant put it, it was possible to get away with a lot, if the minister were senior enough — and in the Country Party. Indeed, such resources, if used judiciously, could be used to prevail over even the prime minister and the treasurer, who in combination were usually unbeatable. This ability did not depend on the possibility of the party's withdrawing from the coalition. This was an empty threat, for the party had nowhere to go. But the Liberals too needed the Country Party, and when Country Party ministers were determined to win a particular battle the Liberals had to calculate whether the price of resistance in terms of friction and discord was worth the advantages to be gained from standing fast.

The period after Menzies' retirement placed cabinet arrangements under considerable strain. The inadequacies in prime ministerial leadership, strife within and between the governing parties, and difficulties in relating political to bureaucratic forces made it hard for any of the central institutions of government to function in a consistent and considered manner. The major political actors lived from day to day without finding a sense of direction either in new initiatives or in a return to old patterns. Both Gorton and McMahon tried frequently to bypass cabinet, and their personal consultations with other ministers were often inconclusive. Both tried to gather small groups of supporters around them, but this produced more opprobrium than an ability to play a strategic role in the direction of policy.

In this context it was not surprising that few institutional innovations regarding cabinet were made. The size of the ministry increased to twenty-six under Gorton and twenty-seven under McMahon, but the size of cabinet remained unchanged. Little information about the working of cabinet committees is available. It is likely that the list of functioning committees was even thinner than it was under Menzies. (In March 1968 Gorton appointed a committee on social services chaired by the minister for health, Dr. A. J. Forbes, to coordinate the work of all departments dealing with social services, but little was heard of it again [*Age*, 15 March 1968].) McMahon experimented with assistant ministers and appointed six of them. However, their duties did not touch cabinet's functions directly, and some of them were appointed to head off electoral contests between the coalition parties rather than for their ability.

After the coalition lost office, a common complaint within the Liberal Party was that its ministers had grown too close to their public service departments and had lost contact with views and interests within the party and among wider groups in society. The truth of this observation, however, should not obscure the point that some ministers had no firm contacts with their departments. Just as their party workers complained that they were hard to reach in Canberra, their departments claimed that they were never in Canberra. These contradictory complaints epitomized the disjunction of actors and institutions within the coalition government up to 1972. Not only was cabinet under Holt, Gorton, and

McMahon not an effective institution, but it was disjoined, as were other bodies also, from the institutions and forces with which it was supposed to be working.

CABINET DURING THE WHITLAM GOVERNMENT

The election of a Labor government in 1972 brought an immediate change to the style, rhetoric, and scope of government activity. While the post-Menzies Liberal governments had appeared to lose their way, Labor promised new and ambitious approaches to policy and administration. Structures of government were to be reviewed and revised; old programmes and commitments associated with sectional and privileged interests were to be scrutinized and cut back; and new programmes catering for what Labor identified as neglected areas of need were to be developed. While some of Labor's actions had a high symbolic content, much activity involved sharp increases in public expenditure. The combination of abrupt shifts in levels of activity and expenditure generated sustained pressure on the central machinery of government. From an early stage in the life of the government its cabinet arrangements attracted vociferous and often contradictory complaints and suggestions for change. Whereas the Curtin and Chifley Labor governments had inherited the arrangements of a disoriented coalition and turned them into effective means of government, the Whitlam government never really settled down. Its own efforts added to rather than reduced the disjunctions evident at the centre of government from the middle 1960s.

Labor took office with no recent experience of government and, it turned out, few procedures for learning as it went or even recalling and adapting the methods used in the immediate post-war years. The burden of learning fell on the ministry and the parliamentary party. Although in the ALP the extra-parliamentary organization determines the platform which the party in office must carry out, the organization is insulated from opportunities of understanding the forces that the ministry encounters. This suits both ministers and members of parliament. It leaves the parliamentary caucus as the main party body with claims to oversee the work of a Labor ministry. But it too has only glimpses of the forces faced by the ministry. Both the extra-parliamentary party and caucus are thus often seen by ministers and by outside commentators as hindrances rather than potential sources of assistance for a Labor government. If such views are too harsh, it nevertheless seems that whereas the advantages to be gained from Labor's domestic arrangements have to be worked for, problems are often self-generating. While the Whitlam government was fortunate in its relations with the extra-parliamentary organization, problems in reconciling the claims of cabinet and caucus recurred throughout its term.

Cabinet's relations with caucus threw into sharp relief the style and preoccupations of the prime minister. Whitlam pushed to the limit the resources his position gave him. Despite his massive talents and creative commitment to social reform through government activity, his wilful style and flawed understanding of his own party exacerbated the structural problems inherent in cabinet's relations with caucus. Whitlam's character and outlook are also relevant to an understanding of relations between the Labor ministry and the public service.

The difficulties faced by cabinet in its relations with caucus and the public service were compounded by its own problems of organization. Under Whitlam, cabinet was not a body that identified and dealt with strategic policy problems on a consistent basis. Cabinet was part of a wider pattern of activity, including members of caucus, senior public servants, and changing groupings of ministers and advisers around the prime minister. Not until the last year of the government was the prime minister able to match up coherent sets of ministers and public servants in a group of ministerial and official committees. The difficulties in organizing cabinet contributed to the government's early insensitivity towards the reactions of community and other interest groups to the rush of activity in 1973 and 1974, and to its inability to cope with a deteriorating national economy. Labor took office assuming that the economic growth of the 1950s and 1960s would continue without interruption. The fulfilment of its most prominent commitments depended on this. The government's inability to identify and respond promptly to a serious economic downturn with severe implications for its programmes raised questions not only about the quality of its political judgment but about the way cabinet and related institutions were organized.

Cabinet Structure

Labor took office with a ministry of twenty-seven sitting as an undivided cabinet. The size of the cabinet was determined by caucus before the election in 1972, and it was reported later that the decision to have an undivided ministry was carried by only one vote (David Solomon, *Canberra Times,* 2 August 1974). The considerations leading to these decisions have not been extensively canvassed, but although electoral victory was in view, caucus does not seem to have lifted its deliberations far beyond the concerns of opposition. In these terms twenty-seven portfolios meant twenty-seven jobs. There may also have been a wish to surround Whitlam with a large and undivided cabinet as a means of moderating the individualistic tendencies in his leadership. If this was the intention, it was not fulfilled. The apparent carelessness with which Labor took over the number of portfolios that the coalition government had established over the years by incremental steps foreshadowed some of the difficulties that were to come.

In electing the members of cabinet, caucus gave preference to seniority. Caucus is a great leveller and is customarily suspicious of newcomers with great reputations. Even newly elected parliamentarians of conspicuous ability and established records in the extra-parliamentary party cannot expect preferment in caucus until they have served long enough to establish a record of caucus performance. Within the Labor Party the only votes for positions of parliamentary leadership are caucus votes.

Accordingly, the members of cabinet elected first in 1973 included members of the caucus executive in opposition. Although the tickets drawn up for the election took regional and factional considerations into account, the main consideration was eminence in opposition. The election of ministers by caucus gives a Labor prime minister both advantages and disadvantages. On the one hand he is relieved of personal responsibility for choosing between competing individuals; on the other he has to allocate portfolios among a fixed pool of ministers. Further, he has limited scope for reshuffling responsibilities and cannot dismiss ministers to make way for new ones. While a Liberal prime minister has to pay careful attention to state, Country Party, and other interests in the balance of the ministry, and cannot without cost replace ministers at will, he has appreciably more flexibility than his Labor counterpart.

The restraints on prime ministerial preferences in the composition of cabinet were apparent throughout the Whitlam government. Although at the outset most of the members Whitlam preferred for cabinet were elected, he had to modify his proposed administrative arrangements to create jobs for   them all. Responsibility for the environment was separated from urban and regional development and for health from social security. Two planned departments became four. Several other departments, including one or two of doubtful significance, were created for the same reasons. Although caucus had no effective say in the actual allocation of ministerial positions, its determinations structured the context in which Whitlam had to work.

Formally Labor's arrangements allowed the prime minister to re-allocate portfolios from time to time, but in practice reshuffles were hard to carry out. Senior ministers resented being shifted to other jobs (the most notable example of resistance came from Clyde Cameron, who was demoted from the senior labour portfolio to the ministry of science), and in any case the choice of replacements was limited to those already in the ministry. Unless vacancies occurred through resignations or electoral defeat, there was no room for new members. The effect of these limits became obvious once the government had been at work for some time. To begin with, one observer thought that the inclusion of a number of departments likely to be rearranged within a year or so, in particular as departmental work was devolved to statutory corporations, would offer scope for future reorganizations of the ministry (David Solomon, *Canberra Times*, 20 December 1972). This proved to be a vain hope. So did the opportunity to review ministerial performance after the election in 1974. Caucus re-elected all ministers except A. J. Grassby, who had been defeated at the polls. This was not simply an example of caucus myopia. Ministers constituted the largest single bloc in caucus, and reportedly one of their number successfully put it to them that they should support one another. Caucus's system of voting assisted this move. Unless supporters of change in the ministry could agree on whom they would promote to it, their votes were likely to be dispersed ineffectively among a large number of ministerial aspirants. For these reasons movements for a "spill", especially in 1975 when the composition of cabinet was discussed incessantly, were also frustrated (for a contemporary comment see Paul Kelly, *Australian*, 30 May 1975). Over the three years Labor was in office, the five new ministers elected (Wheeldon, J. R. McClelland, Riordan, Berinson, and Keating) came in as a result of single vacancies. In the two cases where these arose from resignations from parliament as well as from cabinet (Murphy and Barnard), the political costs for the government were especially heavy.[1] The removal of Cairns after his earlier demotion and the resignation of Connor, both senior ministers whose support had been important to Whitlam early in the life of the government, were also costly. Whitlam's sacking of Cairns after he had misled parliament showed that in an extreme case a Labor prime minister could dismiss a minister. But the dismissal effectively required ratification by caucus and exposed the hazy understandings within the Labor Party about what should be done in such cases — and nothing has since been done to clarify the situation. Moreover, it is doubtful whether caucus would have accepted the removal of ministers merely because of prime ministerial dissatisfaction with their performance.

From the beginning there were misgivings about the size of cabinet, and as the government ran deeper into trouble, proposals for setting up an inner cabinet received considerable attention. The prime minister himself supported the idea and said publicly that a cabinet of half the size would be twice as good (*Age*, 4 June 1975). The logistic difficulties of a gathering of twenty-seven were obvious. The cabinet was far larger than the size regarded as convenient by experienced committee-men; if every minister spoke on an issue for five minutes, over two hours of scarce time was used up. Moreover, the large tail in the ministry suggested that cabinet as constituted was not the place for full and frank discussion of critical policy issues. In 1975 a report by the caucus rules committee recommended the establishment of an inner cabinet of twelve. After the election of the four parliamentary leaders, caucus would elect a further eight members of cabinet and then the rest of the ministry (*Age*, 4 June 1975). However, after extensive discussion of the report, caucus referred the report back for further consideration. Although Whitlam's endorsement of the proposal was supported by the treasurer, Bill Hayden, a number of ministers, including the influential minister for urban and regional development, Tom Uren,

---

1. Senator Murphy was replaced by a "political neuter" after the New South Wales Liberal premier broke with convention and refused to replace him with another Labor man. Barnard's seat of Bass (Tasmania) was lost with a large swing against the Labor government.

opposed it (*Age*, 30 September 1975). Before the proposal could be taken further the government fell.

It is by no means clear that the creation of an inner cabinet in the Menzies tradition would have overcome Labor's problems. It was an available rather than an imaginative solution, and it did not mesh well with established caucus practices. How cabinet business was organized was probably more important than cabinet's size and at least as important as its composition. Recent British cabinets have been only slightly smaller than Labor's cabinet, while federal Canadian cabinets have for several years been even larger. While in both cases criticism of cabinet size has been common, attention has not been focused exclusively on it. The attractiveness of smaller, more authoritative cabinets of senior ministers has been balanced against problems of important departments deprived of cabinet representation or, as in Canada, the exclusion of party elements with acknowledged claims to representation. For a Labor inner cabinet two problems stand out. First, the performance of a smaller cabinet, and especially its working relations with the prime minister, would depend in large part on who was in it. An elected inner cabinet would add further rigidity to an already highly constrained set of arrangements. While within an elected cabinet of twenty-seven there was only limited scope for shuffling portfolios, in a cabinet of twelve ministers those who did not do well would be even harder to shift. This point gains force when it is recalled that some of the most disappointing ministers in Whitlam's cabinet were among those elected to the ministry in the first dozen, not once but twice. These objections would have less force if, within a larger ministry, the prime minister were allowed to choose (and remove) members of cabinet. But even Liberal prime ministers on occasion have difficulty in dislodging members of cabinet whose time to move has come. Second, a Labor minister outside cabinet would be tempted not only to take decisions on his own and pre-empt cabinet discussions, as Liberal ministers sometimes have done, but to appeal to caucus if he thought cabinet had not considered his case adequately. The problems of British ministers who attend cabinet only to put their case and, unfamiliar with the day-to-day working of cabinet, receive inadequate attention, have often been discussed. For Labor ministers in a similar situation, recourse to caucus would be an obvious step. In caucus discussions during 1975 this consideration was used as a persuasive argument against the proposals then put forward. Arrangements that proved satisfactory for Menzies and had been continued by his Liberal successors could well cause more trouble than they were worth for a Labor government.

Standing Committees

More important than debate about creating an inner cabinet was the evolution under Whitlam of thinking about systems of cabinet committees. Although this was slow and uneven by the time the government was dismissed, the elements of an effective committee system were beginning to emerge. The importance of a system of committees for a large and busy cabinet had been recognized by Whitlam before he took office. From the outset, Labor used cabinet committees more extensively and more openly than the coalition. But the experience showed the ease with which apparently admirable arrangements could fall into disuse. Matching up procedural and political incentives supporting a workable committee system proved more difficult than was first thought. Ministers had not only to be convinced of the usefulness and fairness of a committee system but also to find time for committee meetings in schedules of work that were already overcrowded. The longer parliamentary sitting times introduced by Labor combined with meetings of full cabinet, caucus, and caucus committees presented ministers with punishing rounds of meetings each week.

The Whitlam cabinet began work with a system of five standing committees — Economic, Welfare, Urban and Regional Development, Foreign Affairs and Defence, and Legislation. These arrangements followed proposals developed by Dr Peter Wilenski (who when Labor gained office became Whitlam's principal private secretary) while on leave from the public service in 1972. Wilenski's intention was to establish a framework "which [would] facilitate logical ministerial consideration (if ministers wish[ed] to exercise their powers) of all major recommendations, alternatives to them, and their side-effects on other policy areas" (David Solomon, *Canberra Times,* 12 January 1973). His ideas drew explicitly on federal Canadian experience and particularly on the much-noticed outline of arrangements in Ottawa by Gordon Robertson, formerly clerk of the privy council. He proposed establishing standing committees in all policy areas, routing all cabinet business through committees, participation in decision making by all ministers, regular meetings, and the establishment, where appropriate, of co-ordinating committees. At a press conference the prime minister described the proposed system in the following terms:

> The procedure will be that when submissions for cabinet come to me from ministers I will send them to the relevant committee. The committee will hopefully make a recommendation on them. They will then be listed on the cabinet agenda and the recommendation also listed, and unless anybody wants it debated further the recommendation will become the cabinet decision. . . . The members of the committee are under an obligation to attend the meetings of the committee but any other minister will be entitled to attend and hopefully will do so when the documents indicate his department is involved. [*Canberra Times,* 12 January 1973]

The intention was to avoid overcrowding cabinet's agenda without excluding any minister with a valid interest in business before a particular committee. Wilenski recognized that the proposals had disadvantages as well as advantages and specifically listed problems of competing demands on ministerial time, the possibilities of a slowing down of decision making and of excessive public service influence on committee deliberations, and the risk of obvious divergences of view between ministers and their senior public servants. He emphasized that how the system would work would depend on how ministers saw it.

> Whether the system works is finally up to ministers. It is unlikely (after the first month or two) that all ministers will wish to attend all meetings, which would clog up the system. The greater danger is that they may give the committees a decreasing amount of attention — but of course any cabinet has the right to decide what control it wishes to have over policy and what aspects they wish to pass to the Public Service. [*Canberra Times,* 12 January 1973]

As an attempt to provide ministers with opportunities to divide their work without creating closed specialized groups within cabinet, Wilenski's proposals were elegant and persuasive. In the disposition of committee responsibilities, senior ministers received proportionately more positions than other ministers, but most ministers were happy with the way the prime minister allocated the work. During 1973 the arrangements worked reasonably well; however, after the election in May 1974 the system withered. From mid-1974 *ad hoc* committees became much more important than they had previously been. This is illustrated succinctly by comparing the work of *ad hoc* committees before and after June 1974. In the period before June 1974 they met forty-seven times and made 29 decisions; in the period from June 1974 to May 1975 they met sixty-two times and made 117 decisions. From mid-1974 only the legislation committee continued to have an active and effective life. As with similar committees under the Liberals, its functions were mainly technical and procedural. Although the decline of the other standing committees was decisive, it was never the subject of cabinet discussion and none of the committees was ever formally disbanded.

Many reasons may be given for the withering of the system. First, items did not go to a committee unless the prime minister referred them. When explaining the system, Whitlam had made that clear. Thus at his own discretion and without giving reasons he was able to control the flow of business to committees. An indication of Whitlam's thinking by mid-1974 is given by a special meeting he called within days of the 1974 election before it was even certain that the government had been returned. The meeting was held at the prime minister's house in Sydney and was attended by five ministers and a small number of public servants and other advisers. The subject was inflation, which during the election campaign Whitlam had recognized belatedly as a central issue facing the government. In a few hours the issues were thrashed out between all present, ministers had the advantage of immediate and collective access to different strands of advice, and a number of decisions were taken. The meeting cut through the more long-winded processes entailed by the committee/full cabinet approach and included only those people whom the prime minister thought had a real contribution to make. Although when details of the meeting leaked out other ministers were furious, it was clear that the prime minister regarded the format of the meeting as one to be repeated (for an account of the meeting see Robert Haupt, *Financial Review*, 14 June 1974).

Second, when the standing committees were set up there was a failure to integrate the aims of the system with operating requirements, especially with the demanding timetable of expanded parliamentary sittings. At the outset cabinet decided that neither it nor its committees would meet while parliament was sitting. In any case it would have been difficult to hold committee meetings during sitting hours because of the size of the committees (except for one, all had nine or more members) and the rule that any minister was entitled to attend any committee. When other commitments of ministers

COMPOSITION OF STANDING COMMITTEES OF THE WHITLAM CABINET

Economic Committee	Welfare Committee	Foreign Affairs and Defence Committee	Urban and Regional Development Committee	Legislation Committee
Prime minister	Minister for social security	Prime minister	Prime minister	Deputy prime minister
			Treasurer	Attorney-general
Deputy prime minister	Treasurer	Minister for defence	Minister for services and property	Special minister of state
Minister for secondary industry	Minister for the media	Minister for overseas trade	Minister for urban and regional development	
	Minister for repatriation			
Minister for social security	Minister for labour	Treasurer	Minister for transport	Minister for the Capital Territory and minister for the Northern Territory
Treasurer	Minister for education	Attorney-general	Minister for works	
Attorney-general and minister for customs and excise	Minister for tourism and recreation	Special minister of state	Minister for housing	
Special minister of state	Minister for Aboriginal affairs	Minister for repatriation	Minister for the Capital Territory and minister for the Northern Territory	
Minister for northern development	Minister for immigration	Minister for minerals and energy	Postmaster-general	
Minister for labour				
Minister for urban and regional development				
Minister for primary industry	Minister for health	Minister for external territories	Minister for the environment and conservation	
Minister for minerals and energy				

were taken into account (including cabinet meetings) this left little time for committee meetings.

Third, as mentioned above, the arrangements were cumbersome. Although discussions in the committees did clear the way for dispatch of cabinet business, the system was hard to work. Committees could not take substantive decisions, but their recommendations were endorsed as a matter of routine unless a minister raised a specific objection. When a well-attended committee made a decision (attendances could be as large as nineteen), there was a strong desire to make an announcement as soon as possible. This led to the stratagem of declaring that those present constituted a cabinet and could endorse it forthwith. The press of business in 1973 and early 1974 made the arrangements especially hard to operate.

Fourth, the problem of finding suitable times for meetings led to a tendency for committees to meet just before cabinet meetings and for oral rather than written reports to be given by the prime minister. But when committee meetings took place well before cabinet met and controversial topics were discussed, the risk of leaks was high. This raised also the possibility of inspired leaks designed to influence the decisions of full cabinet. Further, the system could not cope with submissions needing urgent decisions. These were taken straight to cabinet.

Fifth, discussion on some occasions was so general and un-specialized that decisions from such meetings had little authority. In these cases committee work was seen as too much effort for too little return. Conversely, the economic committee was often attended by so many ministers that its deliberations were lengthy and resembled those in full cabinet. This caused particular difficulty when for a time it had a far greater workload than any of the other committees. However, after the establishment of the Expenditure Review Committee (discussed later) it had much less significant business to handle.

Sixth, no provision was made either for a priorities or co-ordinating committee or for a general administrative committee which could deal with non-controversial items. One estimate of the proportion of non-controversial submissions (which could possibly have been dispatched by a general administrative committee) suggested that these included 35-40 per cent of all submissions. A later estimate suggested that a general administrative committee could well have dealt with between 50 per cent and 70 per cent of all submissions (see Smith 1977*a*).

This list of reasons for the decline of the standing committee system contains both procedural and political factors and emphasizes the role of the prime minister's changing preferences. While some of the difficulties that emerged had been identified and anticipated by Wilenski at the beginning, others had not, especially the effects of continuing large attendances at crucial meetings, the low level of some committee discussions, and problems of time-tabling. The experience of the standing committees also illustrates the difficulties of institutional borrowing. Transplanted institutions need detailed adjustment to local conditions. The role of the politico-bureaucratic immunologist is a sensitive one. It is note-worthy that Wilenski did not refer explicitly to Chifley's "official family". Commentaries on the Chifley experience made plain the contingency of these arrangements and the difficulty of transferring them to another time and administration. It is relevant also that Wilenski worked in comparative isolation and that his ideas had their influence mainly through the prime minister himself. Although when he drew up specific proposals in the pre-election period in 1972 Wilenski was a rising middle-level public servant, he did not have access to the views and experience of senior officers in the Department of the Prime Minister and Cabinet. Further, he was at some remove from caucus and other Labor Party machinery. Not until he actually joined the prime minister's staff did he have an op-portunity to develop close contacts with relevant bureaucratic and party organizations, and by that time the government was hard at work. Day-to-day matters left no more time for detailed thinking about basic institutional arrangements.

Moreover, two important aspects of his proposals were not taken up in the initial committee arrangements. These concerned the desirability of making provision for a priorities or coordinating committee and encouraging direct discussion between groups of ministers and public servants. Wilenski referred to the Priorities and Planning Committee of the Canadian federal cabinet which, according to an official source, gave "a sense of direction to the cabinet in assisting to develop an overall set of priorities and a plan of action to guide the work of the Cabinet and of the government as a whole" (quoted in Smith 1977*a*, p. 25). Wilenski described it in similar terms but emphasized that it dealt "with long-term issues and not those requiring immediate political action" (*Canberra Times*, 12 January 1973) and was not intended to be an inner cabinet. He observed that the committee was chaired by the prime minister and that attendance was restricted. Although as was noted earlier the committee is often regarded as a *de facto* inner cabinet and its effectiveness has fluctuated, it might have provided an interesting model from which to develop Australian proposals. However, some of its difficulties may have attracted more attention than its usefulness. To the extent that such a committee begins considering matters of immediate moment, it looks more and more like an inner cabinet, and the tendency to retreat to shorter-term issues is strong and often noted. The one early body that might have tested some of these arguments was the Committee on Forward Estimates, which consisted of a closed group of senior ministers and was to be linked with the work of the Priorities Review Staff. The committee met only once, however, and the state of the forward estimates and the attitude of many people towards them did not allow thorough consideration to take place (see Bruce Juddery, *Canberra Times*, 15 August 1975; Weller and Cutt 1976, pp. 114-16).

Since the Chifley government, though public servants had on occasion attended meetings of cabinet committees, they had not been encouraged to take part in discussions. Wilenski advocated more direct discussions between ministers and public servants so that before items reached full cabinet, ministers would have increased opportunities to explore wider ranges of options and information. Other than in exceptional cases he did not propose that public servants would speak in full cabinet. His intention was that ministers should themselves be able to take an interest in matters that were often resolved in interdepartmental committees. But, as he recognized, ministers might not want to do this, and public servants might be embarrassed by the disclosure of differences between them or they might dominate discussions. Recent Canadian experience reinforces conclusions from the Chifley period that the collective intermingling of ministerial and public service considerations has more advantages than disadvantages for most concerned. Canadian public servants appear to have a well-understood set of pragmatic rules about how far they can go in supporting their own ministers, putting others down, or diverging from the views of their official superiors. Despite Wilenski's prodding, the Whitlam cabinet did not face the issue squarely. From an early stage ministers were happy to hand over difficult matters to interdepartmental committees. Although frustrated by the unwillingness of departments, notably the Treasury, to canvass different options, they were unwilling themselves to go out and search for options among public servants. Part of the attraction to the prime minister and his staff of the Sydney meeting mentioned above was that it showed what ministers would do to absorb "the conflicting and normally unrepresented noise which emerges within departments on major policy matters" (*Financial Review*, 14 June 1974). However, even then the search for suitable arenas for repeat performances proceeded slowly. The reason was that at this point several of the organizational problems of the government fused. The prime minister was aware of the need to adjust the government's priorities and wanted to do this by choosing his own teams of ministers and public servants, but ministers excluded from the teams protested vigorously and public service resistance was usually strong; on key economic matters, especially from the Treasury, it was intense. Once having shied away from or failed to recognize the need for some kind of priorities committee (whether to deal with long-term or short-term issues) and for collective ministerial opportunities for seeking and sifting different streams of public service advice, the government found it hard to reach systematic conclusions about what to try next.

Ad Hoc Committees

Whereas Wilenski's work had provided an explicit rationale for a system of committees, the arrangements that evolved from mid-1974 were not shaped to a predetermined pattern. From the beginning Whitlam had made use of *ad hoc* committees of cabinet and informal gatherings of ministers of his own choosing. The relationships generated by this approach went through several phases as particular ministers, issues, and arrangements fluctuated in the prime minister's estimation. However, during 1975 a small number of *ad hoc* committees paralleled by committees of officials assumed increasing importance in the working of cabinet. These were the Expenditure Review Committee (ERC), Resources Committee, and Australian State Regional Relations Committee (ASRRC). Before outlining their responsibilities it may be useful to place them in the context of similar bodies. They were *ad hoc* committees with a continuing existence, and their formation was publicly announced. In many respects they behaved like standing committees but were not given this label or status. There were other continuing *ad hoc* committees, including the Regional Employment Development Scheme Committee (REDS) and Special Assistance to Non-Metropolitan Areas Committee (SANMA). But although these two committees could allocate funds without reference to cabinet, they worked within guidelines established by it and had no substantial role in policy formation. Beyond these committees there were committees of a more truly *ad hoc* nature which usually had a short life. Their existence was rarely made public and their work was regarded as part of the domestic relations of the government. As with previous governments, there was resistance even to saying how many there were at any one time. Their range of work included co-ordination and the resolution of differences, making allocations within specified guidelines, and special tasks which generally did not require sustained committee activity. In all cases their work was far more specific than that of the original standing committees.

Finally, in November 1974 Whitlam established an economic council consisting of a small number of ministers and senior public servants. This body was formally outside the cabinet framework (the Department of the Prime Minister and Cabinet sometimes circulated notices of meetings but did not provide secretariat services) while obviously closely related to it. Besides Whitlam himself its members included the treasurer and the ministers for minerals and energy and social security. At its first meeting Dr J. F. Cairns, as minister for overseas trade and treasurer-designate, also attended. The public servants and officials included the secretaries of the Department of the Prime Minister and Cabinet, Treasury, and Department of Minerals and Energy, and the governor of the Reserve Bank. The functions of the council were not clearly identified, but one commentator reported that they were connected with the prime minister's dissatisfaction with the advice cabinet had been receiving on monetary policy and especially with the consequences for employment of monetary restrictions imposed late in 1973 (Robert Haupt, *Financial Review*, 27 November 1974). Although the council continued into 1975, by August of that year it was reported to be faltering (Bruce Juddery, *Canberra Times*, 15 August 1975).

Of the three *ad hoc* committees that came to prominence in

1975, the ERC was the most important. Its members included the prime minister, the treasurer, and the ministers for social security, labour and immigration, and urban and regional development. In the course of the year Hayden, when he became treasurer, and Jim McClelland, when he became minister for labor and immigration, combined their formal and influential positions on the committee with informal roles as the prime minister's closest ministerial confidants on economic policy. The committee was set up by cabinet in January 1975 when the government had decided that its earlier open-handed approach to public expenditure could no longer be maintained. The committee was to examine all proposals for expenditure both during and outside the budget round. In announcing the formation of the committee, Whitlam outlined its functions in the following terms:

> The committee will ensure that the Government is kept fully informed of the economic and budgetary implications of all its programs, and of the effects of new programs which it might consider . . . .
> Any new expenditure proposals which are brought forward outside the budget decision-making framework would be considered by the committee established by Cabinet.
> The Government has decided that there ought to be a general presumption against further increases of Government expenditure. Any such increase must meet the criteria adopted by Cabinet. [Prime minister, press statement no. 436, 28 January 1975]

The working of the committee conferred considerable influence on a small number of selected ministers. If it rejected a proposal for expenditure, the prime minister tended not to list the item for full cabinet unless the minister concerned persisted. In a time of expenditure restraint, ministerial persistence was not common. Committee decisions effectively became cabinet decisions.

The composition of the committee ensured that some senior ministers from spending departments, notably the minister for urban and regional development, participated fully in and supported the cuts imposed. The committee's deliberations were supported by an officials committee drawn from the departments of ministers on the committee. These officials worked as a task group rather than primarily as departmental representatives. However, like their ministers they were not entirely free from departmental consider-ations. Officials did not meet together with ministers, but the chairman of the officials group (an officer of the Department of the Prime Minister and Cabinet) attended ministerial meetings to assist with recording decisions. Ministers and departments not involved in the committee's work did not attend meetings even to explain their own proposals. This led to critical comment. Had restraining expenditure seemed less important, the committee's authority could soon have come under sustained challenge. However, changes in procedure to allow ministers to defend their proposals would have helped reinforce its position. The creation of the ERC was a limited but definite step towards the establishment within cabinet of a group that could give detailed attention to priorities. Its focus on expenditure was specialized, but this was one of the most important matters on which the government had to make decisions in 1975. Determining where and to what extent cuts would be made gave the committee enormous scope for influencing the shape of government activity.

The other two *ad hoc* committees, the Resources Committee and the ASRRC, had less time to develop their influence. The Resources Committee had been appointed by Whitlam (not by cabinet decision) and was designed to bring some coherence into the government's minerals and energy policy after the initial loans affair had discredited Connor. For a long time Connor had been given almost a free hand. With his permanent head, Sir Lenox Hewitt, he had developed policy in a secretive fashion. Cabinet now wanted a greater involvement. The guiding force in the committee's work was John Menadue, the permanent secretary of PMC. The committee could make decisions without any reference to cabinet; sometimes officials and ministers met together. In this case Whitlam was relying heavily on his department and a small group of ministers to salvage something from what was rapidly becoming a major government disaster.

The ASRRC was less influential and met less often. Between October 1974 and September 1975 it was convened only four times, while the supporting officials met seventeen times. By contrast the ERC met twelve times in the same period, while the officials met twenty-one times. Served by the newly formed policy coordination unit in PMC, the ASRRC was designed to draw together the threads of the government's diverse and often muddled relations with the states. Overlapping grants had been especially common and had become a source of contention. However, the government fell before the committee had an opportunity to develop its capacity. In any case this would have been difficult, for the committee had no clear policy role when compared to the ERC or the Resources Committee.

The *ad hoc* committees had been developed to meet a variety of needs. Their functions included coordination of policy, the resolution of particular policy problems, the review of expenditure, and several special tasks. Their formation indicated the discovery of a need for a more efficient means of drawing together the threads of business; cabinet thus began to establish a three-tier cabinet structure, in which cabinet, cabinet committees and officials' committees each reinforced one another. The relations between these tiers varied from committee to committee, but there was still an indication that new procedures were being considered and that officials were beginning to play a more direct role in cabinet deliberations.

But the new structures also had some quite striking, and potentially divisive, implications. The capacity of the Resources Committee to make decisions without reference to full cabinet, and the *de facto* power of the ERC to prevent new proposals being put on the cabinet agenda, meant that the new structures were becoming more elitist and power was being concentrated in the hands of a few ministers. Perhaps this was a logical result of the size of cabinet and the mediocrity of many of its lesser members. The next logical step might have been the establishment of a general administrative committee to deal with more routine business. Such a committee would have allowed junior ministers some glimpse of what was going on, while allowing the more senior ministers to concentrate on the major problems. The elitist system might not have been acceptable to cabinet as a whole or to caucus in the longer term, but after the forced election in 1974 the government always was operating in an atmosphere of crisis. As such the need to measure up talent with problems was an important step that showed an increasing sophistication, but it was all too late.

Whitlam as Prime Minister

The review of the changing structure of cabinet under Whitlam shows how it tried to adapt in response to failures and emerging difficulties. The workings of cabinet can also be explained by looking at the resources and capacity of the prime minister to direct the deliberations of cabinet and at the comparative role of ministers and their relations with external party members and public servants.

The prime minister has a considerable range of resources. He has his own department which tries to develop a capacity to provide advice on most topics that come before cabinet (see chapter 4). Whitlam himself had a superb memory and worked hard, although his main interests were in the fields of foreign affairs, urban development, and legal and constitutional matters; he knew little about economics and often left the running in this area to others. As leader of the party he could shift ministers between the various portfolios or even sack them if he could get retrospective caucus approval for his actions; but this power could not be used too frequently or without costs. The two sackings that did occur followed blatant examples of misleading parliament, which although not in itself necessarily a reason for dismissal, at least provided the excuse. It remains doubtful whether Whitlam could have gained caucus support for the removal of ministers only because they were incompetent. In caucus, too, Whitlam used his position of prestige to bully his supporters into line. He tended to assert his position and demand support, rather than arrange consensus in the style of Chifley.

His own personality restricted his use of the resources at his command. He tended to make snap judgments, to act hastily without any concern for the victims of his sudden wrath and biting sarcasm. Occasionally his partial or incomplete appreciation of situations and individuals meant that in party terms his was a brittle leadership, sometimes constructive and magnificent in conception, but often erratic. His tendency to surround himself with groups of ministers in favour and to act on advice from a broad range of sources without consulting cabinet meant that he did not always retain the full confidence of his colleagues and was restrained by the limits to their tolerance. Further, as the next chapter illustrates, the public service, and more specifically PMC, had at first only a limited capacity to respond, and Whitlam had difficulty in obtaining alternative options in economic affairs from those presented by the Treasury. This was one of the problems he later sought to rectify.

But the major resource Whitlam had was his capacity to shape and direct the business of cabinet. He could decide what came to cabinet, how meetings were run, and, if controversy developed, what decisions were taken. This control of the cabinet agenda and proceedings is central to the concept of prime ministerial power developed by Crossman.

What is brought to cabinet, and what is not, is a matter for judgment by the prime minister and the ministers concerned. Some general rules have, however, been identified. The following matters are often seen as business for cabinet:

1. Major policy issues
2. Proposals involving employment or large expenditures
3. Proposals requiring legislation or amendments to legislation
4. Proposals having a considerable impact on relations between the federal, state, and local levels of government
5. Senior appointments, including appointments to the first division of the public service and to statutory bodies

These provide general guidelines rather than binding rules, and there are instances from several of these categories where business was not taken to cabinet.

The form of the submissions, the supporting information, and the degree of consultation with other interested parties was also laid down in a paper circulated by the prime minister. The rules adopted by the Whitlam cabinet did not vary much from the Liberal governments that preceded or followed it. The Treasury had to be consulted about financial implications, involved departments had to give their consent, a particular format had to be adopted, and the submission had to be lodged with PMC a prescribed time before the cabinet meeting; it was usually either three or ten days. Decisions were seldom taken without the prior circulation of a submission, except for questions of senior appointments or matters that the prime minister chose to raise himself (see Smith 1976*a*, pp. 207-11).

The lodging and circulation of a submission did not ensure that it would be listed on the agenda; nor did listing necessarily mean that it would be discussed. These matters were decided by the prime minister alone. He could also decide that a circulated submission should be withdrawn. In extraordinary cases, where a minister was trying to get a matter listed or to get it discussed, he could use a variety of approaches to the prime minister. These included: a direct personal approach himself; a personal approach to the secretary of PMC; a personal approach to the prime minister's own staff; an approach to PMC through a member of his staff; an approach to the prime minister's staff through a member of the minister's staff; an approach to PMC by the secretary of his department; an approach by the department direct to the cabinet secretariat. Ministers' appreciation of this process varied as did their skill and success in using it. The prime minister could take advice on the ordering of cabinet business from the secretary or other officers of PMC and from his own staff. However, responsibility for decisions remained firmly his own and, to the extent that any of the supplementary methods above were used, he was not necessarily influenced by them at all.

Suggestions were made that prime ministerial discretion in such matters should be modified by the formation of an agenda committee of ministers. Agenda committees can, however, become bottlenecks, and in any case, no prime minister would willingly share this power. The power not to list submissions was the power to defer deliberation on matters that ran against prime ministerial preferences but which might yet gain majority support in cabinet. Suggestions were also made that the prime minister need not necessarily be chairman of cabinet, but the chairmanship of cabinet carries too many resources for any prime minister to accept its loss.

Cabinet meetings were always chaired by the prime minister. His choice of speakers could be crucial especially, as we will discuss later, when ministers often had a limited capacity to be provided with an effective brief on the submissions of other colleagues. Often Whitlam preferred to ask for objections to a proposal rather than for a directly constructive discussion of it. In most cabinets opposition from the treasurer, with support from the prime minister for his stand, is enough to ensure the failure of a submission. But Whitlam often failed to support Crean, particularly in 1973 and 1974, which led in part to the temporary eclipse of his department, the Treasury. This is illustrated in one of the case-studies.

Records of the decisions of cabinet were taken by officers of PMC. Three officers (including the secretary of the department) usually attended and sat at three small tables in corners of the room. At any one time the three were drawn from a panel of no more than five officers who were known to and accepted by ministers. Some ministers were uneasy that the recording was done by officials. In recording the decisions of cabinet committees, officers were drawn as necessary from within the department. The number of officers who could be called on from time to time was in 1975 about fifteen. The recording officers took notes in longhand, and each officer took notes for most of the time. In the construction of cabinet minutes, memory, note-taking, and shared impressions all played important parts. The whole of cabinet discussions had to be followed closely because the point from which the final decision would come could not always be predicted. This meant that recording officers needed to have read the relevant papers beforehand and to have understood the background to discussions.

In many cases the recording of decisions was relatively straight-forward. The submissions contained proposed decisions, and where they were approved the appropriate part was recorded. Where amendments were made the minister securing the change might have written out a draft decision and given it to one of the recording officers. The prime minister's style in summing up was also important. A clear summation made recording a simple task. But in other cases many amendments were discussed and pieces were assembled and reassembled in debate until agreement was reached. The recording officers then had to satisfy themselves that they had a full and internally consistent decision. This could entail asking the prime minister to clarify points or using breaks in the session to take informal soundings. Problems could also arise towards the end of a meeting as the prime minister tried to deal quickly with remaining agenda items.

Following a cabinet meeting, officers wrote up decisions as quickly as possible. Where recording officers, after consultation with each other, were still in doubt about the terms of a decision, they could consult relevant ministers and other people concerned. In cases where issues were confused they still had to produce something that looked as if cabinet had made an implementable decision. Post-cabinet consultations could involve the prime minister and several ministers and heads of departments. Officers writing decisions could consult ministers orally or produce a draft decision or "forward copy" for comment and possible amendment. Knowledge of this process varied both among ministers and among departments, and extensive post-cabinet consultations were rare. The inclusion in submissions of draft decisions reduced significantly earlier problems of consulting ministers and officials to make sure that the actual language used in decisions was correct.

The prime minister's authority here was decisive. Decisions were circulated before the prime minister had seen them, but if there was any argument about a decision he would have the final say.

However, the prime minister did not usually instruct recording officers. Once a decision was circulated it could not be varied without a new submission; however, amendments of a limited and technical nature could be made. Records of decisions were certified as correct by the senior officer of the cabinet division present at the meeting.

The centrality of the prime minister to the process is illustrated, therefore, by his capacity to control the procedural aspects, to decide what arrives on the cabinet table and, from his position and personality, to influence the actual decisions. Given the significance attached to wording and interpretations both by the press and by the bureaucracy, this prime ministerial prerogative cannot be undervalued. The importance of these resources are reinforced by an account of the more limited resources of the departmental ministers under Labor.

Ministerial Resources

The three years of Labor government saw the rise and fall of several ministers. Cairns is perhaps the best-known example. In June 1974 he was able to challenge and defeat the deputy prime minister, Lance Barnard; in November he was made treasurer and was widely regarded as the architect of the 1974 budget. During the Labor conference held in Terrigal in February 1975, he was a dominant figure. Yet five months later he was discredited, sacked, and a broken figure on the backbenches. Connor's rise, the vote of confidence in his soaring vision expressed by caucus in the ministerial election after the 1974 poll, and then his fall from grace and office were as startling if not as abrupt. By contrast, Senator Jim McClelland won a portfolio in February 1975 and almost immediately became influential. There is no static ministerial position. Positions of influence have to be gained and maintained.

This point is emphasized by the changing structure of the inner group that had access to the prime minister. Some, like Hayden, were first favoured confidants, then outside the pale, and then re-admitted. Others, like Moss Cass, were never on close terms with the prime minister and always had considerable difficulty in getting his support for their proposals in cabinet. The value of that support, for programmes in favoured fields like urban development or education, is indicated by the easier route that major submissions had in these areas.

Ministers were certainly not equal in ability, nor in access to the important resources of the cabinet. These variations were increased by the divergent capabilities of their supporting departments. Relations with the bureaucracy were often a sore point for incoming ministers in 1973. Many ministers were suspicious of the political leanings and doubted the loyalty and competence of senior public servants, but they had given little real thought to the capabilities of their departments and the way they could be used to implement Labor's policy. The senior ministers usually had well-established and competent departments and could benefit from their support. But the tail-end ministers were often at the head of departments that had been created out of Whitlam's imagination as a means of keeping them busy. As a result, some strong ministers tended to get stronger and weaker ones to flounder on in search of new functions.

This variation can be shown by the advice that ministers received. The necessity to keep submissions brief meant that issues were alluded to rather than argued in full. Ministers from other departments often had little idea what the implications of new proposals were.

Submissions were circulated to ministers and, beyond them, to departments on a "need to know" basis. Submissions were regarded as matters for ministers and not as matters for general distribution to departments. The secretariat kept a circulation record for each submission. The Treasury received all submissions with implications for expenditure and economic matters; it thus received most submissions. Many submissions went also to the Attorney-General's Department, the first parliamentary counsel, and the Public Service Board. Submissions were also sent "as appropriate" to departments with head offices outside Canberra. Submissions that were to be considered by the ERC were sent to the departments of the ministers concerned (prime minister, treasurer, and ministers for social security, urban and regional development, and labor and immigration). Within the Department of the Prime Minister and Cabinet submissions were sent to the secretary to the cabinet and deputy secretaries and assistant secretaries of branches concerned.

It was sometimes argued that all departments should receive all submissions. Apart from the logistical problems of producing enough copies (during the period under review, sixty-five copies of each submission were required) there was the possibility that increasing the circulation list would increase the chances of leaks. A further objection was that this could open the way for busybodies to take an interest in matters to which they could contribute nothing. Moreover, departments were unequal in capabilities, substance, and size. The case for sending submissions to all departments would be stronger if there were fewer departments. It should be noted that in addition to normal interdepartmental consultation processes, departmental intelligence networks made many departments aware of activities that interested them and gave them a chance to ask for submissions to be sent from the cabinet secretariat. In such cases the officers concerned had some discretion to grant requests provided a "need to know" basis could be established.

Where departments were not sent submissions by the secretariat they may still have gained access to them through their minister, but only if the minister felt that this was necessary. While departmental support for the successful carrying out of ministerial roles was essential, there were occasions when a minister judged it important for his department (or an agency reporting to him) not to see particular submissions. The capacity to withhold access to submissions was thus for a minister a significant political resource.

Whether ministers sought a departmental briefing on submissions was their own decision. Practices varied widely and depended on relations between ministers and their senior officials. Some departments welcomed the opportunity; others found it irksome; and others simply had insufficient resources to do the amount of work involved. Ministers did not all arrive in cabinet equally well briefed about its deliberations. Nor were they all well informed about the decisions that cabinet had reached. Sometimes there was a delay in circulating decisions that could lead to embarrassing situations. Early in the Whitlam government some ministers announced decisions immediately they had left the cabinet room, only to find later that their recollections were faulty.

The dissemination of information about cabinet decisions is therefore important. Traditionally the formal decisions contained simply what was decided, although sometimes an attempt was made to convey the "flavour" of the discussion. British practice of producing an austere summary of arguments for and against a cabinet conclusion has not been adopted in Australia. It might be argued that producing decisions in the British style would be useful, but writing decisions in this way is time-consuming and a skilled art. Once arguments were reproduced, even in dry prose and without attribution, names could be inferred by the knowledgeable. Moreover, ministers who used foolish arguments and were defeated would have no interest in embalming even a hint of their experience in a written record. Nevertheless, during the Whitlam government some amplification on an informal basis was available concerning cabinet decisions. In special circumstances recording officers could give discreet and selective briefings, making use of official cabinet papers and their own notes, to certain heads of departments. This could be initiated either by officers of PMC or by officers from interested departments.

Decisions were circulated to all ministers and to relevant departments on a "need to know" basis. Ministers varied in the interest they took in decisions, especially ones that did not concern their own responsibilities. It was argued by some that abstracts of decisions should also have been distributed to departments not immediately affected. Although departmental networks were alert for information affecting them, the authority of cabinet decisions was such that departments should have been in no doubt about the existence of decisions of even marginal relevance.

In addition, ministers always had to watch the reaction of caucus. Legislation approved by cabinet was explained to caucus before its introduction in parliament. There was not necessarily a connection between other cabinet business and caucus. The consultation of caucus committees on cabinet business was not a straightforward or consistent process. When parliament was not sitting, cabinet business proceeded without any caucus consultation. Whether (and when and how) caucus committees were consulted depended on the skill and judgment of ministers. The involvement of caucus was an irregular and unpredictable stage in the processing of government business, and it was not the responsibility of anyone except ministers to see that it was carried out in a manner compatible with the working of cabinet. Prudent departmental officers made sure that appropriate items were routed through caucus, but cases occurred where officers did not do this and the minister and his staff failed to pick them up. Ministers could use caucus support as a resource to push proposals through cabinet. Some, like Hayden and Kim Beazley, usually took the relevant caucus committee into their confidence and ensured a smooth passage for their bills; others tried to bore caucus into submission, while a few told them nothing and later regretted the fact. Caucus could often be a safety valve, and some of its members had a keener eye for the electoral impact of policies than more remote ministers who often held safe seats.

Ministers who were unable to secure cooperation from their colleagues or to short-circuit the system adequately often found it frustrating. One, who had been told to obtain the approval of other ministers before a submission was relisted, pointed out the dramatic consequences of the continued delay and commented: "If this happens we can hardly expect to escape if we allow the next few months of precious time to be squandered by self-imposed red tape about pre-cabinet consultation with over-worked ministers who just can't find the time for extra-cabinet consultations." A minister who wanted action but could not get his item listed for cabinet consideration, let alone secure approval, was stalled. Consultations were necessary, but indeed took time.

The comparative impotence of individual ministers to affect the broad topics is well illustrated in our case-study on the making of the budget. It is sufficient here to point out that cabinet is not an easy arena in which to operate (which is one reason why public servants prefer to settle areas of dispute within the bureaucracy rather than taking them to cabinet), that ministers have only limited resources there and that some never learn even how best to use those resources. What emerges, then, is a picture that is far from co-ordinated and coherent, as ministers generally argue their departmental cases, for which they may be well briefed, and are often only poorly informed on the intentions of other departments.

Initially there were some proposals to brief cabinet collectively. This was one of the reasons for founding the Priorities Review Staff. But ministers were usually far too busy; when individually they sought advice, two or more ministers were embarrassed when they found that they were about to make the same comments in cabinet itself. The PRS soon became a fire brigade outfit, designed to put out the policy bushfire rather than to discuss strategy or to give collective advice. Ministers were left to their own devices, to whatever support their departments could provide, and to the often erratic assistance of their ministerial advisers (see Smith 1977a).

THE WHITLAM CABINET: AN OVERVIEW

The most notable feature of the Whitlam cabinet was its lack of coherence. All cabinets must suffer from this problem to some extent, but this one seemed to have more problems than most precisely because it was trying to effect major change at great speed. At no stage was there an attempt, or even apparently an expressed desire, for cabinet to take a clear view of where the government was going. The pace was always too hectic. As a result, obvious overlap and a lack of coordination were the features most often remarked upon, as policy at times seemed to lurch from crisis to crisis.

Cabinet simply had difficulty organizing itself. Because everyone wanted a voice in full cabinet, the workload of cabinet was not reduced by the establishment of a successful set of cabinet committees until it was too late. There was little coherent debate about the organization of the public service and what should be done about the monopoly of economic advice from the Treasury which was so often considered unsatisfactory; the establishment of commissions and departments, the creation of so many IDCs continued until there were signs that with the formation of the policy-coordination unit these questions of incoherence were being tackled. But the turbulent economic conditions made such concerns irrelevant.

Yet the success or failure of a cabinet depends largely on the prime minister. If Whitlam's cabinet did not work well, he must take much of the blame. While Whitlam was without doubt the government's greatest asset, he was also one of its greatest problems. He was often not willing to work to ensure smooth relations with caucus or to orchestrate the deliberations of cabinet. At the same time, as a Labor prime minister he could be outvoted in cabinet or have his decisions overruled by caucus. He had to work within a structure that depended on consultation, among a group of ministers who had no ingrained tradition of consultation. Whitlam alone had the capacity to make the system work; he did not always put his mind to it.

A cabinet is not self-stabilizing; and the Whitlam cabinet was less so than most. Ministers and the prime minister had different resources and often divergent ambitions which led to a lack of coherence at the centre, particularly when the traditional co-ordinators of policy, the Treasury and PMC, were temporarily uninfluential. Certainly ministers had to account to one another, but cabinet became a battleground precisely because many ministers were concerned only with their own portfolios. The prime minister alone could provide coherence; too often Whitlam failed to do so, and the inevitable failings of any cabinet became even more marked.

THE FRASER CABINET

Fraser went into office publicly committed to the concept of collective cabinet government. He had written that "how" things were done was important (Fraser 1974) and indeed when destroying Gorton had claimed that Gorton had made decisions without consulting cabinet. He reinstated the inner cabinet and insisted from the beginning that ministers adhere to a rigid code of discipline. Statements could be made only after they had been approved by cabinet or cleared with the prime minister himself. This procedure was later simplified when each cabinet submission was to be accompanied by a draft press statement.

When first elected, Fraser announced the formation of six cabinet committees; he himself was to act as chairman of the four most important — those on planning and coordination, economics, foreign affairs and defence, and machinery of government. The choice of members of these committees indicated how far the members of cabinet who were less sympathetic to the prime minister were isolated from political power. After the 1977 election most committees were reappointed and a new committee concerned with intelligence and security was also created. But the economic committee of cabinet was abolished; as Fraser pointed out, it had "touched on so many portfolios that it became akin to cabinet itself. For that reason cabinet as a whole normally deals with economic issues" (Fraser 1977). In its place two smaller committees to deal with economic affairs were appointed — one responsible for interest, bank and currency exchange rates and the other for industrial and wages policy. Yet it still seems unlikely that these committees can overcome the traditional problems that face cabinet committee structures and so ease the burden of cabinet. Indeed in the early months there was a tendency for hard decisions to be delegated to the inner leadership of five — Fraser, Anthony, Lynch, Sinclair and Withers; at times, especially when Anthony was ill, Fraser and Sinclair made many of the major decisions.

Fraser is still clearly not satisfied with the central machinery of government or with the public service. He has tinkered consistently with them, creating a Department of Productivity in October 1976 and then splitting the Treasury. He has shown a desire to use other ministers as troubleshooters, especially John · Howard, who was made responsible for the abortive wages and prices freeze before he knew it was on, was then made the prime minister's personal trade negotiator to the EEC, and is now treasurer. At the same time Fraser has continued to increase the influence of his own department. For a time he continued with Menadue as permanent head, then replaced him with Alan Carmody, a bureaucrat with a "can do" philosophy. The department was restructured, and a second secretary to cabinet, G. J. Yeend, was appointed. On Carmody's death Yeend became secretary of the department. PMC was clearly at the centre of political events.

Cabinet procedures have been tightened too; the circulation of decisions and submissions has been restricted and the security agencies have on occasion been called in to try to trace leaks. Effective secrecy has been reimposed on most cabinet matters. At the same time public servants have been asked to make more deliberately political judgments. In drawing up submissions, the minister was once required (and in the preparation of submissions, this means his department) to indicate how he "expects the community to receive the proposals recommended and what longer term consequences there might be in terms of government public relations. There should be a list of those persons or groups who could be expected to favour the proposal and those who could be expected to voice opposition to it". Care for political impact of decisions is obviously important, even if still not demanded precisely in this form.

Fraser's personal position of pre-eminence cannot be in doubt. He has honed prime ministerial power to a much greater level than Whitlam could ever aspire to. He himself denies that he is excessively powerful. In the Garran Oration he asserted:

> If the commentators [claiming the existence of presidential government] are implying that all power lies in the hands of the prime minister, then I can dismiss such an assertion simply by referring to the essential features of my own cabinet. Strong ministers taking responsibility daily inside and outside the parliament for their individual actions and decisions within the framework of collective responsibility and mutual support between ministers.
> The attribution of untrammelled power to a prime minister shows a lack of understanding of how an effective cabinet system functions. It falsely

assumes that the prime minister's views always prevail, because when cabinet confidentiality operates as it should, a prime minister is never seen to adopt views at variance with those of cabinet. [Fraser 1977, p. 4]

But as prime minister he has frequently become deeply involved in economic and foreign affairs, relegating the official minister to second place. He makes the running in many policy areas that have been previously wholly the province of one minister. One report in October 1977 listed half a dozen important decisions that had been the result of Fraser's personal direction, not based on the advice of responsible ministers. They included tax cuts in the 1977 budget, the decision on the uranium mining, the splitting of the Treasury and the increase in oil prices to half world parity in four years. Further, the report argued that the government's antagonism to the IAC is founded on the prime minister's own high protectionist views (*National Times*, 5-10 September 1977). The 1976 devaluation was another one that bore the prime ministerial stamp, and the decision to re-open a tender for a major computer contract in early 1978 was the result of his intervention.

Cabinet is certainly consulted frequently. The list of items that must come to cabinet under the Fraser government (see Fraser, 1977, Addendum 1) are essentially the same as under Whitlam (see above p.88). But what is important is not whether cabinet is consulted or whether it formally adopts certain lines of action. What is important is the way in which cabinet is manipulated. It is probable that under the Fraser regime *too much* comes to cabinet, so that ministers have little opportunity to read or understand the initiatives of their colleagues, let alone discuss them. An excessively busy group of ministers with a very full agenda allows a dominant prime minister considerable scope to manipulate the agenda and the discussions. It is not that Fraser is never overruled in cabinet; there are some acknowledged cases when he has been; it is simply that as a Liberal prime minister he starts with more power than his Labor counterpart and his style has been to develop his power, both as prime minister and as cabinet chairman. Frequently cabinet may be provided with a *fait accompli*, so that the decision is an endorsement of actions already adopted. Quite clearly Fraser not only keeps tight control over cabinet proceedings, summing up the feeling of the meeting to provide the decision (and not by taking a vote); he also, as every prime minister must, tries to ensure his view is adopted. In particular he attempts to receive the support of leading members on important issues — particularly the top Country Party members. If the prime minister, the leader of the Country Party and the treasurer are opposed to a submission, there is little that the rest of the cabinet can do.

A Liberal prime minister, and especially an activist one like Fraser, is not restricted like a Labor prime minister by the need for a vote. He may not be able to get his way all the time, but when he dominates his party as Fraser does and can do much of the business in the environs of cabinet, he is unlikely to be overruled often. One reporter described it as follows:

> The concentration of political and bureaucratic power around the prime minister means that his ideas are quickly translated into government policy, and the chief explanation for the government's changes of direction are almost always related to Mr Fraser's change of mind . . . One of the chief problems facing the Fraser government is that is has almost no checks and balances upon Malcolm Fraser. [*National Times*, 5-10 September 1977]

Cabinet government and prime ministerial government are not polar alternatives. The forms of cabinet government can be observed while the procedures and results are still dominated by the prime minister. Unlike the other post-Menzies Liberal prime ministers, Fraser has created a situation where he can manipulate his cabinet successfully.

CONCLUSION

It would be incorrect to suggest that cabinet works "better" under Fraser than under Whitlam, for this suggests there is some standard against which both can be judged. Intuitively the idea of somehow getting the centre of government "right" is attractive. But to get it right means deciding first on the proper role of cabinet. Is it to co-ordinate policy, to strengthen the party in power, to allocate resources, to cope with crises, or any one of innumerable other functions? Cabinet is, of course, all these at different times, hence what is right for one occasion is not right for others. The only criterion by which to judge a cabinet's activities is that of political success.

If one thing is clear it is that cabinet cannot do everything. The limits are not simply organizational; they are also related to the ability of the relevant actors to participate in and comprehend the immensely complex situations at the centre of government. Decisions can almost never be taken in isolation. Other factors, extraneous to the topic under discussion, will always be involved. Solutions and problems can very easily become decoupled.

The reasons are not simply to be found in its structure but in the very problems that cabinet must face. It must be understood as the arena in which combatants with a variety of resources meet and often compete. Cabinet may find decisions hard to reach because puzzling about policy is hard and there are no easy or immediate solutions. Ministers compete fiercely, whether for funds, position, or ideology, for they come to cabinet primarily as departmental spokesmen, and if they cannot always be constructive, some may be content to restrict or spoil the plans of others. The evidence presented to cabinet in submissions is designed to persuade, not to enlighten; obfuscation and misinformation are among the weapons of cabinet debate. If it is difficult to maintain coherence in the formulation of policies, it is just as difficult for cabinet to ensure co-ordination and cooperation of departments in the implementation of policy.

If cabinet can ensure central political direction, that is, unity and will and a sense of purpose among ministers in the exercise of power, it may be able to obtain a degree of integration in the formation and execution of policy. But it does not always manage to do so. While the evidence is not available to show cabinet in the process of shaping policy, it is possible to make some broad comments about its capacity. At the lowest level, cabinet can sometimes make effective decisions on particular items of policy and can review their political impact. There is no doubt that cabinet can strike hard and pointedly on occasions, where political sensitivities are on edge. But cabinet finds it less easy to pull together the threads of sequential policy decisions to prevent overlap or the more blatant contradictions, to relate the particular policy to the more general strategy, and, above all, to control the economy in such a way that its broad attempt at management does not make policies in other areas unattainable. Unable consistently to control its environment, usually unwilling to set clear objectives in anything but general terms, cabinet is often isolated at the centre. Further, if cabinet is not always coherent, then the administration is unlikely to be well integrated. The corollary of lack of direction at the political level is the ceding of direction to other central agencies and the replacement of cabinet's aims and priorities by theirs.

What coherence cabinet does have depends heavily on the personality and style of the prime minister. It has only the most modest organizational support of its own to aid its decision making. As the next chapter will show, the changes in the Department of the Prime Minister and Cabinet were always designed to help the prime minister, not cabinet as a whole. In the past thirty years, leaders have used their resources in differing ways to give cabinet some political direction. Chifley developed his "official family" as a means of gaining access to the necessary information about available and existing policies. Menzies relied heavily on his personal position in cabinet. Gorton tried to develop PMC and used it to try to dominate cabinet, rather than to facilitate better cabinet discussion or decision making. Whitlam at first made no attempt to impose a sense of direction on his cabinet; when the initial arrangements failed, and as his government faltered, he began to introduce experiments like the ERC and to require his revitalized department to keep a log on the action taken on cabinet decisions. Like Menzies, Fraser dominates his cabinet, and such coordination and coherence as it has is guaranteed by his involvement in the taking of important decisions.

To consider the capacity of cabinet to give political direction is to ask simply whether cabinet can maintain control of the policies it proposes and understand their implications. Clearly, as this chapter has shown, this capacity is limited. Cabinet has difficulty in maintaining a long or consistent view, and its performance as a unit depends largely on the methods adopted, with greater or lesser success, by prime ministers and on the degree of cooperation it is able to win from the other central agencies, PMC, Treasury, and the PSB, especially in such matters as economic management and in coordination of the other departments.

4

The Coordinating
Agencies

The chief coordinaging agencies of the public service are the Department of the Prime Minister and Cabinet, the departments of the
Treasury and of Finance (Treasury's recent child), and the Public
Service Board. They are not the only influential agencies, or the only
ones to lay claim to a coordinating role. But historically they have
had a degree of influence which makes them crucial to the processes
of coordination. All but Finance have existed for the last fifty years,
and they have important resources always at their disposal: their
controls over people, money, and decisions. The prime minister has
always been responsible for the PSB as well as PMC, and sometimes
he has had responsibility also for the Treasury; in any event the
treasurer is usually a senior minister. These agencies are closely concerned with the work of the cabinet and of the government
generally. Ambitious public servants aspire to transfer to them.
Chances of promotion in them are thought to be high, and a capacity
to influence policy is also thought to be more likely there.

Notwithstanding their general similarities, each is nevertheless
distinctive and all have been undergoing changes. PMC has changed
most. For many years it acted as a secretariat along the lines of the
British Cabinet Office. It was the "coordinating department" *par
excellence*. It brought the work of the various other departments
together and saw that new tasks were distributed properly. PMC was
the honest broker which could bring opposed views into concert, its
own hands unsoiled by sectional interests. The dividing line between
arbitration and advocacy was always uncertain, however, and recent
prime ministers have found it necessary to look to the department
for advice to counter or supplement that coming from the "line"
departments. In particular, the capacity of the department to offer
economic advice has been greatly increased, and it would be difficult

to go back to the PMC of the past. PMC was always central in the general policy process, but now it is gaining a new part.

Treasury has experienced sudden change. In 1976 the Department of Finance was carved out from Treasury to do the financial and general accounting work of government, leaving Treasury as the economic manager. For the most part we refer just to "the Treasury", since the division of the department is so recent that most of our remarks apply to the undivided department. But the division was an important event. The powers of both Treasury and Finance severally are still considerable, as those of the old Treasury were. But the split revealed some of the tensions that exist between the coordinating departments, as well as between themselves and their environment. Some reasons for this development will emerge from the following section on the central machinery of government, and other reasons will be shown the case-study on the making of the budget of 1974.

The PSB, like PMC, has been changing fundamentally if gradually; but its course is less certain than that of PMC. Federation coincided with the emergence in the Australian colonies of independent personnel authorities to do the work of establishment control which in England had been handled by the Treasury; and the new commonwealth agency followed the emerging pattern. Because the PSB exercises statutory power independent of the government in certain personnel matters, it is in a different position from the Treasury and PMC, both formally and informally. It controls important resources, but many of them are used by the public bureaucracy itself and are less likely to become a public matter of political dispute than are the concerns of PMC and Treasury. The PSB's work is sometimes a matter of public controversy, as numerous industrial disputes and arguments about public service numbers show, but on the whole governments have been anxious to avoid an involvement with questions that can hardly ever return a political profit. Over the years, however, the PSB has tended greatly to extend its charter of operations. This has presented governments and the board itself with problems.

CONFLICT AT THE CENTRE

The puzzling problems of integrating the process of policy

formulation and decision have become recently more intractable and have been felt throughout the public service. Economic hard times have given added sharpness to eternal questions about the allocation of financial resources. Even the management of the public bureaucracy itself has become a prominent issue, with troubling implications for the central personnel agency. The authority of ministers to deal with these problems is not necessarily enhanced when their departments take on new roles. They may find themselves in new conflicts, as may their departments. These problems are especially acute for the central coordinating agencies, for their functions are closely intertwined; change in one calls forth response in the others. When the capacity of governments to command events seems to be in doubt, attention focuses on these central agencies where problems of coordination are at once most pressing and most complex.

Policy processes under stress are likely to produce new institutional arrangements, or at least a redistribution of influence, but in Australia these have not been easy to bring about. Stability and the increasing concentration of power at the centre is as characteristic of the institutions of central government as of the polity in general. In an obvious sense, the central institutions have taken shape simply through the consolidation within the commonwealth government of the functions taken over from the former colonies in 1901 and of the functions that have been added piecemeal ever since. Seventy years ago the commonwealth bureaucracy was made up of small and scattered units, doing tasks that varied from place to place and which were organized in different ways. Now it is integrated through a network of fine regulations covering most aspects of service life; a managerial class of common origins and outlook has been created; and the upper levels of the public service have been concentrated in Canberra. These tendencies have strengthened the capacities and increased the power of the central agencies that promoted them. At the same time the existence of strong and long-serving officials at senior levels has both hastened and reflected these centralizing tendencies. This was most obviously true in the late Menzies years when tired ministers were seldom disposed to question the proprieties of centralism and strong formal controls which have increasingly come to characterize Australian government.

The organizational strength of the central agencies is considerable. PMC, PSB and Treasury share with a few other departments a higher level of classification (and remuneration) for their senior officers. They all have many functional divisions spread across wide areas of work. All these departments are heavily represented on interdepartmental committees, those bodies established to facilitate work across departmental boundaries which are the points of transaction for so much business within the service. They also attract good staff. All have a high ratio of senior to junior staff and a disproportionate share of university graduates.

Their strength relative to other departments has undoubtedly grown. Still, these trends have always had their opposites. Co-ordination is a dynamic process and it often finds expression in differences between agencies about what their tasks are and how they should do them, differences which must be settled if partnership or cooperation between departments is to survive. The "line" departments have constantly disputed the territory or the capacity of the central coordinating agencies. Sometimes they have been successful for a time. The Department of Trade, for instance, under a strong minister in the 1960s, presented views on the economy which differed fundamentally and consistently from those of the Treasury; and it sought to develop its bureaucratic weight as it did so. The years of the Whitlam government revealed old differences very clearly, and some new ones besides. Finding the powers of the co-ordinating agencies irksome, the ministers challenged their established roles by the creation, sometimes deliberately and sometimes not, of alternative institutions for policy advice. The government sometimes criticized the existing capacities of the central agencies and sought to alter them: by giving them new tasks, by altering their institutional procedures, and by rearranging their personnel. Other bureaucratic agencies took a hand in this activity, which they welcomed. The central agencies themselves were not insensitive to their changed circumstances. They tried to defuse criticism, sometimes even to respond to it, and to define new roles for themselves.

The style and substance of their various responses was complex. But this is not the whole story. Whatever the pattern of change, the central agencies have maintained great authority over crucial resources of policy. Maintaining authority while yet changing its application: this is not just an Australian experience.

OVERSEAS PERSPECTIVES

Dissatisfaction with the performance of the central institutions of government has been evident in Canada and Britain in the last decade. Demands for change, suggestions for innovation, and experiments with new procedures are continuous, although both countries have different central structures. It is clear that there is no perfect distribution of functions that can satisfy the needs of government and that the problems of the centre are common to all countries with Westminster systems of government.

In Britain the three main central institutions are the Treasury, the Civil Service Department, and the Cabinet Office. The Treasury provides economic advice and controls departmental expenditure. It has developed a system of five-year rolling estimates, called the PESC scheme after the Public Expenditure Survey Committee that reviews them. The estimates are published annually in a White Paper debated in parliament. In the past, established programmes received automatic increases to meet demand, but this built inflationary tendencies into public spending. A new system of cash limits has now been imposed to bring these tendencies under control; but generally there is a view that, despite the sophistication of the techniques, the Treasury had not managed to maintain a tight grip on spending. This charge is made even though by the standards of other countries it has considerable resources it can use. Discussion of the best methods of control and experimentation with new techniques appears to be continuous (see Heclo and Wildavsky 1974; Diamond 1975; Pollitt 1977; Wright 1977).

One common excuse provided for the Treasury is that it no longer controls the allocation of manpower. The Civil Service Department was created in 1969 following a recommendation of the Fulton Committee. Its personnel and establishment functions were taken from the Treasury. The CSD also advises the cabinet on the allocation of functions between agencies. Since its inception there has been a continual debate about whether the division of financial and personnel controls has been justified. Several, including the secretary of the cabinet office and two former prime ministers, have argued that it might be desirable to split the Treasury again and so reunite the financial and personnel functions in a new budget-bureau organization. Most critics have agreed, however, that it would not be desirable to put personnel controls back in the

Treasury because it would then become too large, too centralized, and too powerful. The debate about the possible changes is lively and unresolved.

The Cabinet Office is also under review. It is not a department, though it acts as the central coordinator of cabinet proceedings and provides secretariat services for all cabinet activities. The Cabinet Office is available to the prime minister, who on occasion has relied on it heavily, but it also has responsibilities to the cabinet as a whole. It has included units like the Central Policy Review Staff, one of whose original functions was to give strategic advice to ministers as a collectivity. But prime ministers have often wanted more. Harold Wilson, for example, created a policy unit in 10 Downing Street that was independent of the Cabinet Office, and in anticipation of success, Margaret Thatcher made similar plans. Indeed, because the Cabinet Office is not the prime minister's own department, the prime minister may be forced to seek advice from diverse sources. This may become an advantage, especially if his advisers do not become part of the official framework that predigests cabinet material. It could increase his range of advice, if only because he has at times to work around, rather than through, the Cabinet Office. Proposals for the establishment of a prime minister's department in Britain have generally received little attention.

The problems facing British government since the early 1960s have led to a searching and often sophisticated review of how influence can best be distributed at the centre. But the problems are still there, and as the search for the ever-elusive solution continues, in the form of institutional rearrangement, the distribution of influence is continually in flux.

In Canada there is a different distribution of functions. The Department of Finance advises cabinet on economic management. The Treasury Board secretariat, which was hived off from it in the mid-1960s, controls the government's resources. It maintains controls on manpower and departmental spending and monitors the efficiency and effectiveness of departmental programmes. The Treasury Board draws up a public expenditure budget, while the Department of Finance presents a fiscal outlook to cabinet. In this respect the Treasury Board has more united control over the resources of the public sector than its equivalents in Australia and Britain (Johnson 1971).

But the Treasury Board's controls have been criticized for being too loose. In the Glassco Report on the Canadian civil service, the main theme was "let the managers manage". The view was that considerable initiative and control over resources should be decentralized to departmental managers. Some critics now believe that this decentralization has gone too far. The auditor-general has argued recently that departments have been too lax in their checks on spending and that in practice there are almost no effective central controls. At another level a former head of the Treasury Board has questioned whether the philosophy espoused by the Glassco Report is compatible with some of the tenets of collective responsibility (Johnson 1971*a*). If departments make savings, for instance, he has argued, it should be cabinet and not the department that determines how those savings should be allocated. When compared with Britain, there have been no sustained attempts to plan ahead; the Treasury Board projects trends in public spending three years ahead, but little more is done.

The structure of the Privy Council Office, the Canadian equivalent of the Cabinet Office, has also changed since the 1960s. Under John Diefenbaker the central organizations were fused, personalized, and passive. Since then the support available to the prime minister has grown in two directions. On the one hand is the Privy Council Office, staffed by civil servants. It was set up to serve cabinet as a whole but is geared primarily to the requirements of the prime minister: it provides secretarial service to cabinet and advice on machinery of government and appointments; it plays a quietly political role. The Prime Minister's Office, on the other hand, is staffed by political appointees and combines personal service to the prime minister with a "hit and run" advisory capacity. In Canada advice and support for the prime minister come from two institutions, both of which are large enough and flexible enough to meet a variety of challenges. Moreover, the division between them, while existing formally in functional terms, does not depend on a rigid compartmentalization of jobs. The prime minister can, if he wants, ask both bodies for suggestions on how to tackle the same problems (Doern 1971).

Despite different functional arrangements, the central institutions in Britain and Canada fulfil similar roles. They control expenditure and manpower by dealing with cabinet and the departments, and they service cabinet and the ministers. In both Britain and Canada there is heated debate about how best the cabinet and key ministers can be supported and how the controls should be exerted. These are important questions because these institutions are powerful. The immense potential influence of the British Treasury, for instance, was neatly summarized by one former secretary. When Sir William Armstrong was asked if he was influential, he responded:

> Obviously I had a great deal of influence. The biggest and most pervasive influence is in setting the framework within which the questions of policy are raised. We, while I was in the Treasury, had a framework of the economy basically neo-Keynesian. We set the questions which we asked ministers to decide arising out of that framework and it would have been enormously difficult for any minister to change the framework, so to that extent we had great power. I don't think used maliciously or malignly. I think we chose that framework because we thought it the best one going. We were very ready to explain it to anybody who was interested, but most ministers were not interested, were just prepared to take the questions as we offered them, which came out of that framework without going back into the preconceptions of them. [*Times*, 15 November 1976]

How do central departments use such influence in relation both to ministers and to other departments? How have their structures and procedures changed? How do they influence policy processes? These are the questions that must now be considered in relation to Australia's central departments.

PRIME MINISTER AND CABINET

In Australia, PMC has confined itself to high-level paper shuffling for much of its life. Its position and prestige have depended on its role in recording and circulating cabinet business in particular. This has given its senior officers status in comparison with officers in other agencies, including the Treasury and the PSB, but the department has nevertheless depended on a narrow base of work. The government's strategic view, its adaptive capability, and its capacity for coordinating and integrating its activities are now, however, especially important. How PMC can add to the capacities of government in these fields, if at all, has become a key question. It is not a new question. There is no one best way of organizing things for a prime minister. The role of PMC has to be related also to the disposition and roles of other central authorities. Departmental support for the prime minister may provide him with new opportunities once it goes beyond paper shuffling. It also poses problems, often in an acute way, for existing institutions and arrangements. PMC is a late comer to the exercise of bureaucratic power. Treasury and the PSB are already entrenched. Debates about PMC reflect not only the doubts of those who value old roles but also the anxieties of other interests. Further, there is the fear among both politicians and public servants that the processes of government will become even more focused around the person of the prime minister. Similar debates are taking place in some of the states as the roles of premiers' departments are becoming more overt — and more contentious.

From the establishment of PMC in 1911 until after the Second World War, departmental roles were largely formal. The Chifley government planned to reorganize the department after the elections of 1949. It would have included a secretariat servicing not only the cabinet but the whole network of cabinet or ministerial committees, senior officials' committees, the Premiers' Conference, and perhaps some other important Commonwealth-state conferences and major international conferences held in Australia. Thus all policy making at these levels would be reported and the record coordinated at the centre under the control of the prime minister. The secretariat would also contain a core of able, trained officers making it their daily business to be in touch with the key points of the service and the current policy plans of key departments and able to brief the prime minister on all matters likely to reach him. Finally, there would have been an economic policy division, along the lines of the then economic section of the British Cabinet Office, to share in the formulation of the principal economic plans, priorities, and guidelines of the government.

The defeat of the Chifley government at the elections in December 1949 meant that these plans were not put to the test by those who had formulated them. The economic policy division withered, and the department did not develop significant responsibilities in handling the business of the principal interdepartmental committees or in following up decisions of cabinet or its committees. However, especially during the secretaryship of Sir John Bunting (1959—68), the department did improve the nature of its secretarial services for cabinet and extend these services to cabinet committees. It also developed capabilities for briefing the prime minister, for checking the policy implications of departmental proposals, and for encouraging consultation and coordination.

In discussing the proposed developments under Chifley, L. F. Crisp has pointed to the potential tension between the facilitating approach that developed and the plans for an assertive economic policy division with a capacity for developing policy proposals of its own. Crisp preferred the idea of quarantining the established functions of the old department against the infections that the new one might bring (Crisp 1967). It is precisely this tension that lies at the heart of the debate on what functions PMC should and can perform.

In the last decade, the development of the department has been anything but smooth. What may be seen as the first in a series of more or less continuous readjustments was made shortly after Gorton became prime minister in 1968. Under Gorton the department was divided between a small Cabinet Office (with a total staff of thirty-eight) and a Prime Minister's Department. The Cabinet Office assisted the prime minister with the organization of cabinet business and the keeping of minutes. The Prime Minister's Department was to provide the prime minister with a broad range of policy advice and assistance. This episode in the growth of the department is difficult to disentangle from the personalities of the principal actors. Gorton moved Bunting, the incumbent head of the department, to the Cabinet Office and installed C. L. S. Hewitt in the Prime Minister's Department. Gorton's relationship with Hewitt, Hewitt's legendarily abrasive personal style, and the slight deemed by many to have been inflicted on Bunting do not make for a straightforward story (see Mediansky and Nockels 1975).

Several points may be made, however. First, the line of division between the Cabinet Office and the larger department cut through two principal functions which, following Crisp, we might identify as the facilitation of policy making, on the one hand, and the capacity actually to develop policy on the other. Recording cabinet decisions was separated from general advising. As one observer noted:

> The principal source of the prestige and power now held by the secretary of the Prime Minister's department is the Cabinet secretariat. Through his presence at Cabinet meetings, his knowledge of Cabinet committees, the secretary of the Prime Minister's Department enjoys the unique privilege of being the only public servant privy to the process of decision reaching, knowing what facts have influenced the government in reaching its decision on each policy matter. [*Financial Review*, 27 February 1968]

Hewitt was supposed to be the adviser, but since Bunting and not he attended cabinet meetings, Bunting had the job that gave the access to the critical information that the prime minister's principal adviser needed.

Second, the terms of Hewitt's brief were not clear. Early press commentaries made much of Hewitt's previous association with Gorton and Gorton's desire to have his own man "build up the policy side" of the department (*Financial Review*, 29 February 1968). It was pointed out that Bunting had neither wanted to increase the department's capability in the provision of policy advice nor been encouraged to do so by Menzies. The department did not initiate policy or comment incisively on proposals put forward by departments. This left the role of critic largely to Treasury. Except for the Department of Overseas Trade, Treasury had no serious rivals. To the extent that policy evolved from debate between departments, it did so mainly on matters in which Treasury and Trade were both interested. Many observers welcomed the possible emergence of an augmented Prime Minister's Department. But what Hewitt was to do and how his department was to be organized were not specified.

Third, the way in which the prime minister achieved the division of the department combined with Hewitt's approach to his job made it easy for critics to find fault. Public servants and others were disturbed by the way Bunting had been treated. Although in Britain the head of the Cabinet Office is not the head of the civil service, a courtesy given to the head of the Treasury until the creation of the Civil Service Department, it was accepted in Canberra that Bunting was the senior man. Displacing him made waves. Moreover, Hewitt introduced no innovations to earn him credit. Within the department, divisions were shuffled around but no institutional innovations were made. Lines of responsibility were unclear and efficiency suffered. A great deal of the department's work in fact related to correspondence. This was not inspiring for junior officers or for their seniors who had to check the drafts of replies before they were sent out. In commenting on policy proposals, the department was reactive rather than creative. As the *Canberra Times* (21 October 1970) pointed out, other departments objected to Treasury no less than Prime Minister's commenting on their proposals. But the difference was that they did not question the competence of Treasury officers. Further, Hewitt tended to monopolize communications with the prime minister. Items had to be put in writing, submitted to Hewitt, and transmitted as he judged best. This slowed down the flow of business.

The reasons for Gorton's dissatisfaction with the department as Bunting ran it are not hard to find, but his experiment with Hewitt yielded no solutions. Problems confronting a central policy advising and coordinating department were not posed in a sharply defined way. Splitting the department irritated people without giving the prime minister an increment in performance. The emphasis on policy advice raised expectations which were dashed as soon as Hewitt began work.

When McMahon succeeded Gorton as prime minister he reinstated Bunting as head of the Department of the Prime Minister and Cabinet and made Hewitt secretary of a new department containing bits and pieces formerly in the Prime Minister's Department. These concerned principally Aborigines, the environment, and the arts. The reshaped PMC had more senior officers and wider responsibilities than the pre-Hewitt department, but Bunting's style was reimposed on it and the Cabinet Office was reintegrated with the other divisions of the department. The reintegration was not, however, complete. A feeling of separateness remained, and this was reinforced by rules about the internal availability of papers relating to cabinet. The department continued its coordinating and note-writing activities much as it had done earlier.

Once the initial redispositions had been made, McMahon did not tinker extensively with his department. But he did not find it congenial, and he made unsuccessful efforts to build up his personal staff.

Whitlam and PMC

When Whitlam took office in 1972 he did not make major changes in the department. Bunting remained as head, though Whitlam enlarged his own staff, headed by Peter Wilenski as principal private secretary. He was influenced by the model of the Canadian PMO, but his own staff never approached the numbers in the PMO and did not have the resources to second guess the department. They settled into the role of providing personal support for the prime minister, making occasional wider forays, and leaving PMC to follow its own path.

The department did not make the running with suggestions for changes. It did not see itself as a major provider of substantive advice. As one senior officer put it, "The PM's advisers are his ministers, not his department." Although under previous prime ministers the department had become the repository of miscellaneous reponsibilities which seemed to need prime ministerial attention, Whitlam did not load the department with new tasks. PMC did set up, for a time, a protection policy division to oversee the government's early emphasis on lowering tariffs, but in the first two years of the Whitlam government more attention was given to a new department, the Department of the Special Minister of State (SMOS), as a possible bureaucratic home for such responsibilities. Thus when the Priorities Review Staff (PRS) was created in 1973 as a policy "think tank", it was located in SMOS rather than in PMC. It was noted at the time that whatever the problems of putting the PRS in SMOS, PMC as constituted did not provide a congenial home for it either. These arrangements began to change late in 1974 with Whitlam's announcement that from February 1975 one of his former private secretaries, John Menadue, would replace Bunting. Bunting became high commissioner to the United Kingdom. Menadue's appointment provided encouragement for people in the public service and in the Labor Party who believed that the department needed to play a more assertive part in the management of bureaucratic support for government policies. Changes came slowly, however, despite a spate of activity behind the scenes late in 1974, also involving officers of the newly appointed Royal Commission on Australian Government Administration, to which Wilenski was appointed special counsel. Menadue brought to the task the benefits of a close relationship with Whitlam. While working with the Murdoch group of newspapers he had maintained the links formed during his seven years as private secretary. His appointment nevertheless had costs. Although he had been a public servant before joining Whitlam's staff in the 1960s, Menadue had not held senior positions. His party affiliation was well known and had been reinforced by his candidature with ALP endorsement for a seat in 1966. His appointment was widely criticized as "political" even though both Whitlam and he maintained that it was within the normal conventions for senior appointments. But because of criticism he had to move slowly. He had to establish his credit with senior officers in PMC and in the rest of the service. He did this with considerable success, establishing himself as a moderate but active administrator — by no means an incautious radical, but rather an executive concerned with management and procedures. Indeed, he managed to combine some of the ability to win personal respect that was so much a part of Bunting's strength with a cautious but consistent activism at the centre, something from which Bunting had shied away.

Proposals and Changes

When Menadue took over, there were a number of streams of thought about what might be done with the department. It is not possible to be comprehensive in any account of them; nor is it possible to distinguish with any certainty Menadue's own distinctive contributions. What is clear is that Menadue indeed won control of his department, established a firm working relationship with Whitlam and senior ministers, and made a number of important changes.

One set of proposals listed six functions that PMC might perform. These were (1) to assist the prime minister in managing the work programme of cabinet and its committees and to handle cabinet papers and record decisions; (2) to brief the prime minister on submissions; (3) to follow up strategic cabinet decisions to ensure implementation; (4) to assist in legislative programming and management of government activities; (5) to provide continual supervision of government programmes and liaison with departments and state governments; and (6) to analyse and review particular programmes.

The first two of these functions were said to be work for a cabinet office or secretariat, and the third was also seen to be associated with them; but methods for checking on implementation were unspecified. The fourth function was to be carried out by a reorganized group of projects divisions. Emphasis was placed on coordination, intelligence gathering and bureaucratic diplomacy. The intention was to turn the projects divisions into more than post-boxes or agencies providing amateur estimates of what was going on in particular policy fields. To some extent this function could be seen as overlapping with the third. The fifth function was to encompass the work of the PRS which late in 1974 was transferred to PMC.

Further comment on the problems and potential of these kinds of operations will be made below.

The sixth function was an attempt to break new ground. The PRS had done a number of programme evaluations, but there was no systematic basis for organizing such work. The specific proposals drew on British experience of Programme Analysis and Review (PAR) without, however, going into the problems that had been identified with PAR. Making PMC responsible for devising workable arrangements for programme evaluations was an attempt to give the department a substantial new role going far beyond the paper processing and discreet coordination of the Menzies-Bunting style.

These proposals did what the Gorton-Hewitt experiment had failed to do. They suggested ways of enhancing the department's capability to advise the prime minister on substantive matters of policy within the framework of an integrated department. They also emphasized the need for the department to have a close working relationship with Treasury and for political backing for the department when disputes with Treasury took place. The proposals began to work towards a redefinition of the relations between the central coordinating departments, and they generated further ideas.

One concerned interdepartmental committees (IDCs), which the proposals did not discuss. It was suggested that PMC should have a role in managing their work, not only in recording decisions but in preparing papers for discussion and acting as a catalyst in the speedy conclusion of their business. Another concerned the provision of economic advice for the prime minister. It was recognized that this was not a problem to be resolved simply by institutional tinkering; rather was it a matter of bringing together the substantial talents of economists already within the department in such a way that the prime minister could have regular briefings on economic conditions (and on the divergent views about what these were and what should be done about them). However, a notable difficulty was that Whitlam, like Menzies, had no real interest in economic policy. He did not have Chifley's intellectual interest in the discourses and diagnoses of professional economists. Thus economic advice had not only to be procured from the right balance of competing institutions but had to be packaged in a way acceptable to a prime minister who did not do much analytical thinking of his own in this field.

What happened in PMC during the remainder of the Whitlam years did not lead to a neat set of institutional solutions. The economic division gained in influence; the official in charge of it, for example, chaired an officials' committee which paralleled a ministerial committee set up to review public expenditure and actually attended the ministerial meetings "to record decisions". The PRS continued its work, but the ambiguities surrounding its role remained. The plans for systematic programme evaluation machinery were not fully realized. The department placed much more emphasis on its roles in federal-state relations. Two new structures were set up: the Policy Coordination Unit (PCU) and the Information and State Relations Division (ISRD). The PCU worked on a number of specific "fire brigade" tasks, tackling problems as they emerged, but its role had not crystallized when the government fell. There was some rivalry and overlap between it and the PRS. The PCU had no responsibility for operational matters; it was in a sense an ideas unit with a short time range. But it did have ambitions to play a major role in the coordination and implementation of policy. Thus its lack of operational responsibilities might be rephrased as a desire to get others to practise what it preached. While it operated, the PCU worked on renegotiating the general revenue assistance arrangements with the states and served as a resource and servicing unit for the cabinet committee concerned with federal-state relations. The ISRD gave divisional status to the department's continuing work in relations with the states. Its connection with the PCU on this subject was not entirely clear, though one aspect did emerge prominently. The "information" component of the division's work involved preparing information on a systematic and readily retrievable basis about the distribution of federal spending in states and regions. This allowed the initiation of a major bureaucratic drive to "get the credit for Canberra".

In the area of processing cabinet papers and briefing the prime minister on cabinet business, Menadue was associated with a number of measures aimed at streamlining procedures. Stricter and clearer instructions on the submission of proposals were issued. Note writers were given new instructions about points on which the prime minister needed to be briefed.

More generally, the department took the lead in tackling tough political issues. The role of the economic division has been mentioned already, and Menadue himself was personally concerned with redirecting resources policy after the resignation of Rex Connor. The broad efforts of PMC were integrated with those of the prime minister, his personal office, and his chosen inner circle of ministers. Throughout the government, Whitlam had picked and chosen among his advisers and confidants. But with Menadue in PMC an attempt was made to put the chosen few to useful work. A conscious effort was made to recreate an "official family" along the lines attributed to Chifley by L. F. Crisp.

Whitlam's reliance on Menadue had one unfortunate effect. He became so dependent on PMC that his private office no longer maintained detailed files of his activities. When the government was dismissed in November 1975 Whitlam was immediately cut off from some of his closest advisers. His private office did not have the expertise to make up the loss. These circumstances, however, were so exceptional that they need not be given further discussion in a general treatment. Their importance is specific to a particular episode.

Fraser Carmody and Yeend — The Rise and Rise of PMC

Under the Fraser government, PMC was reorganized three times (to June 1978), but its activist role was undiminished. Fraser, the "Menzies man", did not want a Menzies-type department. Menadue was kept on as head for nearly a year before being dispatched to a prestigious and important diplomatic post — Tokyo. He earned the ire of some Labor partisans and the grudging admiration of some Liberals for his ability and determination to serve a Liberal prime minister as well as he had served a Labor one. In the first reshuffle in PMC after Fraser took over, the PRS and the PCU disappeared; a new projects division was formed and some staff from both the PRS and PCU joined the new division. The former head of the PRS became the department's consultant economist working in collaboration with, but separately from, the economic division.

The second reshuffle (in 1977) was primarily the work of Alan Carmody, Menadue's successor as permanent head of the department. Carmody was a well-known bureaucratic imperialist and activist and he sought to meet Fraser's demands by increasing his department's influence and by changes to its style and to its formal structure. The department introduced a more senior classification structure for its officers in the second division, something hitherto reserved for a handful of other departments. (Curiously, in the context of the government's concern with federalism, the ISRD disappeared and no single element in PMC was given responsibility in this field.) Security and intelligence were emphasized, and other divisions were rearranged, although it is not clear what principles of organization, if any, were followed. The projects division was expanded and seems to have been allocated ambitious tasks in programme evaluation discussed but not followed through under Whitlam and Menadue. A few months later a second "Secretary to Cabinet", (in effect a second permanent head) G. J. Yeend, was appointed. The appointment allowed PMC greater flexibility in representation on permanent heads' committes and also indicated the broader role that the department expected for itself.

Longstanding trends in the department were strengthened by the appointment of Carmody — a concern with secrecy, a desire for greater central involvement and coordination and a "can-do" philosophy. Problems and pressures were identified. But the "can-do" philosophy, however welcome it may be to activist prime ministers, can create difficulties, especially as the department seemed undecided whether it was a policy adviser or cabinet facilitator or both. PMC is still a small department, and if unrealistic deadlines and ever-increasing responsibilities are taken on, then eventually, as on senior officer put it, the department simply "can't-do". Not only will the standard of policy advice be suspect but the capacity of officers to perform under pressure — created often by the uncertain and disparate nature of the work — will also be in question. The death of Carmody himself from a heart attack in April 1978 tragically illustrates this point. Indeed, officials in other departments have suggested that as PMC tried to take on more responsibility, so its effectiveness and the standard of its contribution declined. There may have been more activity, but less purposive action.

As the rise of PMC has been due to the conjunction first of Whitlam and Menadue and then of Fraser and Carmody, the change of permanent head may change its style. The new secretary, G. J. Yeend, has spent his career entirely in PMC; he has long-standing links with the facilitating role that Bunting perfected. Pragmatic, cool, effective, and dedicated to the concept of a neutral but flexible service, he may be able to met Fraser's demands without generating the frenetic activity that Carmody seemed to favour, because he may moderate those demands to administrative feasibility. He quickly proposed a restructuring of his department which plays down the "efficiency review" activity and returns much of the policy analysis to the operating sections of the department. He seems likely to combine the facilitating style of Bunting with the substantial policy role of Carmody.

But more important than the formal changes is the increasing influence of the Fraser style. The prime minister uses his department as a primary source of policy advice, especially about foreign affairs and economic management, often to the exclusion of the traditional departments. PMC has become, in effect *the* overseeing department on policy matters. It has gone beyond a coordinating role to become interventionist, responding to a prime minister who wishes to exercise control over all sectors of government. The outcomes of this control have not always been auspicious. The PMC has become perhaps the most powerful of the coordinating agencies.

Summary

The seventies have taken up what December 1949 killed off. PMC is now indisputably not simply a prestigious department but one that is trying to command the strategic points of bureaucratic influence. It is not a large department — it has a core of about four hundred officers — but it has added to its earlier functions concerning cabinet business important claims to the coordination, review, and evaluation of programmes and policies. Its growth has not been un-challenged. Other bureaucratic forces have guarded their own flanks, as Treasury prepared to do in 1949. Moreover, there has been an influential view, crystallized under Bunting, that PMC should conduct its affairs with a certain passivity. It has been argued that if ministers are well chosen and departments well organized, then a prime minister does not need to be supported by more than a facilitative department. Coordination could be a gentle process. Prime ministerial leadership would not need to be aggressive. This view depends on cabinet functioning as an efficient clearing house and point of resolution.

In this picture, central coordination and control at the bureau-cratic level is carried out by treasuries and central personnel agencies. As government became more complex, such bodies often took on added functions and disguised the extent to which they covered new territory. In the federal government, PMC became subject to demands for a wider coverage but was not keen to satisfy them. Arguments resisting change were based on custom and notions of the proper way to run a cabinet system. Unfortunately, this approach had the effect of safeguarding the department's position at the expense of leaving tasks undone. Problems were shuffled off but not disposed of — redirected but not resolved.

The growth of pressure on PMC can be seen as the impact of more complex governmental problems, tendencies to more and more government activity, and a consequent overstretching of existing resources and procedures. Guiding a government needs more than one astute man manipulating political and bureaucratic colleagues, even if he is prime minister. He has to have support. Once an attempt is made to organize this, the reality of a new centre of power is not hard to recognize.

How support should be organized has proved troublesome. One particular problem is that there are still arguments about how much of a "boss" a prime minister should be. Hence there are arguments about the extent of his bureaucratic support in case it is too great. One idea has been to set up bodies like the British Central Policy Review Staff (CPRS) to assist cabinet collectively. This was the idea behind the PRS too. But any new coordinating initiatives that help cabinet probably help the prime minister more. Further, the problems to be addressed by a department like PMC cannot be addressed with routinized responses. Economic doctrines are in conflict; social problems have many faces; analysis can start with many questions; techniques of analysis are not neutral. Pluralism in advice is still a disputed notion, and how to organize it, although long discussed in the United States, is a new question in Australia. Getting and keeping the attention of politicians is always a problem. The CPRS and PRS "solution" is especially precarious. The routine and the immediately pressing drive out the strategic, the speculative, and the problematic (see Plowden 1973; Pollitt 1974).

One way of specifying the elements of a prime minister's department has been to specify the roles of prime ministers. This is attractive but dangerous. The problem is that the roles of a prime minister are bundled together, and different elements in the mixture can be emphasized or played down differently by incumbents. Moreover, prime ministers can switch roles rapidly. When this is put together with the bureaucratic suspicions of other central departments and the political wariness of their ministerial masters, it adds up to an environment for a prime minister's department which is hostile and — in both long and short terms — changeable. The leaders and followers in a prime minister's department have to be both nimble and flexible. Static institutional arrangements come under real pressure.

A further problem is that such a department has few resources, though these may be powerful. It does not have access to routinized resources like a public service board or a department of finance. It does not have a solid concentration of economic expertise like a treasury. PMC depends on the narrow resource of control over cabinet papers and decisions and the potentially fickle resource of prime ministerial support. Thus its reputation and involvement in government can be subject to booms and busts.

In particular, a wedge can easily be driven between PMC's role in servicing cabinet and its wider roles in policy development and co-ordination. Once this is done the cabinet papers may still flow smoothly, but performance of the more nebulous and more important tasks of the department will tend to fall off. What this suggests is that the servicing of cabinet calls for staffing on the basis of policy and political capacity rather than merely on skills in high-level paper shuffling. Internal departmental arrangements have to be flexible; personnel have to be shifted in and out of the department as required. Further, while with a small cabinet office only a few top officers have to have the trust of the whole cabinet, with a larger, more active department the core of recording officers has to grow and such officers must fulfil other tasks as well. Purity and trust can no longer be ensured by aloofness and insulation.

TREASURY AND FINANCE

The chief controllers of that scarce resource, money in all its forms, are now two: the Treasury, which advises the cabinet on the management of the economy; and the Department of Finance, which is the keeper of the government's books and controls departmental expenditure. From 1901 to 1976 the two departments were one. They were divided by Fraser, officially in the hope of improving the capacity of Finance to control expenditure. Previously the conjunction of their tasks was a major source of power. The economic managers in the Treasury used the information gained by the divisions which are now in Finance as a means of getting a general view of government activity; less often their forecasts were used in arguments with departments over the financial aspects of particular programmes. It is too early yet to determine what impact the split will have; at least two or three budget rounds will have to be completed before they can be examined. Most of our comments will therefore be directed at the way the system has worked over a long period of time with comments later on the possible effects of the split.

The Treasury has long played a key role in Australian politics. Its advice, its views, and its relations, good or bad, with ministers and other departments have all had an important effect on the government's policy. Its influence is of course variable. The control of expenditure, now exercised by Finance, is reactive: for example, Finance does not decide what should be considered for action or what problems should be tackled, but it does give its views on what the government can afford. Departments propose, Finance disposes. The officers in Finance comment on the feasibility of programmes, on their hidden and future costs, on their compatibility with other programmes run by other departments. It tries to ensure that there is no fat, that the money can be spent and that all expenditure is properly authorized. Every year the expenses of existing programmes are considered, with the previous year's performance taken as the main indicator of need. New programmes are examined in some detail to ensure that they are needed, properly costed, and authorized. When a government embarks on a cost-cutting programme, it is Finance that has to find the places where cuts are to be made. Often it does so arbitrarily, with across-the-board cuts. Ministers find it difficult to monitor the consequences of decisions of this kind (for detailed treatment see Weller and Cutt 1976).

They also have found it difficult to control Treasury in its role as coordinator of economic policy. Economic policy is, at least these days, the classic wicked problem which defies definition, let alone solution. Yet in Australia the Treasury has maintained a near-monopoly on economic advice, and its influence can be powerful when it shapes the formulation of the problem put before ministers, for if all the options are determined within the boundaries of one such formulation then they are options only within very specific limits. Treasury has claimed that it is geared to presenting alternatives (Wilson 1976), but other departments believe that many alternatives are ignored. Certainly, in presenting proposals to ministers, the Treasury acts monolithically. Treasurers usually find it extremely difficult to discover whether or not there are divergent views within the department. This position is exacerbated by the existence of what is regarded as a "Treasury view". This has been described by one writer as —

> opposed to attempts to control prices and incomes directly, because it is "interference" which distorts the market mechanism in ways that are ultimately self-defeating; it is opposed to indexation as the "*quid pro quo*" for wage restraint, though it advises a strong government line against wage increases in the Arbitration Commission; it is temperamentally opposed to government spending, particularly to higher government spending at this time as a solution to unemployment; it is, or was up to September last year, in favour of demand deflation through higher taxes and lower government spending; it dislikes barriers against foreign investment; it is in favour of lower tariffs and more competition, though it maintains that these decisions should be made slowly and with proper provision for the consequences. [Edwards 1975, p. 6]

What is more, such a view is transmitted from generation to generation of Treasury officers. Promotion in the Treasury has largely been internal, so that many of those promoted succeed because they accept the proper mores of behaviour. A special recruitment programme is run to cream off the better products of the more conservative university economics departments. Those who do not perform well or differ in their assumptions are encouraged to join other departments (Weller and Cutt 1976, pp. 36-39). Basic Treasury attitudes therefore last throughout the changing political times and are far more persistent and more powerful than individual mavericks.

What develops is not necessarily that the Treasury is pro-Liberal or anti-Labor, but that its solutions are likely to be the same whatever government is in power. As long as it retains its monopoly on economic advice, no government or group of ministers has the time, the access to information, or the expertise to develop an alternative model or a coherent alternative policy. Nor in the last resort is it possible for a government to direct the Treasury to develop a policy to achieve particular objectives, since the Treasury can simply argue that these objectives cannot be achieved. And it has often so argued.

Because the Treasury does important things, it is involved in difficult choices; what it does nearly always matters. It has not, accordingly, always been popular as an institution with governments or other departments. That is inevitable and necessary. At times, departments have sought to contest its powers or to rival its capacities. But for many years the Treasury resisted attacks on it with considerable success. Its powers could not be lightly overturned.

Background

The Australian Treasury was one of the original departments established after Federation in 1901. It had a continuous and unbroken existence until 1976, although its functions and influence waxed and waned as permanent heads, political circumstances and the state of the economy changed. In the first thirty years it was little more than a ministry of finance, balancing the government's books and keeping a check on government expenditure. The power of its position was increased, in peacetime at least, by the affluence of the Commonwealth, but its economic responsibilities were limited by the Constitution. As Crisp remarks, the boundaries to the power of the federal government and the Treasury were best illustrated by the inability of either to find any realistic solutions to the Depression. The Treasury had to stand by, on the sidelines, as the national economy was supposed to regulate itself (Crisp 1961, p. 317).

Gradually the role of the Treasury became far more complex. The 1944 agreement by which the states temporarily gave up their right to levy income tax gave the federal government virtually complete control of the purse. The successful referendum in 1946 enabled it to take a new role in social welfare. Keynesian ideas influenced especially the young economists who were rising rapidly to the top of the expanding federal public service. The new trends were symbolized by the publication of two White Papers in 1945. The first, *Full Employment in Australia*, explained the government's commitment to the prevention of the high levels of unemployment that had prevailed before the war. The second was the initial annual White Paper, *National Income and Expenditure*. These papers, Crisp explains, acknowledged that the federal government had a general role of leadership of, and intervention in, the Australian economy. They also recognized that its own revenue raising and expenditure had become so large that they helped to determine the condition of the national economy as a whole. As a result, all the government's activities had to be deliberately reconciled and coordinated to help achieve the government's economic objectives of stability, high employment, continued economic expansion, and social welfare. The Treasury became the centre of the process of wide-ranging governmental supervision of the whole economy. It had to develop a new capacity to undertake these responsibilities, especially in the increasingly important division that was concerned with economic management. Financial control remained one, but only one, of the functions undertaken by the Treasury to govern the national economy, and in many ways it became subordinate to the demands of economic management (Crisp 1961).

Under Chifley, and in its newly developing role of economic manager in the late 1940s, the Treasury was especially powerful because Chifley was both prime minister and treasurer, a combination of roles that has not been repeated since in federal politics. To some extent the Department of Post-War Reconstruction, under the leadership of John Dedman and Dr H. C. Coombs, challenged the Treasury's monopoly on economic advice, but it was already being phased out by 1949 and was abolished by the incoming Liberal government. During the 1950s and early 1960s the Treasury retained its hegemony under Sir Roland Wilson. Despite the failure of such policies as the credit squeeze of 1961, which almost brought down the Liberal government, and despite challenges from the Department of Trade, under Sir John Crawford and Sir Alan Westerman, the Treasury's position as the premier department and the main adviser on economic affairs remained undisputed.

One example of the department's influence can be seen in the government's reaction to the report of the Vernon Committee of Economic Inquiry in 1965. Established in 1963 in the aftermath of the 1961 economic crisis, the Vernon Committee had been appointed to examine the government's economic decision-making machinery; the committee included Crawford, former secretary of the Department of Trade. His old department's influence could be seen in the final report. Among its recommendations was a proposal for the establishment of an independent Advisory Council on

Economic Growth, which would prepare an annual review of the country's long-term prospects. After the report was published, it was vigorously opposed by the Treasury because, among its other effects, this new council would have ended the Treasury's monopoly of advice on macro-economic policy. Aided by Treasury's advice, Menzies denounced the proposal as leading to government by technical experts and suggested that it would introduce a degree of planning and direction of the economy that would be inappropriate in Australia. The report was buried and the Treasury's economic hegemony was safe (Spann 1973, p. 343). Seldom has its bureaucratic power been better illustrated.

The first major reduction of influence of the Treasury occurred in 1968, when Gorton was elected prime minister. It was not that the expertise of the Treasury was reduced; instead, its position was challenged, and the challenge had the support of the prime minister and the deputy prime minister. Gorton also tried to use the re-arranged PMC as a counter to the Treasury and its minister: he was sceptical about the advice emanating from the Treasury and his relations with the treasurer, McMahon, were usually strained and distant. Gorton occasionally rejected the Treasury's advice. In 1969 he ignored the proposal for a "tough" budget and emphatically discarded a suggestion that the sales tax on petrol should be increased. He devised new guidelines to regulate foreign takeovers and co-operated with McEwen to establish the Australian Industries Development Corporation, despite the Treasury's opposition to both proposals.

When McMahon became prime minister the situation changed, because the new advice-oriented structures in the prime minister's department were dismantled. McMahon, as treasurer, had been fully advised and had performed competently. But as prime minister he left himself almost without advice and soon began to flounder. He recalled that when he tried to change the direction taken by the 1971 budget, he was unable to get any response from the Treasury for six months. Further he was never told that opinions in the Treasury about the original strategy were divided. Indeed, soon after the arrival of Sir Frederick Wheeler as permanent head of the Treasury late in 1971, the Treasury was again "riding high". The temporary reduction of the Treasury's influence is not therefore a phenomenon that occurs only during the tenure of Labor governments; it is part of a long-running dispute over departmental influence that will occur under any government.

The Treasury under Labor

Under the Labor government the periodic storms increased, although they were by no means continual. Labor members entered office with a deep-seated suspicion of the public service as a whole and of the Treasury in particular. They believed that after serving a Liberal government for twenty-three years the public service must inevitably be conservative. In their first year the Labor members energetically set out to implement their electoral pledges. Whatever was included in the platform or the policy speech was considered sacrosanct, and the Treasury's belief that public expenditure was being increased too rapidly was ignored. Even though it may be true that no Labor treasurer could have slowed down the rush of re-formist and expensive programmes, it is certainly true that in 1973 and 1974 the incumbent treasurer was not willing to fight his colleagues and was very easily overruled. Yet at the same time the government implemented several other measures, notably the re-valuation of the currency, which the Treasury had advocated for some time.

The government's opinion of the value of Treasury advice varied. In March 1974 when McMahon criticized the Treasury, Whitlam defended it as the best-equipped department to handle the financial questions that were being discussed. The Coombs Task Force, established in early 1973 to examine existing government programmes and to recommend where cuts could be made, had been the brainchild of a deputy secretary of the Treasury, John Stone, who then served on it. Yet by December 1974, when the Treasury was being criticized by Gorton and McMahon to the RCAGA, Whitlam also attacked it, stating that in future he would require better and quicker advice than had so far been provided. His dissatisfaction sprang in part from the arguments that had developed over the formulation of the 1974 budget strategy, the subject of one of our case-studies.

Then came the loans affair. Its very origin indicated the suspicion with which the Treasury was regarded. Rather than use the Treasury to raise loans through the usual channels, the select group of ministers involved preferred to work through a variety of shadowy middlemen whose capacity was unproved and whose loyalty was later shown to be lacking. As the story began to break in the press, and as the opposition seemed to be kept supplied with a regular flow of documentation, the suspicions of the Treasury among ministers grew. They were further boosted by evidence suggesting that Wheeler, the permanent head, was acting without consulting his minister, although the evidence was ambiguous and provided by the Department of Minerals and Energy, then engaged in a bitter bureaucratic feud with the Treasury. In an attempt to remove Wheeler from the secretaryship of the Treasury, he was offered the post of governor of the Reserve Bank. He declined the offer, opposed all moves to replace him, and retained his position. During June, discussions over splitting the Treasury were held, with Connor and Cairns, the treasurer, urging that it be done. Then the loans affair finally blew wide open, and the treasurer was sacked. June 1975 proved to be the low point of the Treasury's fortunes. In 1972 and 1974 the Treasury had argued that government spending should be restrained; in 1975 the budget was shaped on the lines that it advocated. The Expenditure Review Committee of cabinet, appointed to oversee the levels of spending, and with a committee of officials acting as its executive arm, began to operate more effectively. The Labor government fell at a time when, in the view of many Treasury officers, it was becoming responsible for the first time.

Resurgence and Division under the Liberals

Under the Liberal government elected in December 1975 limits were immediately placed on government spending. Rigid guidelines and instructions were announced within two weeks of their taking office, and Sir Henry Bland was appointed to head a committee responsible for finding any excessive or duplicated expenditure, although, interestingly, there was no Treasury officer on the Bland Committee. The Treasury was again seen as very influential.

Then, in November 1976 the Treasury was suddenly split. The decision was sudden, but in one sense it should have surprised no one. Alternative institutional arrangements had long been under consideration by both Labor and Liberal ministers. The immediate reasons for this particular institutional rearrangement must be sought in the interplay of personality, irritation, and spontaneity. The particular case was unique, but the general situation was not. The Labor government had considered splitting the Treasury but left its thinking so late that other more pressing questions took its attention. Labor had, however, shuffled other institutions quickly around; this did not make the process easier or more successful, but it did evidently make it more acceptable to governments.

The Treasury's Activities

In the past it has been the conjunction of the Treasury's several roles that has made it so powerful. It had three main functions: it advised on economic management, it acted as overseer for government expenditure, and it was the government's bookkeeper. This meant that for every proposal put forward by spending departments the Treasury's opinion was presented at three stages at least and often more. As economic manager, the Treasury advised cabinet about the boundaries of government spending and whether in broad terms costs of a particular proposal could be afforded. As financial controller, the Treasury reviewed most new proposals before cabinet considered them and commented on the worth of the proposal, the accuracy of the forecasts, the possibility of overlap with other government programmes, and a host of other factors. Once a programme had begun, the Treasury negotiated with the sponsoring department about the level of funds required to continue it. In doing so, it made judgments about the effectiveness of the programme in the preceding year, and it was prepared to argue for a reduction in expenditure on the basis that the programme should be carried out differently. Its expertise in these areas may have been limited; its involvement was not. Fourth, as the national bookkeeper, the Treasury was often responsible for the payments of funds to states or other bodies under a programme. Its involvement was therefore both continuous and crucial; if the Treasury wished to question the validity of a programme, it could do so frequently and this could very easily delay policy implementation.

Formally the Treasury is involved in the development and administration of policy because of its concern with financial accuracy. But traditionally its interests have been much broader and its influence has usually helped to shape the content as well as the cost of a departmental proposal. The Treasury always had a greater capacity than any other department to fit together the various segments of government policy because it alone was continuously involved. Hence, it often became by default the only coordinator of government policy (albeit from a financial stand point).

At times it questioned whether or not a programme could be

better done by a different department. It was also an insistent guardian of cabinet responsibility. If a department wanted to spend money on an item that was not explicitly covered by a cabinet decision, the Treasury could and often did refuse to give approval until it was referred back to cabinet.

Since cabinet rules usually require that the Treasury should be consulted about the financial implications of a proposal before it is presented to cabinet, the Treasury can force departments to accept its views before it will give its support. Often this takes time. The same may be true of the administration of a programme. Most acts include a clause that allows the treasurer to make advances to state governments "at such time and in such amounts as he sees fit". This power is delegated to officials in the Treasury, but before they "see fit", they may ask for a range of detail that may not be easy to provide and in the views of the departments may not be necessary.

These methods are *ad hoc* and vary from officer to officer and from division to division. There is no set list of criteria applied to all proposals, nor as yet any serious attempt to ensure any consistency in the application of controls. The treatment of departments depends much on their "track record", that is, on whether the department is considered trustworthy or reliable. If it is not, then Treasury/Finance has a number of ways to exert pressure and to cut expenditure. There is no doubt that the Treasury has in the past used its financial control powers to assert its bureaucratic ascendancy. One officer claimed that he sometimes asked for information to "assert our right to know". But on other occasions the requests may be essential to allow the centre to know what is going on. It is generally impossible to say which demands are obstructive and which are necessary, for on different occasions the same question may fulfil different functions. This capacity of Finance to exert uneven controls on departments led one officer in 1975 to make the sour comment: "Is there a Treasury view? Yes, it is no!"

The Treasury's great power was based on the conjunction of its several responsibilities. If its advice was not taken at one point, it could press the same argument at a later stage of a programme's development. Further, it had in the past a monopoly of these functions. It had been the only department to make calculations about the effectiveness of existing programmes, although these were often guesses rather than detailed analyses. Its minister was, apart from the prime minister, the only minister briefed on every item with financial implications that came to cabinet. The Treasury was the only department with the information, capacity, and skills to develop on a regular basis forecasts of the country's economic future and to advise cabinet in these areas. It has fought hard to maintain this monopoly and has at various times had to defend itself against others like Trade and DURD, which have claimed a similar capacity. PMC is its latest rival.

Treasury argued that it could only fulfil its functions properly if all its functions remained united. The argument was based more on a desire to retain its bureaucratic hegemony than on any functional logic, for the Canadian situation has shown that different structures can work adequately. In the past the economic managers dominated the Treasury's strategy and advice. They found the support of the supply divisions who controlled expenditure invaluable as an intelligence service to find out what other departments were doing. But, partly as a result, expenditure decisions about particular policies became subordinated to general economic demands.

Now the conjunction has been broken. As a result there are bound to be some overlapping functions and possibly demarcation disputes. The most obvious area in which these may occur is federal-state relations. The Treasury retains responsibility for loan raising and the general level of assistance; the Department of Finance will examine and supervise all special purpose grants and developmental projects. How policy and supervision can be separated in this area is not clear.

The necessity to maintain a regular flow of information between the departments will probably ensure that, contrary to the prime minister's assertions, the workload of many officers will be increased. The old Treasury operated very hierarchically. Communications to other departments were sent out at a high level. If this practice continues between the two departments it could easily lead to a paper-jam, as memoranda go up rather than across. Further, the fact that the Treasury gives its economic forecasts to another department, however close a relationship the two may have, could easily lead to demands from other departments for similar access. If this pressure grows too great, the record of the Treasury suggests that it would withdraw access rather than increase it, and Finance may become more isolated. In the past the economic section of PMC has had difficulty in getting information on economic trends from the Treasury, even though some of its officers formerly worked there (see Weller 1977).

However, the greatest problem may be caused by something far more intangible — the growth of a new independent bureaucratic empire. All departments develop their own identity and interest. They have responsibilities they want to keep, power they want to preserve, influence they want to extend. Departmental officers seldom want to be another department's poor relation. Even though relations between the two departments may remain close, the Department of Finance will ensure that it is not dominated by the Treasury in the way that the old general financial and economic policy division used to dominate the supply divisions. The Department of Finance will develop its own ethos and attitudes, will compete for individuals, functions, and influence, and a gradual separation of ways must follow. This development will be speeded up as a separate minister of finance was appointed after the 1977 election.

Since the two departments now report to different ministers, they can no longer always ensure that their advice is coordinated before it reaches ministerial level. Duplication of advice will gradually grow. As a member of cabinet's monetary committee, the minister of finance wants to be able to make his own contribution, and therefore relies on his department for comment on the accuracy of Treasury's macro-economic proposals. How the appointment of two ministers will affect the preparation of the budget will take some years to emerge. Yet it does mean that the new general expenditure division of the Department of Finance is looking at ways of introducing greater consistency in its application of financial controls.

The Treasury has always been an important central actor in the bureaucratic game. It will probably remain so. The creation of the Department of Finance will reduce some of its influence; so will the accretion of power to the revitalized PMC. The major factors in determining how the Treasury worked were always institutional. Personalities may have varied the performance and other departments may have been temporary rivals, but the conjunction of economic management and financial control within a capable organization always in the final resort ensured the Treasury's success. That power now has been split; the two departments together may never be as consistently powerful, but the joint influence will be more important than any other department.

Despite the changes, the Treasury has shown no indication that it is altering its methods of procedure. PMC has been searching for new functions with vigour and initiative, but the Treasury has continued to apply existing procedures. Change in those methods is introduced only gradually. Functional classification of budget outputs is one change that has occurred. Forward estimates have also been introduced, but for a variety of bureaucratic and political reasons they have not been successful as a planning device. Since 1976 they have been used as a means of collecting departmental proposals together to allow cabinet to see an early budget picture. Finance has used these opportunities to exert increased controls and impose new cuts on the general lines accepted by cabinet on its recommendation. The Treasury is proud of being a hard-headed and conservative department. Despite its occasional loss of influence — in 1969 and 1974, for instance — its variety of controls can ensure that any decline in influence is temporary.

The development and administration of every programme is likely to have some unique features, not least because the Treasury's (now Finance's) control procedures are essentially *ad hoc*. Nevertheless, an example, based on one particular programme, will show how the Treasury can shape the programme's content and progress.

Treasury and the South Australian Lands Commission

In March 1973 the Labor cabinet decided in principle that it would establish land commissions in each state in cooperation with each state government (for detailed treatment of this programme, see Troy 1978). The purpose of such a commission was to improve the allocation of land by government involvement and, if possible, to reduce its price. Only one state, South Australia, was prepared to act quickly enough for funds to be spent in the 1973-74 financial year. Even then, only $8 million was used.

Nevertheless, in 1973-74 the Department of Urban and Regional Development, which sponsored the proposal, negotiated with the Treasury at least four times over this programme — during negotiations for budget cabinet in 1973; over the legislation to establish the scheme, the Lands Commission (Financial Assistance) Act 1973; over the terms of the agreement with South Australia; and over the actual payments of the funds to the state. On every occasion the negotiation with the Treasury was prolonged and difficult.

In the submission presented to budget cabinet, DURD put two proposals, one seeking funds for $60 million, the other for $120 million. The Treasury, which was sceptical about the value and objectives of the proposal, and believed that DURD did not itself know what it could spend, opposed such high figures. Cabinet eventually agreed to appropriate $30 million for the programme, and that amount was formally included in the budget.

The next two stages — the legislation and the agreement with the state — occurred almost simultaneously. The first meetings with the Treasury on the legislation were held in August 1973, and drafts of the instructions being prepared for the parliamentary draftsman were later sent for comment. The Treasury provided detailed comments on the instructions on 24 October and on the principles on which the land commissions were to work. As some of the land to be used was to be freehold, whereas the original submission had spoken only of leasehold, the Treasury argued that DURD should prepare a further submission for cabinet to clear up this and several other problems.

In early November a further cabinet submission was thus lodged. It proposed acceptance of changes to the condition of tenure and the terms of finance. The Treasury refused to give its support because it did not have time to consider the latest drafting of the bills. Three days later the Treasury commented in detail and suggested that all action on legislation should be delayed until cabinet had approved the use of freehold land. Such a step would probably have made passage of the legislation in that session extremely difficult. DURD argued that the bills already had sufficient flexibility.

Cabinet duly accepted the proposals in the submission, and the next day the legislation committee of cabinet approved the introduction of the bills "subject to final settlement of the financial terms by the treasurer and the minister". Unaware of the condition, Tom Uren, the minister for urban and regional development, introduced the legislation in the House on 21 November. The next day, at the IDC on urban and regional development, a Treasury officer blandly declared: "If the legislation is introduced, then in terms of cabinet decision 1612 it will have to be amended." A rapid series of meetings between the permanent heads of the two departments was then held to settle the outstanding points of difference, especially differences over interest rates. The amendments to the legislation were introduced into the House by Uren on 29 November.

At the same time, negotiations on the form of the agreements were in progress. On 28 September, Uren had sent to the prime minister proposed documents for the Lands Commission agreement with South Australia. On 9 October PMC asked the Treasury for comment on these documents and received a detailed and lengthy reply on 28 October; in particular, the Treasury argued that the draft agreement added in several respects to the draft model that had been approved by cabinet. On 9 November the prime minister asked DURD to refer the documents to the appropriate IDC, a view that (not surprisingly) was also espoused by the Treasury. On 5 December the permanent head of DURD wrote to PMC, asking to see any comments that the Treasury might have made to PMC on the draft proposals. In other words, the department was still officially unaware of the detailed objections of the Treasury to the draft proposals, although informally it had access to a copy. The IDC on urban and regional development met on 12 December — and decided to establish a working party which met a week later. In the meantime DURD decided to take the points of contention to cabinet in a further submission. Negotiations with the Treasury on acceptable financial terms continued, but remained unresolved until early February. The dispute was finally settled at a bilateral meeting between Uren and the treasurer, when notes to be read into the cabinet record were finally agreed on. The actual terms had been settled by two meetings of the permanent heads, and the compromise was accepted by cabinet on 18 February.

The financial agreement with South Australia was finally executed on 11 April. But the money had to be paid over by 30 June if it were not to lapse. Under the terms of the legislation the treasurer could make such advances as he saw fit. But before the Treasury was prepared to make the advance, it demanded more information and detail about the blocks of land that were to be bought. DURD argued that the information was simply not available; the Treasury argued that the department had not fulfilled the requirements of its own schedule and that the payments would not be legal. Eventually, direct prime ministerial intervention ensured that the money was paid — on the last possible day.

Doubtless this case was an especially stormy one. DURD was a new and active department, staffed in its early stages by activists in a hurry. They argued that the Treasury was invariably unhelpful and obstructive, that it never provided information unless specifically asked and failed to comment exhaustively on a proposal at first sighting, and that it never tried to speed up a policy that the government clearly supported. In other words, the situation in which the Treasury's comments to PMC on the South Australian drafts were not communicated to DURD for a further six weeks was not an uncommon one. For its part, the Treasury saw DURD as hasty, erratic, and inexperienced, ignorant of proper procedures, prepared to bend the rules of cabinet government and to take undesirable short cuts too often. And its treatment of DURD was little different from its treatment of many other departments. Information, in particular, had to be carefully husbanded; it was a weapon to be used when most effective in achieving ends of which the Treasury approved.

Conclusion

The main point of this brief outline is to show the centrality of the Treasury to the policy processes. It had the opportunity to become involved on several occasions in the one programme; it had the capacity to delay action until it was satisfied, even to the point of insisting on amendments to legislation already introduced in the House; it could raise more detailed queries before paying out the advances to the states. The case emphasizes the capacity of the Treasury to coordinate and perhaps even to frustrate policy. It pulls together the various departmental proposals in the annual budget, which is at least intended to express a consistent view. The Treasury attempts to ensure that policies do not overlap and are not inconsistent with one another or with the cabinet's general approach. It maintains control of the payments made under many of the programmes, and can force agreement on all legislation and state agreements. Treasury and Finance between them, then, are the *only* central agencies with this continuous and detailed involvement, the *only* agencies to have such detailed information and such frequent input into the administration of policies. Further, by providing the advice and analysis of economic management, they also provide the general framework into which the details must be fitted. No other agencies, whether central or spending, can challenge their position.

But how well do they fulfil it? There is no doubt that, in fulfilling the responsibilities as they see them, they are competent, hard-working and vigorous. The main outside criticism is of their lack of imagination, their conservatism and their insistence on judging all policies almost exclusively in financial terms, with little account for their "policy" implications. The creation of the Department of Finance will probably gradually change this situation, but it is unlikely to do so quickly. Change has in the past come only slowly. In the meantime, Treasury and Finance have such general and pervasive involvement in policy that their influence will always be important and usually (but not always) decisive.

THE PUBLIC SERVICE BOARD

The PSB has a crucial task: to maintain and control the personnel resources of the public service. It has statutory authority to create offices in the public service and so to decide what sorts of, and how many, public servants there will be and how they will be fitted into organizational structures; to act as the wage-fixing authority in the public service and as the "employer" of public servants in negotiations about conditions of employment, especially with arbitral bodies; and to ensure that personnel resources are being properly used through reviews of the efficiency of departments (Caiden 1967). In carrying out these statutory functions the PSB coordinates some important activities of other departments: it establishes rules to guide the articulation and settlement of establishment, personnel, and industrial disputes, for example, and it balances departmental needs against the limited resources of government. To coordinate is to evaluate and to allocate, and the maintenance of the personnel resources of the public bureaucracy, no less than management of the financial resources, is a major element and condition of the policy processes at all times.

But it is hard to define the board's functions in a fixed way. It has some responsibility for recruitment to the public service, promotion, job evaluation and grading, pay and other conditions of employment, grievance procedures, the resolution of industrial disputes, staff development and training, retirement benefits, machinery of government, overall limits on staff numbers, automatic data processing, and for the managerial and technical efficiency of departments; and we will see that the board has attempted to widen its role even further in recent years. Not all of these functions can be related easily to the board's statutory charter. Other government agencies sometimes believe that the PSB is involved in "policy" beyond its proper province, and certainly the board influences the policy processes in ways that go beyond any narrow definition of its "coordinating" role. It is no longer possible, if it ever was, to see the PSB as simply a "central staffing and pay authority" which operates "as an all-wise authority issuing its fiats on the staffing and remuneration of the commonwealth service" (Wheeler 1967, pp. 7, 8).

Since we cannot review all the PSB's activities, we concentrate on one issue of crucial importance to illustrate the way in which "coordination" becomes intertwined with "policy": the control of public service numbers. It is at the heart of the board's activities and our case-studies at times rely upon the growth or decline of staff numbers to explain or illuminate the wider policy processes. Here we refer essentially to the creation and abolition of offices (the "establishment" of the public service) rather than to the growth and decline of officers (the "staff"). The two matters are closely related, though they are not the same. Later we will see that attempts to control the number of public service *officers* has, in fact, made it difficult for the board to exert its accustomed control over *offices*.

The Board's power over *offices* in the public service derives from section 29 of the Public Service Act, which provides that:

1. The Governor-General may, on the recommendation of the Board, after the Board has obtained a report from the Permanent Head —
    (a) create an office in a Department; and
    (b) abolish an office in a Department

2. The Board may, after the Board has obtained a report from the Permanent Head —
    (a) raise or lower the classification of an office; and
    (b) alter the designation of an office, other than an office of Permanent Head.

The board's control of offices resembles the Treasury's control of financial resources. Departments with work to do must seek not only money but also positions for the public servants who are to do it. Each kind of control enables the coordinating agency concerned to evaluate a programme in the light of available resources as it sees them, and thus in effect to judge the values of the programme itself. The board can get to know the business of other departments through its knowledge of where positions and people are allocated, just as the Treasury knows departments' internal financial logic. In other ways, however, the two controls are not at all the same. Offices must be defined in terms of people and skills, and people are less tractable than money. Personal skills and organizational fit can be used to sustain long-running arguments. The imperatives of the budget cycle and the failure as yet to establish a manpower cycle also establish quite different relationships. Departments retain more capacity to resist the pressure of the board. Moreover, a number of statutory authorities are formally outside the board's jurisdiction and have varying degrees of freedom over matters associated with establishments (including such complex conditions of employment as remuneration). These patterns of responsibility are not stable. Coordination is, as always, a question of shifting relationships.

Even if the business of government were unchanging and even if public policy could be divided up into discrete programmes with staffing needs unambiguously specified for each programme, the PSB would still have important and difficult work to do. It would still have to recruit the right number of people at the right time, for example, and would have to match them to appropriate tasks. The board does much work of this sort, and it must accordingly grapple with problems about the composition of the workforce (for example, Are the right skills available as required?) and about how individuals can best be used (for example, How should staff be trained and developed?). Such questions, even about long-running and stable programmes, can involve the board in disputes with other departments about "policy". The board may doubt the capacity of some senior public servants, or even of whole departments, to manage their existing programmes. It approaches with special caution any suggestions that such departments should extend their tasks.

This happens often, for the business of government is always changing in both scope and intensity. Changing circumstances create new pressures on old functions of government. New pressures can to some extent be foreseen and systematically dealt with. Where the board has good relationships with an agency, for example, it may become accepted that increases in the agency's work should lead to an increase in staff according to some mutually agreed formula. But policy-related difficulties can still enter. The Auditor-General's Office, for example, is seeking to develop a capacity to mount reviews of government effectiveness, which involves it and the PSB in the troublesome definition of new tasks and skills. This cuts across old agreements, for the Office can more readily get staff to do work of an established type: an increase in the volume of conventional compliance audits, for example, will almost automatically, if slowly, lead to the creation of new offices. Accordingly, there are incentives for both sides to proceed slowly and perhaps to ask whether new policy is worth the effort of justifying new offices in new ways.

The expansion of existing functions alone can create problems for the board. In 1975, for example, it was taken by surprise when a sudden rise in unemployment resulted immediately in fresh demands being placed upon the counter staff of the Department of Social Security (which pays unemployment benefits); the board was asked to provide more staff, albeit to do more work of an accustomed kind, at the very time it had launched an exercise (discussed below) to limit staff growth in the whole public service. In this case, as in countless others, the board had to consider not only whether new offices should be created but whether additional officers should be found and also whether different working methods might be an alternative to increased numbers. It was involved, in other words, with problems about industrial relations and about the efficiency of another agency.

Moreover, public policy changes the scope as well as the intensity of its demands. Governments constantly think of new things to do (though they are unlikely to discard the old), and so the board has pressure forever upon it to create new positions so people can do new work. Through parliament a government can make funds available, as certified by the Treasury, for the creation of new positions. But it is the board which has the difficult task of interpreting and translating such decisions into types, levels, and numbers of positions and so into numbers of people. Public policies are developed on the basis of objectives and financial costs rather than on the basis of the personnel resources needed to implement them. Cabinet submissions, for example, rarely have staff requirements attached to them, and even less frequently does cabinet make decisions in these terms. It suits both ministers and departments to act in this way. Departments that are unsure about what personnel resources they need to tackle a new problem, for example, do not want to be bound by a precise cabinet decision. Ministers typically do not want to be bothered with apparently petty matters which seem so fragmented as to be beyond their understanding or control; dollars are easier to summarize and make decisions about than people.

It nevertheless is the task of the board to staff the departments that have charge of new programmes. Cabinet decisions have to be assessed to determine their implied staff requirements; and assessment requires consultation with affected departments, which may have different interpretations to offer. This is a matter of classifying work, of determining tasks, of allocating them between offices and between levels of a hierarchy, and of matching individual skills to official needs. It should be technical or neutral work, or so it is said to be. Certainly the board represents these processes as being almost objective in character. To the professionals of the board, there should always be one best answer to the problem of establishments, and it is true at least that some answers are better than others. Since human resources are limited, it is important that the board should not be profligate in any particular case; there will otherwise be less to be shared later. It is also important that the board should not be miserly; the business of government will then be skimped. It is natural, then, that the board should have statutory power to recommend the creation of offices in the public service. The decisions of the board can be overridden by cabinet, but it makes too many decisions for this to happen very often. In any event, ministers and departments alike also have reasons for leaving the board alone.

This is not because the board has statutory powers. The board's autonomy does not, of course, result from this charter. The reverse is true. Questions about establishments and staffing are highly charged politically, and it is the board's statutory charter which legitimizes the discretion it needs to manoeuvre between the competing claims upon the resources it controls. This discretion is universally, though not equally, valued. To some extent all participants have an interest in seeing that the board maintains a middle way, for they would prefer their own changing situations to be dealt with in a regular and predictable manner, not erratically as the result of uncontrolled pressures. Just as the failure to specify programmes in terms of personnel resources allows departments and ministers to redefine their needs as circumstances change, so does the board's statutory authority allow it to adjust the answers that it gives. But this general understanding often breaks down when particular cases are at stake. Staffing is not an uncontested exercise of authority but rather a continual process of negotiation and compromise between the board, departments, and ministers. The board always must make judgments about the best way to translate policy intentions into establishment outcomes. The interesting questions concern the ways in which those judgments are contested, and whether the board's role might be contested in such a way as to undermine it altogether.

The board has learned — perhaps it always knew — to make its judgments sceptically. It doubts the ability of departments to seek new offices in a disinterested way. More than a government's intentions are involved, it feels. Departmental empire-building may also be at work, or even plain inefficiency. As the board has said, in its careful way, "certain centralised controls . . . are an essential and inescapable need, to protect those overall interests which go beyond the area of a particular department or other agency" (Public Service Board 1974a, p. 93). From the viewpoint of particular departments, however, things look very different. The caution of the board can be interpreted as hostility to the proper aspirations of an agency or its minister. New agencies, having almost no resources at all to begin with, may feel this strongly. The Social Welfare Commission, established by the Labor government in 1973 as a research and advisory body, thus argued that the "powers" (by which it meant the slowness and unhelpfulness) of the PSB had "compromised" its independence through the PSB's agreeing too slowly to create the positions the commission thought it needed (Social Welfare Commission 1976). The "professional" detachment of the board's officers can seem like indifference. One permanent head could thus "see a case for a Board representative virtually in permanent residence in some departments at least. . . . this would be welcomed and protect the Board from a reputation of making decisions in isolation on the basis of superficial inspections by people who do not understand enough about the policy" (Defence 1975a). Especially to the RCAGA, departments and their permanent heads vented their frustrations trenchantly about a PSB which seemed to be more and more a brake on their own proper responsibilities. Sir Lenox Hewitt put the anti-board case most pungently: the board seemed to him "to proceed from an assumption, an inverted onus of proof, that the permanent head is a prolific [sic] lunatic, reckless, and must be ground down and given a half, a third or a quarter of what they say from their day to day desperate experience they need to stay alive" (RCAGA 1975, p. 1757).

The board seldom has the luxury of dealing with such antagonists in isolation. Instead it must deal with departments and ministers who have overlapping and conflicting claims upon it. Cabinet decisions may not specify clearly who is to perform new tasks. In any event, the programmes of government are seldom entirely new; they usually have some relationship to older tasks and, perhaps, to the contentious disposition of staff between agencies. To the board, its own decisions in one case may appear an unwelcome precedent in another.

The PSB has not always seemed helpful to departments and certainly not to politicians. They find that the intractability of the board's operations makes action slow for them. Money can be voted to create new offices, but that is only the beginning of the problem. Animosities are most intense and room for disagreement greatest when new agencies are created, for their charters are usually broad and call for correspondingly wide exercises of discretion to be made in deciding about their establishment and staff.

The board's role was questioned sharply by ministers during the years of the Whitlam Labor government. From the outset, the PSB was required by the government to create and staff the new agencies that were intended to put new policies into effect. This was not easy to do. Not only had the staff to be found, but the organizations into which they were to be placed had to be carved from existing institutions or newly constructed. Existing institutions watched the process jealously, and the board never had a free hand. An especially protracted dispute arose between the board and the new Department of Urban and Regional Development, which argued for an organizational weight equal to that of the Treasury; the particular issue upon which judgments of weight turned was the second division structure of DURD. Were its ascending levels to be staffed at the 2, 4, and 6 levels of Treasury, or was it to have the 1, 3, and 4 levels of nearly all other departments? This was not simply a dispute about numbers of staff. The permanent head of DURD specifically claimed to want only a small, but expert, department. The board did not think the higher-level structure was justified. It was a question of how the numbers were to be disposed. Upon such complex issues — more than symbolic in the status-conscious world of Canberra — the board was forced to fight. It was fighting not just about its judgments on job content. It was fighting also to preserve relativities of status and capacity in the public service as a whole (and in this case it won).

The board could never expect to please everyone. The board's protests that new departments and new offices could not be constructed overnight went largely unheard. Ministers were frustrated and at times openly expressed their hostility towards an agency that seemed to them thoroughly and pejoratively "bureaucratic". Statutory powers notwithstanding, ministers occasionally tried to override the board on questions that went beyond establishment issues. In 1973, for example, the minister for labour belaboured the PSB as the protector of the highly paid "fat cats" of the public service and attempted to appear in opposition to it during wage hearings before the Conciliation and Arbitration Commission. In 1974 the prime minister announced his intention to disregard any decision the board might reach in a dispute then being heard between a permanent head and a prominent subordinate, an Aboriginal official.

More lasting injuries were also suffered by the board in this period. Its jurisdiction over staffing was, for example, reduced. A number of statutory authorities have always put their establishment proposals to cabinet independently of the board, but until 1974 their significance had been slowly falling, and in that year some two-thirds of federal government employees fell within the board's ambit. A larger number of agencies also set certain of their employees' conditions of employment independently of the board, but the board had also been moderately successful in reducing anomalies and encouraging consultation between agencies. While recognizing the need for certain government agencies to have control of their staff (to preserve judicial independence for example), the board had carried the centralization of the public service some considerable way forward. In 1974, however, the Department of the Postmaster-General was abolished and two new statutory authorities were created in its place, with their staffing authority outside the board's ambit. The department had employed nearly half the total number of public servants, and the proportion of federal government employees under the PSB declined at once to about one-third. The board made strenuous efforts to reverse the situation. Together with the Department of Labour and Immigration (which had related though distant interests in manpower planning), the board tried to establish a committee to consult with the new commissions about staffing needs. For their part, the commissions saw the attempt as further evidence of the "delaying and inhibiting" role of the board (Postal Commission 1975, p. 3).

Staff Ceilings

The decision to establish the commissions was taken with little regard to the board's views, but that decision became, ironically, one of many indications that the government needed the board, however troubled the relationship. Ministers had their own programmes to promote and consequently their own departmental staffing needs, but they also were collectively concerned at the politically damaging consequences of the rapid growth in public service numbers. During 1973-75, the senior levels of the public service grew rapidly, and this growth was colourfully reported in the media. The growth of the postal and telecommunication commissions after their separation from the public service was especially, though not uniquely, alarming. The autonomy and technical skill of the board in assessing establishment requirements came under greatest pressure precisely at the time when it was most needed and demanded. As the board said, "complaints about growth of the Public Service often fail to recognise that the growth is a consequence of demands generated by the community for new or improved services and for new initiatives in public policy". It added, however, that there was "a constant need, at all levels of the Service, for critical review of activities, and where possible, redeployment of staff from activities of lower priority". And it warned: "Each function of the Service requires Government approval and it is then the responsibility of the Permanent Head and the Board to keep staff increases within proper limits" (Public Service Board 1974, p. 2).

The response of the government to these problems was to impose (at the suggestion of the board, it was reported) a "ceiling" upon the growth of the public service. This was expressed as a percentage figure above which the number of public servants was not to rise during the following year; the board had the task of breaking up the total percentage into absolute figures for each department. The device, apparently unique to Australia, had been used by Menzies in 1951, and again in 1970-71 by Gorton and in 1972 by McMahon as a way of curbing the growth of the public sector. Whitlam announced in July 1973 that the growth of the public service was to be kept below 5 per cent for the following year; in June 1974, suddenly at a Premiers' Conference, he announced a new figure of 2.6 per cent. It seemed that here was a rigid instrument of control, the more powerful because individual departmental figures were confidential to the board and to each department. Once the total figure was settled, the board might enjoy the luxury of bilateral relationships with departments. And once a departmental figure was agreed on or imposed, the disposition of staff within departments to meet new or changing needs might become merely a task for departmental management (Wiltshire 1976). The board still claimed to evaluate establishment proposals on their merits, but a ceiling upon numbers seemed to pre-empt much of this delicate work.

But the work of the board was not so straightforward. Ceilings changed many of the rules of the staffing game, but old conflicts simply took new and more complex forms. Old functions of government still expanded and clashed with the staffing demands raised by new programmes; negotiations between departments and the board were no less fierce when hope for marginal improvement was less; and the board could not escape basing its staffing judgments upon what it knew about internal departmental operations. Indeed, ceilings gave the board new problems. The board's best judgments of what a department needed could not always be accommodated within the ceiling, and its own staff resources were greatly strained by the negotiations entailed by ceilings. The board felt that its sophisticated control had been reduced by the crudeness of the device, whatever impact it had on the total staffing figure. For example, departments tended to fill senior rather than junior positions when forced to make a choice to keep total numbers static, but the PSB saw that the balance between "chiefs" and "Indians" was sometimes thereby harmed. Its appreciation of these delicate points was the more acute because the overall ceiling figure was derived politically; it seemed reasonable to the ministry because it sounded right and compared well with growth rates in other employment sectors. It could be defended, even could be made a positive point electorally. But the board knew that its own figure would have been different and would have been derived by using better methods.

Then, in January 1975, the policy was reversed. With school leavers entering the labour force and with unemployment rising, ceilings were lifted and departments were instructed to recruit staff rapidly. The rush of pent-up demand, the need to assess claims quickly, the relaxation of inspection procedures, the acceptance of long-discredited justifications for staff expansion — all made this period difficult for the board. Its difficulties were altered though not eased when ceilings were reimposed in July 1975 and subsequently retained in modified form by the Fraser government. The very rapidity with which ceilings were imposed, removed, and altered made planning seem futile. Then in 1976 the board found its role as the sole bureaucratic adviser on staff ceilings sharply reduced; an interdepartmental committee was established, with Treasury as an active participant, to recommend numbers to the government. Not only did the board have to contend with bureaucratic competitors in what had been its exclusive preserve, it found also that the new government was capable of overturning old decisions about ceilings without consulting it. In January 1977, for example, the treasurer agreed with the board that ceilings should not be reduced further during the year; but without warning to the board they were reduced in May.

In an extraordinary frank assessment in its 1977 annual report, the board laid down its claim to independence and authority: "The Public Service Act makes clear . . . that the Board's involvement is one of partnership with ministers and permanent heads in the processes determining the size and nature of the permanently established service and in improving the efficiency with which it operates." But the board added:

> The extent to which staff restrictions have been imposed has led to problems. The board has been informed of difficulties in providing prompt and efficient services to the public, maintaining professional and technical services, meeting peak work loads and in the expeditious handling of correspondence. There are also indications that the restrictions are adversely affecting the efficiency of the service in the longer term. [Public Service Board 1977, pp.3-4]

The board warned, accordingly, that "low-priority tasks may have to be dropped or a lower standard of performance accepted" (Public Service Board 1977, p. 2). Ministers did not welcome the implications of this for their own departments. Though supposedly responsible collectively for the ceilings policy, ministers could turn on the agency that implemented it. When the auditor-general severely criticized the Department of Social Security for the overpayment of unemployment benefits in 1977, for example, the minister responded publicly that the fault lay with the PSB, which had not given the department "as much as we want" to do its job properly, despite her "strong representations". The prime minister, prompted by the minister for social security, maintained: "In no case did the PSB advise me that staffing levels would result in inadequate controls of payments." He went on to warn: "In addition to that, the Public Service Board knows very well that there is an overriding requirement, in relation to the administration of staff ceilings of the Government and of the Board, that services to the public are not to be prejudiced as a result" (*Canberra Times*, 15 September 1977).

It is not so easy for the board. The apparent simplicities of staffing control have always been difficulties, and the changes of policy in recent years have not generated solutions but have compounded the problems they were supposed to solve. The board, as its chairman said at the height of the wrangle over ceilings, "has certain independent powers and there is nothing the Prime Minister's department can do about it" (*Age*, 15 September 1977). Yet the PSB had originally supported and may have suggested the imposition of staff ceilings. It had little choice, for some response had to be made to political demands, and other instruments of control were not available or were not acceptable.

The PSB and Change

In these circumstances, the PSB has sought to develop its own alternative ideas. The growth of public service numbers makes it difficult for the board to sustain its old attention to staffing detail, apart altogether from recent "political" difficulties. Consequently, the board has been prepared to experiment with delegating some authority to departments; for example, one important scheme, the "bulk establishment control scheme", has attempted to allow departments some flexibility in classifying and transferring officers within specified limits, subject to the board's audit. At the same time the board has tried to increase its long-term control over staffing by supporting the development of manpower planning, and especially by promoting the development of forward staffing estimates. Departments are now required "to submit annual estimates of staff needed for the following three years, identifying each programme or activity and its staff requirement and priority" (Public Service Board 1975, p. 71). The board has attempted not to lessen its control but to exert it in a new way. However, these changes have been jerkily undertaken and have by no means won the full-hearted support of ministers and departments. If they succeed, they may reduce departmental autonomy; if they fail, perhaps because of financial stringency, then time and effort are wasted. Yet the reforms promoted by the board have raised hopes of further reforms which the board is reluctant to gratify.

Such hopes go much wider than staffing. The centralizing and professionalizing tendencies of the public service since the Second World War have a definite connection with the development of the PSB. Now the tide may be running the other way. At its height in the late 1960s the tide was certainly strong. In its effort to extend uniform regulations throughout the public service, for example, the board was influential in creating a carefully defined class of superior officers known collectively as "the second division". These officers, some thirteen hundred of them in 1977, stand between the permanent heads and the vast number of government employees concerned with lesser tasks. They are a division of general management and policy-advising capacity. The idea of such an administrative elite was suggested by an inquiry into the public service which reported in 1958 (the Boyer Report) but the creation of the new "class" was mainly the achievement of Sir Frederick Wheeler, chairman of the PSB from 1961 to 1970 and later secretary to the Treasury. As the structure of the new division was put together, the occupational categories of the public service, which had become fragmented and overlapping, were simplified, and graduate recruitment was greatly increased to feed the new arrangements.

Concentration of function was given another dimension by concentration of geographical location also. The top levels of government agencies, modelled closely on the board's plan, have been gradually grouped together in Canberra. These senior levels have also slowly become relatively more senior than the state or regional representatives of the Australian government, a development the PSB has promoted. In one of its reviews of workloads in the service, the PSB thus noted that "certain areas of policy advising and administration and management in the Central Offices of Commonwealth departments . . . have shown a significant increase in complexity of work and functional responsibilities. However the indications available to the Board do not suggest that there has been a similar increase in the State Offices of Departments" (Public Service Board 1971, p. 46).

Under the chairmanship of Wheeler, these changes had important reflections within the board itself. Its senior positions grew rapidly and were reorganized to accommodate the new functions we mentioned at the outset. Wheeler attracted talented officers to the board who remained after he departed and who were not disposed to regard modestly the role of their institution. Where new tasks in the public service have arisen, as in the purchase and application of ADP technology, the Board has moved vigorously to assert its capacity to make a contribution. Centralizing and rationalizing tendencies within the public service have owed much to the board, even as these tendencies have strengthened the capacity of the board to apply uniform rules across the service affecting conditions of service, rewards and sanctions.

In other ways, however, different standards have emerged. In particular, as a result of continuous reviews of classifications and work values, Canberra has had concentrated within it more and more of the "rewards of the service"; there is now, as one critic has put it, a "bi-polar distribution" of incentives within the public service and, perhaps, some signs that a "mandarinate" is beginning to emerge at the centre (Schaffer 1976, p. 28). This has disturbed other agencies, politicians, and even voters, and the board itself has attempted to grapple with the problems of centralized, now perhaps overcentralized, control. But these problems are not easy to define, let alone solve. One of our case-studies shows how uneasy the board had become about its range of work and about how well it did it, just before the appointment of a committee of inquiry into the public service. It said then, for instance, that there was a "need for review of overall performance in relation to programs with the object of advising Ministers on long-range planning and priorities"; but how to do this was not clear. "There is", the board also said, "an important contribution to be made by the central administrative machinery which may be complemented or supplemented by the views of those who have not traditionally been a key part of that machinery" (Public Service Board 1974a, p. 79). While being unable to suggest ways in which reform of the public service might be undertaken, the board was aware that changes might indeed need to be made: but it wanted to discover as well how to ensure the continuance of its own position.

In loosening its grip upon such matters as the control of numbers, which it will not be allowed to sustain or cannot sustain in any event, the board has sought other tasks which seem likely to be of strategic importance in maintaining its eminence as an institution. Its efforts have increasingly been directed towards identifying issues which are of great importance, which are related to the present functions of the board, and which yet are not within the bailiwick of another powerful department. Several have been found. The issue of forward staffing estimates has been mentioned. A related issue is the board's attempt to take a more active part in arranging interdepartmental transfers and promotions of senior officers. Traditionally this has been a matter of individual or departmental initiative; now the board is trying to develop acceptable systems which will identify the human talent of the public service and direct it consciously, under the board's guidance, to the places where it is most needed. An enhanced role for the board in staff development schemes might follow.

Another example concerns the appointment of permanent heads, traditionally a matter for informal agreement among ministers and key bureaucrats. The board has now attempted to secure a formal place for itself in any consultations, and recent legislation in fact provides that the chairman of the board will be consulted formally by the prime minister about certain top appointments (RIPA 1977). The board has also sought a new role in advising governments about machinery of government questions; the creation and abolition of agencies and sections of agencies were always bound up with decisions about staffing, but now the board seeks a more active part. It has, however, found it difficult to recruit a politically sensitive staff who might be useful for this work, and its hurried advice has often been ignored by governments (Hawker and Carey 1975). The appointment of a special officer to run the cabinet side of PMC, mentioned above, is an example of how governments can act without regard to the board. Other issues are more difficult to manage. Ministers and departments have frequently contested the operations of the board, as we have noted, and they are more likely to do so when the role of the board is changing.

The board has changed its own structure to meet new demands. A minor reorganization in 1975 was followed by a major streamlining of the organization in May 1978. The number of divisions then were reduced from nine to five and, following the precedent of PMC in 1977 and the Department of Overseas Trade in early 1978, the levels of its second division officers were adjusted upwards. The 1978 reorganization was very much the work of the new chairman, K. C. O. Shann, a career diplomat who has quietly been marking out the Board's traditional territory since his appointment. He has remarked that he would not want "anyone to go away with the impression that the Board has lost its teeth" (Shann 1978, p. 1).

The board remains the most cogent — and indeed virtually the only public —bureaucratic defender of the traditions, customs, and present strengths of the public service. In its public statements over recent years (many to the RCAGA, but also in its uncommonly useful annual reports) it has argued for the maintenance of a bureaucracy which is expert, impartial, and adaptive to political and social change. Yet it has also made plain the difficulties experienced by a public service which has been less than adaptive, and the problems associated with its own role have become more apparent. The board is no more open to sudden change than the rest of the public service, least of all at a time when uncertainties about the policy processes are apparently at their height. Like the other central agencies, its adaptations have brought it new problems with the departments it is supposed to control. The coordinating functions of the board have never been accepted as being neutral or disinterested; in times of stress, as we saw with the imposition of staff ceilings upon the Department of Social Security, the activities of the board are seen to touch directly upon the capacity of another department to formulate policy and carry it out. That is not an unusual position for the board. If its problems are unusually severe it is because the diverse powers of the board are exercised on so many changing fronts.

CONFLICT AND THE CENTRAL AGENCIES

In a brief survey it is not possible to explain in any detail how the central departments interact with "lesser" departments. That would require a further volume in itself. The foregoing surveys have given some hints in particular cases, and the relationships obviously vary with time and from department to department.

But if the central agencies retain much of the bureaucratic power, they do not have a monopoly. The departments that have to run the government's programmes and deal with the clients also have voices and resources. They may not be able to determine their own levels of expenditure and staffing, but they have crucial information so that other people can make judgments about expenditure, effectiveness, and so on. They do not readily accept the more coercive aspects of central coordination and consistently argue that they should have greater independence and freedom to manage their own resources.

When, for example, PMC sought comments on the RCAGA's proposal for a system of efficiency audits, the permanent head of the Department of Defence replied in scathing terms. He suggested that PMC should also look at the RCAGA's proposals for greater authority and responsibility to be ceded to permanent heads of departments. If that did not take place, he argued —

> it may well prove of doubtful validity and value for the efficiency audit to assign responsibility for merit or criticism to departmental heads who, despite 25 (2) of the Public Service Act, retain a managerial responsibility inextricably interrelated to the performance of the relevant coordinating authorities. If there is to be no prior significant change in the Permanent Head's power then coordinating authorities will need to be willing to be more forthcoming and innovative than coordinating authorities have been in the past, if the efficiency audit is effectively to examine departmental performance. [*Financial Review*, 13 May 1977]

Coordination is not policy or value free. If the centre is to gain greater control, the "line" departments must lose some of their independence, or so they fear. Jockeying for power and influence is continuous; there can never be a "proper" balance or one that is undisputed for any length of time.

The functions of the central agencies have always brought them into close contact with one another, and frequently into conflict. They have roles that impinge upon one another. The case-studies show how this can happen. More generally, the part of PMC in setting and interpreting cabinet agendas is always of importance to the PSB and Treasury; the PSB has statutory responsibilities, which, in the field of industrial relations, may concern the others too; and Treasury, with its watchful eye on the cost of government, may find both PMC and the PSB engaged in expensive operations. In any event, the three agencies are in competition for such resources as staff and ministerial time. Their organizational and political roles overlap.

If ambiguity has always been present, it seems now to be increasing because new problems have sharpened old disputes. As we have noted, PMC seeks to rival Treasury in the provision of economic advice to the prime minister and to ministers generally, though these two departments have an interest also in maintaining a common front against other departments which seek to make an unwelcome economic input. Because the cost of government has become an issue of some public importance — as for example, in polemics about the number of government employees — the attempt of the PSB to exert new staff controls through forward staffing estimates has been regarded with some reserve by the others. Treasury has taken a leading part in the implementation of staff ceilings, and PMC has sought an involvement too. The efficiency of the public service has traditionally been the PSB's province, even if only in a formal sense, but PMC now has a more positive capacity. In a broad sense the efficiency of the public service and the effectiveness of its programme activity involve all three central agencies. They are not the only agencies involved. Disputes about the effectiveness and capacity of government occupy the cabinet, parliamentary committees, and many other agencies, as we have noted at length in chapters 2 and 3. The central agencies are as important as ever, but they are as much part of the problem as givers of answers. There is no unity at the centre.

CONCLUSIONS

In this part of the book the importance of procedures and structures has been emphasized. How things are decided will in part determine what is decided. Efficient procedures do not — indeed cannot — make difficult problems easy, nor do they remove the burden of government; the need to think out solutions is continuous. But effective structures can make the identification and solutions of problems more manageable. A study of institutions can show how the influence of actors and procedures affects the way that the policy processes are developed, the kinds of pressures that can be applied and the factors that are important.

But there are other things that such a study cannot do. It cannot predict precisely how powerful the Treasury will be in a particular case, or how cabinet will deal with a problem, or how the prime minister will interact with his colleagues. At most a study of institutions and processes can explain the environment within which such debates or actions will take place and the factors that might influence these processes. That bureaucratic politics and positional politics matter is proved beyond debate, and writers will inevitably be inaccurate if they try to ignore them. But that contention does not suggest that bureaucratic politics is the only important factor, for clearly it is not. The difficulty in determining in particular cases what factors influence the processes of policy making is that each has a unique mix of factors, and this can be illustrated only by case-studies.

The exclusive use of case-studies can be misleading. Case-studies may lend order to a snapshot that is in reality confused and incomplete. But case-studies are useful for illustrating the dynamics of the policy processes; they bring together a number of actors as issues are defined and settled, redefined, and fought over anew. They also show that a stable state is never reached, and in that sense none of the case-studies has a "natural" ending.

We have chosen case-studies which illustrate a wide variety of influences. This focus gradually narrows towards the centre of policy making. The first has a broad view, looking at the development of the policy for funding schools over a decade. In the second we examine a department manipulating the interest groups in its environment to facilitate the introduction of wheat quotas. The third concentrates on the bureaucratic scene, examining the attempts of the Department of Foreign Affairs to expand its functions and explaining the reactions from the central agencies; it is a study of bureaucratic politics at work.

The last two case-studies concentrate on policy making at the centre. The decision to establish the RCAGA was made in the environs of cabinet, with various actors coming on and off the stage, and shows the crucial part played by the prime minister's office. The case that examines the formulation of the 1974 budget looks at cabinet itself in action and shows the problems it faces when traditional procedures are found wanting.

All the case-studies, whether looking at broad or narrow topics, at departmental or cabinet action, capture the complexities of their subjects. They are designed to concentrate on the policy-making processes and to show how the system of government works; they can thus add another perspective from which our conclusions can then be drawn.

Case-Studies

5

Funding Schools:
Policy and Incrementalism

Incrementalism is characteristic of most policy-making processes, especially those in stable and mature administrative systems. Reformers are often sceptical of incremental change, because they fear that existing arrangements are simply adapted without major alteration to changed circumstances. It becomes very easy to argue that as a result vested interests, unsympathetic administrators, and the like may deliberately prevent radical change by reducing it to incremental steps. But even if it is possible to talk in radical terms about changing some policy processes, it is also necessary to understand what it is that makes incremental change possible, and even at times desirable. The case we describe in this chapter is one that is strongly marked by incrementalism, even though some elements may be regarded as non-incremental and others as the result of interaction of interest groups and vested interests with administrators.

Three aspects of policy making in stable systems are especially important for explaining incremental change. First, because policies are the result of interactions between groups and individuals in institutions who invariably draw on existing knowledge and established procedures, policies are never developed wholly *de novo*. It is often easiest and wisest to redirect established resources from old projects to new policies and to make use of existing experience and procedures; it would be wasteful to do otherwise. Second, policies are seldom worked out in detail, especially if they are to extend far into the future. They are left vague, perhaps with gaps, to be redirected by later decisions. Options unforeseen at the time may present themselves later. With the benefit of hindsight, it may seem as if each step in the development of a policy was logical or inevitable, foreseen or provided for, but in practice this is seldom the case. Most policies leave room for hard future choices which make more or less difference to their effect or to the ends they serve. Third — and this is the reverse side of the second point — decisions set precedents, preclude some options, and result in changes of situation so that later when a new starting point seems to arise from which new initiatives may be developed, those changes will occur within constraints imposed by what has already taken place.

This case-study surveys the development of the federal government's aid to schools from 1963 to 1975. It does not pretend to be a history of the aid policies (see Bessant and Spaull 1976; Birch and Smart 1977; Smart 1974) and it relies heavily on existing sources (especially Smart 1975). Nor does it evaluate the educational justification or success of the programmes. It simply illustrates how, over a decade or so, each proposal has been based on earlier precedents. Three themes are central to the discussion: the types of pressures that lead to policy proposals, the administrative process that turns those proposals into programmes, and the way in which old policies are readapted in new directions.

Over a fifteen-year period the increase in the government's funding of schools has been dramatic. Even given recent rates of inflation, table 1 shows how large and sudden the jump was in federal involvement.

Table 1 Federal Expenditure on Schools
(In millions of dollars)

	Government	Non-Government
1966–67	16	3
1968–69	22	6
1972–73	50	39
1974–75	406	139
1975–76	523	199

Bureaucratic growth was fast. In 1963 there were two main institutions responsible for education: the Commonwealth Office of Education (COE), founded in the mid-1940s to advise the government and to serve as a central point of reference for international contacts and the collection of statistics (Smart 1975, p. 29), and a section of PMC. In 1967 a Department of Education and Science was established, and in 1972 a separate Department of Education. The staff numbers involved were:

Table 2. Staff: Department of Education and Science (1967–72) and Education (1972–76)

	Division			
	1	2	3	Total
1967	1	7	231	239
1969	1	12	584	597
1971	1	15	937	953
1973	1	23	2,321	2,345
1976	1	35	1,681	1,717

In the joint departments the science function was always secondary; in 1970, for instance, seven of the eight branches were concerned with education.

There is one major conventional problem in the discussion of incrementalism — how large must a change be before it ceases to be incremental (Simeon 1976; Wildavsky 1975). Quantitative tests are irrelevant in some cases, where a major change of policy might entail no large change in funds or staffing, but it is a question that plagues discussions of incrementalism in budgetary studies. However, it is not an important question here, as we are concerned with processes, not outcomes and costs. We describe incremental aspects of the policy-making processes and show how each administrative step which led to massive increases in expenditure used earlier precedents as a starting point for debate, if not actually as a guide for action. Routine administrative procedures directed both major changes in expenditure and the policies the funds were to serve.

BACKGROUND

Constitutionally, the funding of primary and secondary schools is the responsibility of the states. Before 1963, federal assistance had been granted to students but not to schools under the 1946 amendment to the Constitution. The COE was the main body that administered migrant education, the Colombo Plan, postgraduate scholarships, and the commonwealth retraining schemes. Student assistance could be politically useful. Education had been considered important by the Labor government of the 1940s but the number of programmes was not increased by Menzies.

Change began in the late 1950s. First the Commonwealth gave some assistance to the independent schools in the ACT, a relatively small and unnoticed change at the time which was later to be regarded as a significant precedent. Then Menzies established the Murray Commission to examine the funding of universities. He had only gradually been persuaded to make such a move in the face of widespread demands for increased educational spending and reputedly was alone in supporting it in cabinet, where he sat out the opposition of his colleagues and, especially, of the Treasury. But once the Murray Commission had been formed, the eminence of its members ensured the acceptance of its recommendations. The establishment of a permanent Australian universities commission and the increase of federal funds for tertiary education were the main results.

Nevertheless, Menzies still argued that historically there was a difference between federal involvement in tertiary education and direct federal funding of schools. He denied that the precedent of the Murray Commission would later be extended to what, he argued, were the states' clear responsibilities for secondary education.

In 1960 he claimed: "If the Commonwealth starts to interfere with the educational policies of the States, with the way in which they go about their job in the educational field, that will be a very bad day for Australia" (Smart 1975, p. 47).

THE SCIENCE BLOCKS SCHEME

In his campaign speech for the 1963 election Menzies announced that, if re-elected, his government would introduce a scheme to finance the building of science blocks for both state and independent schools. The promise was made without any prior consultation with cabinet, with the Liberal Party, or with the public service.

What caused this complete reversal in Menzies' actions? In 1958 he had defended his position, claiming he did not want to interfere in state affairs and had not been asked to do so; but in 1959 he lost that excuse when the Labor premier of Western Australia sought federal support for the teaching of science. By 1961 there was considerable and diverse pressure for such involvement (see Smart 1975, pp. 49-70). A report on scientific and technical manpower had illustrated the need for increased training in these areas; the launching of the sputnik made the country science-conscious, and the Murray Commission had pointed to the pressing need for improved science education at both university and school level. At the same time parents and citizens' associations, the Headmasters' Conference, and the Australian Education Council (AEC), made up of the state ministers of education, demanded assistance.

Yet the activities of groups are not a sufficient explanation for the sudden change of mind. There had been similar demands for state aid during 1958 which led to several parliamentary debates and stirred both parties to mention education in their federal platforms. But Menzies stood firm and refused to change his stand. In 1961, during the credit squeeze election, education had been scarcely mentioned. But in 1963 Menzies had a majority of one in the House of Representatives and needed the electoral support of the Catholic-oriented DLP which strongly favoured financial support for Catholic schools and could be expected to welcome the proposal readily. They did. The Liberal Party's electoral opportunism took the shaping of policy one step further.

At the time, divisions within the ALP made a promise of state aid politically desirable. Early in 1963 the New South Wales Labor conference, at the instigation of the state cabinet, had decided to give aid to independent schools. In a politically tactless move the state government was then censured by the national executive of the party on the grounds that its actions were contrary to the federal platform. Opposition to state aid had grown in the party after the bitterness of the 1955 split and because of the latent anti-Catholicism in many sections of Labor. The immediate furore caused by the federal party's criticism of state government policy led to a speedy retraction of the motion; it was replaced by another whose wording indicated that the aid would be given to students, not to the schools (Freudenberg 1977, pp. 24-38; Smart 1975, pp. 98-109).

But the damage was done. Within two weeks of the Labor dispute, Menzies had decided to call an early election in the hope of enlarging his majority. One tactic was to promise state aid in the expectation that it would exacerbate the divisions within the Labor Party and also win him DLP support. Menzies quickly promised to fund the science blocks; the cost was negligible, only £5 million a year. The proposal had another advantage: bricks and mortar were tangible evidence of what federal politicians and federal money could provide.

There was an administrative precedent in the private sector of which Menzies was aware and which he undoubtedly used as a model. In 1958 a group of businessmen had established the Industrial Fund to finance the building of science blocks for those independent schools represented in the Headmasters' Conference, all of which were boys' schools. The Industrial Fund was able to distribute a total of about £600,000; but, more important, it was to provide a model on which the federal scheme could be based (Smart 1975, pp. 56-58).

Menzies had not consulted anyone about the proposal, for traditionally the formulation of the Liberal policy speech is the prerogative of the leader. The topic had apparently been raised in cabinet on 15 October, but inconclusively. The feasibility of the proposal was not discussed with the public service, although this was not unusual where policies were designed for political appeal.

Once the government had won the election, the administration was under pressure to inaugurate the system quickly, because Menzies had promised the scheme would start on 1 July 1964. Fast action was required if the machinery was to be ready and workable in time. It was — just. The federal government decided that the programme would be administered from Canberra, through the education division of PMC. Gorton was appointed minister assisting the prime minister in education matters and in effect ran the education division of the department as a separate entity.

The Industrial Fund was a model for implementation. A committee was established under the chairmanship of L. C. Robson, one of the founders of the Industrial Fund and formerly a headmaster of a leading Sydney private school. His job was to define the standards required for buildings and to determine the necessary priorities, in consultation with the state departments of education and state advisory committees. The committee also had to establish two sets of arrangements for the provision of funds to independent schools, one with the Catholic school system and the other with the non-Catholic independent schools. The main arrangements were made by March 1964. Then Gorton announced that one condition of granting the funds was that the money was to be additional to existing state levels of expenditure on science buildings. Later, at the Premiers' Conference in July, this condition was changed to require that state educational expenditure as a whole be maintained, but the principle which was to be included in all future schemes was established (Smart 1975, pp. 170-71).

The scheme was officially introduced in the State Grants (Science Laboratory and Technical Training) Bill in April 1964. The science scheme was coupled with new expenditure in technical education primarily as a tactical manoeuvre to appear to minimize the amount that would be going to independent schools.

Although the scheme started officially on 1 July, it soon ran into problems that illustrated the lack of control of the federal government over the implementation of such programmes. Independent schools were quickly off the mark, in part because some schools had already made applications to the Industrial Fund which could now be transferred to the federal government. But they were also able to hire their architects and start building more quickly. The state departments were highly centralized. Building had to be arranged through the Public Works departments, which were notoriously slow and in one case began designing buildings to the wrong specifications. As a result, Victoria spent a large proportion of its grant for the first year on equipment because its buildings could not be planned in time to ensure the expenditure of funds in the 1964/65 financial year. Further, state-built laboratories also proved to be about 25 per cent more expensive than those which were privately built (Smart 1975, p. 253).

There was no system of evaluation built into the science programme. In part the speed with which the whole scheme was introduced made it impossible. There was no attempt to decide whether science blocks were needed more or less than other educational facilities; that decision had been pre-empted by Menzies. Nor was a survey of existing science blocks completed before the grants were started. The only evaluation could be in terms of money spent and the number of blocks, rooms, and equipment provided. The judgment could be in bricks and mortar but not in education.

The science blocks scheme was politically convenient, but the limitations on the capacity of the Commonwealth to spend the money had quickly become evident. Further, the administrative position of the division within PMC also became difficult. PMC's permanent head, John Bunting, had a conception of this department's role which did not include major policy analysis and implementation. But the bureaucratic machinery needed to service the science blocks grew and, as it was Gorton's responsibility rather than the prime minister's, it became increasingly separate from and uncomfortable within PMC. It was not surprising that during the 1966 election campaign Holt promised that he would establish a new Department of Education.

THE LIBRARIES SCHEME

Early in 1967 a new Department of Education and Science was founded and Gorton was appointed its minister. Its permanent head was Sir Hugh Ennor, an eminent scientist, but from the beginning the education division, headed by K. N. Jones, the first assistant secretary who had been responsible for education in PMC, was the more important part of the department. Science programmes tended to be more long-term and less electorally attractive, while education was becoming a nationally important issue. In 1970 only one out of eight branches in the department was concerned with science, and its ministers were far more concerned with education policies than with scientific matters.

After the success of the science blocks programme, and in the context of continuing internal tensions within the Labor Party throughout 1966, the question was not whether new programmes of state aid would be introduced, but which ones and when. Several possibilities were discussed, including the teaching of Asian languages in schools. Eventually it was decided to fund secondary school libraries. It was a logical decision, in that the need for libraries was undeniable, although there was no search and evaluation of possible alternatives. The scheme was introduced because the department and minister were looking for new initiatives while a group in the community was demanding government support. The conjunction of these forces was vital (Smart 1974).

In part the decision was a response to a coordinated campaign organized by the Libraries Association of Australia (LAA). It had established a subcommittee which had publicized the needs for libraries, contacted MPs, and been in touch with senior members of the bureaucracy. The committee had started campaigning for government funds in 1965, when one of the members of the committee had discussed tactics with a senior bureaucrat involved in education affairs in PMC. The memorandum describing the meeting illustrates both the usefulness of contact with bureaucrats and the way that tactics must be shaped by political reality. The memorandum in part read as follows:

1 Would this be a good time to make an approach to the Federal Government? It couldn't be better: this year's election would undoubtedly act as a spur. Libraries have already been in Senator Gorton's thoughts (he [the bureaucrat] was emphatic that Senator Gorton was the key person in the whole situation, and as Minister in Charge of Commonwealth Education would be responsible for presenting a case to Cabinet, as well as its implementation). Even if nothing could be done this year it certainly could be next year or the year after.

2 Would it be sensible to approach state ministers and directors of education to get a statement of need? No, this is quite unnecessary. It was not done with the Science Grants or the Technical Education Assistance from the Commonwealth. The need is well documented. If further evidence is felt by the L. A. A. to strengthen the case, simply mention that bodies such as A. C. E. R. , professors of education, etc., have indicated that they support the idea. The states would never reject a Commonwealth offer, such is their need for assistance in monies for education. It would prejudice the case in federal eyes if the state authorities were approached first.

3 Secondary school libraries only, or all school libraries? The officer said here, that in order to give Senator Gorton room to manoeuvre in Cabinet, it would be better for the L. A. A. to recommend that initially the aid be given to secondary school libraries only, with the suggestion that primary school libraries be assisted after, say, two or three years.

4 Should the L. A. A. recommend amounts and method of grants? No, rather suggest they be administered along the lines of the science grants. He seemed to think that $10 million per annum, the current expenditure on science laboratories, not an impossibility. Some mention of the U. S. $100 million grant should be made.

5 Should we ask for a deputation immediately and present the submission then? No, simply offer to meet with Senator Gorton should he wish to discuss the matter with us further, as the L. A. A. could give further professional advice should he require it. Deputations first tend to scare ministers off the subject. Better to submit case, let them consider it, and then discuss personally.

6 Method of presentation? a short, simple statement, devoting one paragraph to the need for remedy of situation, the authoritativeness of the *Fenwick Report*, its objectivity. One paragraph on the practical sense of the *Standards*, and that experts such as state supervisors of school libraries, practising school librarians from all types of schools, governmental and independent, etc., considered the situation for four years, etc. The officer indicated that this statement should be calm, objective and well researched, and that arrays of figures would not be

necessary as it was policy that would be considered coming out of it. Include copies of *Fenwick* and *Standards*. Probably it would not take more than four or five paragraphs, and fit on one foolscap page. [Quoted in Smart 1974, pp. 112-13]

Using an MP as intermediary, the committee presented its proposals to Gorton after he had become minister for education and science. Initially he promised nothing, although he was sympathetic. But he became prime minister before any action was taken. He was succeeded as minister by Malcolm Fraser, whose ambitions and competence as a minister were already marked. He was well aware of the potential political importance of new programmes and was especially sympathetic to the needs of the non-Catholic independent schools. He was quickly persuaded of the case for aid to libraries and sent a senior officer to visit the states to inquire into their needs. In February 1968 the AEC, which then consisted only of the state ministers for education, also requested assistance for school libraries, but specifically wanted funds for primary and secondary schools and for books as well as buildings.

The programme was announced in the budget speech in August 1968. It was intended to begin on 1 January 1969. Speed once again was essential, although some preparatory work had already been done by the department. While procedures for the science blocks scheme were adopted, there were efforts to avoid some of the problems of the initial scheme. In particular there was a desire to ensure that equipment was used properly, because in the past some items had been left idle as there was no one trained to use them. The libraries scheme was therefore devised to provide for the training of staff as well as for the provision of equipment, and was allocated funds for running short courses for school librarians during school holidays; the first such course was held in Sydney in January 1969.

A Secondary Schools Library Committee (SSLC) was appointed with a member of the Department of Education and Science as its executive officer and hence its key member. The SSLC initially had two tasks: to decide on standards for new buildings and to work with the state committees. Following the system adopted for the earlier programme, the claims of the independent schools in each state were considered by two committees, one for the Catholic system and one for the other independent schools. The state committees listed the schools in order of priority, thus removing from the central body the political unpopularity that any decisions about priorities might bring. When funds became available, a member of the committee simply visited the school that was next in order of priority and assessed its needs. The credit therefore came to the federal government; the state bodies shielded it from blame.

The SSLC published in roneoed form *Standards for Libraries*, which was to provide guidelines for state committees. It was to be a condition for the provision of the grants that funds would only be given for libraries that would meet these standards. The SSLC was alert to prevent any reduction in these standards.

In devising the scheme, some consideration was given to evaluation, but this proved difficult. The concept of the scheme, according to the LAA, was to make the library the central unit around which the school was to operate. But whether such changes really had taken place would always be difficult to evaluate. Bricks and mortar and the number of volumes purchased with federal funds were much easier to document — and were regarded electorally as far more effective than any change in educational philosophy.

But if the process could work smoothly with the committees of independent schools, this was not true of state departments. The AEC resolution of February 1968 had emphasized the need for the libraries scheme and had held discussions with the federal officials about the means of implementing it. But the Victorian and New South Wales governments in particular were concerned that a programme might be foisted on them and that their priorities might in effect be pre-empted unilaterally by federal decision. In August, before the scheme was officially announced in the budget, the New South Wales minister proposed that the states should agree on a suitable plan before one was imposed on them (Smart 1975, pp. 284-85). But, pleading lack of funds, Fraser did not accept the suggestion that the scheme should apply to primary as well as to secondary schools and only agreed to provide basic books. As with the science blocks programme, grants were divided between states on a per capita basis — although in 1971 this was changed to secondary enrolments — and buildings had to meet the standards determined by the federal government.

The latter conditions caused dissension between the federal and Victorian governments. The Victorian minister argued that he should be allowed to spread the funds further and more thinly. Initially he proposed to build twenty-four libraries, instead of only the twelve that could be constructed if the commonwealth standards were to be maintained (Smart 1975, p. 286). He was finally forced to withdraw his demands after pressure from teacher associations, parent groups, and library bodies, but the dispute led to long delays in Victoria. The minister also tried to use the federal grant as a means of constructing libraries as the first buildings for new high schools. This procedure did not, as intended, grant libraries to existing schools that needed them most, but helped to alleviate the classroom shortage (Smart 1975, pp. 308-10). This practice continued until 1974, when the minister finally agreed to accept the direction of his federal counterpart.

The disputes between Victoria and the federal government indicate the strengths and weaknesses of federal involvement in education. With its financial strength and the capacity to use section 96 tied grants, the Commonwealth could dictate what should be done and could in effect ignore the demands of the states. It could not ensure the rapid implementation of its programmes if the states were unwilling to cooperate or slow to act. The federal department could supervise the general scheme, but not assert its authority in areas where it had no constitutional powers (Weller and Smith 1976a).

After 1968 the federal Liberal government gradually became more heavily committed to the independent sector. In 1967 the Headmasters' Conference had approved in principle the receipt of recurrent funds from the federal government. With the 1969 election as the immediate catalyst the L-CP government promised that it would introduce per capita grants to all independent schools. This was a major, if expected, change. The science blocks and libraries schemes were deliberately limited in their concept; their aim was to bring schools up to an acceptable standard, after which the programme could be terminated. But the new promises gave a permanent role to the federal government in the funding of independent schools. This was expanded in 1971 and 1972 when the electorally harassed McMahon government not only increased the per capita grants but provided $215 million for a five-year capital aid programme for state and independent schools. Again the change indicated a commitment to recurrent, not merely specific, expenditure and coincided with concern about electoral defeat. In ten years the Liberal government's commitment had risen rapidly — from $5 million in 1963 to $215 million in 1972.

LABOR AND THE SCHOOLS COMMISSION

State aid to independent schools has been described as "the oldest, deepest, most poisonous debate in Australian history" (Freudenberg 1977, p. 24). It was an especially divisive issue for the Labor Party in the 1960s. Menzies had taken advantage of its divisions on the issue to call the 1963 election. The New South Wales Labor government's defeat in 1965 was also attributed to this issue. Then in early 1966 the federal executive passed a series of resolutions that rejected all forms of state aid, including those already in existence. When Whitlam, then deputy leader of the party, opposed these decisions, he was almost expelled from the party. Finally, two special conferences in 1966 agreed to allow support for existing forms of state aid. ·

In 1969, after a long and bitter campaign, Whitlam persuaded the national conference to accept the idea of a schools commission, a body of experts which would determine what aid was required by both government and independent schools on the basis of need. This plan had constructive aspects. As Whitlam argued, it would bring regularity to educational funding instead of the uncoordinated and unrelated initiatives taken by the Liberals. But it also had the advantage that most sections of the Labor Party were prepared to accept it as a necessary compromise. The one exception was the self-consciously radical Victorian branch. In 1970 the state executive tried to censure a leading parliamentarian who had advocated the federal policy during a state election. He appealed to the federal executive and, after a protracted and tortuous debate, the federal executive took over the affairs of the state branch and reconstructed it on the basis of proportional representation. By the 1972 election the ALP was publicly united on the need for federal involvement in the funding of schools. But by this time it had gone further. Education had become a major electoral issue. It was one of Whitlam's greatest achievements to turn a subject that had been so divisive into one of the central planks on which Labor's election campaign was founded (see Smith and Weller 1976 for a detailed study of the development of the schools commission plank).

Within two weeks of his electoral victory, Whitlam announced the establishment of an interim schools commission with Professor Peter Karmel as its chairman. When promising this action in his election speech, Whitlam had explicitly sought a precedent and stated that he would follow the example of Menzies' appointment of an interim universities commission under Sir Keith Murray in 1956. He also stated in December 1972 that all funds provided by the Commonwealth would be additional to existing expenditure and that the state governments were required to maintain their existing efforts, as Gorton had demanded ten years before.

Within six months, as requested, the interim committee had published its report, *Schools in Australia* (Canberra, 1973) which is regarded as a watershed in discussion of education in Australia (D'Cruz and Sheehan 1975; Allwood 1975). The report detailed what it understood as the concepts of equality of opportunity and of needs and explained how it would satisfy these needs. Then on the basis of these concepts which had been included in its terms of reference, it recommended the expenditure of $660.1 million, in six main categories — general recurrent, general buildings, libraries, disadvantaged schools, special education, and teacher development. These grants were provided for both state and independent schools, so that the Commonwealth was now directly involved in the recurrent expenditure of the state system of education. The money was to be provided by tied grants so that although the state departments had some flexibility within the six categories, they could not transfer funds from one category to another. The tenor of the report centred on the belief that all schools should be brought up to an acceptable and predetermined standard, as the science and library schemes had tried to do in more specific areas; it rejected the concept of per capita grants.

The Karmel Report depended on the earlier precedents we have discussed and on available information: it could not have reported so quickly if it had operated any other way. In 1969–70 the state departments had surveyed what financial support they needed to upgrade their education systems. At the time the federal minister refused to accept the figures presented in the report which had emerged from the surveys, arguing that these were unreliable. In fact they were simply too large. This report now provided the basis on which state departments could respond rapidly to the requests of the Karmel Committee. The interim committee's report also proposed administrative arrangements that were similar to those of the libraries scheme.

In December 1972 Whitlam had created a separate Department of Education, splitting the old Department of Education and

Science. The change indicated the high priority that the Labor Party gave to solving educational problems. The new department had the responsibility of giving the Karmel Committee's proposals legislative effect. Two bills were required — a Schools Commission Bill to establish the machinery and a States Grants (Schools) Bill to appropriate the necessary funds: both relied on precedents.

The officer responsible for the Schools Commission Bill took as his model the act that had earlier created the Australian Commission on Advanced Education. He adopted the clauses of this act wherever possible, since it had already been the subject of discussion with the parliamentary draftsman, and changed it only where it was necessary to meet the new demands of the government. The major change was in the section that spelt out the terms of reference of the commission, requiring it to give priority to aid for state schools and to pay attention to several specific categories of students (Smith and Weller 1976, pp. 30-35).

The States Grants (Schools) Bill was modelled on the State Grants (Independent Schools) Act of 1972 by which the Liberal government had increased the per capita grants to independent schools. But the 1973 bill was more detailed and also more broad-ranging. It proposed new requirements for reporting on expenditure, listed the programmes under which money could be spent and how programmes like the one for disadvantaged schools would operate. The final act was substantially different from the original.

The main difference between the educational legislation introduced by the Labor and Liberal governments was in the detail. The Labor government wished to spell out its philosophical goals in the bill, to include specific terms of reference and to try to ensure that their funds were spent as directed, a requirement that entailed more complex reporting arrangements. By contrast, the Liberal cabinet preferred to have more general terms of reference and more flexible administrative arrangements and seemed less concerned to check on how the money was spent, so long as there appeared to be some electoral impact.

Yet some state governments were still far from content. While they welcomed the funds, they were often less happy about the conditions. In their view the requirement that they maintain their levels of educational expenditure limited their capacity to set their own priorities at state level, while the Labor government's demands for more detailed accountability and for information about such subjects as disadvantaged schools put considerable strain on their already creaking state bureaucracies. The Victorian government was especially critical of the bureaucratic demands the new system imposed. Indeed, in its report for the 1976–78 triennium the Schools Commission agreed to reduce the number of different programmes under which funds were made available.

The Labor Party did not always accept the recommendations of the Schools Commission. In the 1975 budget discussions, cabinet decided to suspend temporarily the system of triennial funding, and it rejected the report of the commission. It made special arrangements for 1976 and asked the commission to redevelop proposals for the 1977-79 triennium along as yet unfinished guidelines. However, the cabinet did not try to direct the commission's conclusions (Smart 1978).

By the time the Labor government was dismissed, the Schools Commission was well established and was regarded as electorally popular. Its involvement and importance were accepted as legitimate, even though there was controversy about the effectiveness of the massive increase in funds it had orchestrated.

THE FRASER GOVERNMENT AND THE SCHOOLS COMMISSION

During the 1975 election the Liberals had promised that the Schools Commission would be retained and that educational spending would be maintained. Nevertheless, in their first few months in office rumours about its abolition were common and educational pressure groups campaigned noisily and consistently to keep the Liberals to their promise. The minister for education, Senator J. L. Carrick, then reaffirmed that the commission would not be abolished. But lack of harmony between the government and the commission was not surprising. The commission was essentially organized to oversee increased spending, while the cabinet was trying to reduce the size of the deficit. Further, its whole approach, designed to develop a national educational policy, contradicted many of the tenets of the Liberals' "new federalism" which Carrick had been responsible for designing.

The government was therefore committed to maintaining the form and structure of the commission, and even its terms of reference, but was largely unsympathetic to the concept of aid according to needs, to the desire to increase educational expenditure, and to the commission's vision of a consistent national policy. It reacted by trying perceptibly to impose tight guidelines within which the commission's recommendations should be formulated.

The process was gradual. The cabinet accepted the spending proposals foreshadowed by the Labor government, although it introduced more flexibility for the state governments by allowing them to transfer funds between capital and recurrent programmes. It also decided to impose financial guidelines within which future commission proposals should be designed. Initially these guidelines were not published, but in the 1976 budget it was claimed that expenditure on education would be increased by a real amount of 2 per cent per annum in the next three years. The commission was instructed to develop its recommendations on that basis within the structure of a three-year rolling triennium.

In February 1977 the cabinet told the commission "not to set aside state education department priorities simply because the Commission wants to develop a uniform approach throughout the country" (*Canberra Times*, 18 February 1977). This instruction was regarded in some quarters as an infringement of the independence of the commission and as a means of making it a rubber stamp for the wishes of the states. But the charge, even if not welcome to the commission, was consistent with the political stance of the government.

Although the commission occasionally sniped at the restrictions being imposed on it, the real dispute about its independence occurred in May 1977, when Carrick announced the new guidelines for the 1978-80 rolling triennium. Not only were the funds to be allocated for 1978 below the increase proposed in the 1976 guidelines, but Carrick also *instructed* the commission to transfer from the reduced amount a further $13.8 million to independent schools, including $2 million for the richest private schools (*National Times*, 27 June — 2 July 1977). These orders were resisted by the commission. Its chairman acknowledged that cabinet must make the final decisions but claimed that "prior to end of 1976 the government did not feel the need to substantially pre-empt, through detailed guidelines, the advice of the commission on priorities within the total of funds which could be made available for a period" (*Sydney Morning Herald*, 18 July 1977).

The commission's opposition to government instruction was expressed strongly in its 1977 report. It did not comply fully with the demand of the minister. It agreed to the transfer of $8.8 million to independent schools in order to bring some of them up to government standard, but it argued that to transfer a further $5 million to private schools could not be justified in the then existing financial situation. It wanted to protect its programme for aid to disadvantaged schools which was central to the concept of needs. The report also attacked the decision of the government not to abide by its 1976 guidelines; it argued that to reduce the minimum figure was to negate any benefits of the rolling triennium (*Sydney Morning Herald*, 9 September 1977).

The commission's advice was rejected by the government, which stated that the private schools had suffered financially in the previous three years. The redirection by the government of the commission's recommendations was a natural political response and clearly indicates the embarrassment that a symbolic administrative structure can pose for a government that wishes to alter policy. The Liberal government thus used the guidelines as a means of restricting the initiative and limiting the independence of the commission. The procedures and formal structures were not changed, but they were redirected, with some difficulty, to push policy in a marginally different direction.

CONCLUSION

In less than fifteen years the role of the federal government in education has changed completely. Bessant and Spaull argue that the 1963 decision "was the culmination of the struggle to bring the federal government into the schools. This in itself is one of the successful political campaigns in the history of Australian schooling" (Bessant and Spaull 1976, p. 115). But at the time the decision was as much a means of embarrassing Menzies' political opponents as a response to pressure group activity. Yet once that initial step was taken and the Liberal Party's electoral success was credited to it, reasons and opportunities could more easily be found for meeting demands for more funds. Labor had to accept the inevitable and, given Whitlam's political skill, was able to turn the issue to its own advantage. The situation in 1976 was never imagined by Menzies in 1963; it emerged from a series of discrete decisions by separate governments. No single decision was critical, but each built on the foundations that its predecessor had created. The disjointed actions which led to the existing situation were political, not educational, in their objectives; the changes in funding arrangements before 1972 combined administrative ease, political relevance, and cheap commitments. The policy was not thought through as an integrated whole in the beginning or at any later stage.

The way that the various steps were taken shows how policies are developed incrementally. The Department of Education learnt from experience and developed the new initiatives along routine lines, working initially from the example of an organization outside the public service; each stage was based on precedents of earlier programmes, with changes to circumvent any problems that were identified. The legislation itself was cumulative, as a successful form was adapted to new demands. Such an incremental procedure is not only a sensible way for public servants to work; it is proper for officials to build on past experiences and learn from past mistakes.

One result was that the steps that were taken were limited by the past actions and past plans. Once the science blocks scheme had been introduced successfully, it was probable that the next scheme would follow similar lines. Once state and private schools had accepted the idea of federal funds for specific purposes, it was a small step to accepting money for recurrent purposes. After 1963, the environment had changed, new political initiatives were available, and there was never a possibility of reviewing afresh the whole question of the advisability of federal involvement. Even when the government changed after 1975, it only brought a gradual redirection of existing administrative procedures.

But, even if options are constrained by precedents and by the procedural style of public servants, the choices available are still broad and difficult. It was not inevitable that libraries would receive funds or that the Schools Commission would allocate resources on any concept of needs. The amount of money, the personalities, the allocation between states may all be marginal, but they are important decisions for recipients. The fact that policy making is directed by incremental means, that the processes follow predictable lines, as we have described here, does not mean that the outcomes of these pressures are predetermined, even if they are within the constraints created by the incremental system.

6

Introduction of
Wheat Quotas

In 1969 both government spokesmen and industry officials presented the introduction of delivery quotas for wheat as an industry response to problems of overproduction. The Australian Wheatgrowers' Federation (AWF) took responsibility for formulating the scheme and recommending it to the federal government. Specifically, it also took responsibility for recommending to the federal government the size of the national and state delivery quotas. But the case was not as straightforward as this. It was not simply an instance of a well-organized agricultural interest group inducing a desired reponse from a government. On the contrary, the federal government played an active, but publicly understated, role in introducing the scheme. The government used the resources at its disposal, which included its lack of formal constitutional responsibility for agriculture and its financial control of the level of the advance paid to growers on delivery of their wheat, to produce a scheme acceptable to itself while minimizing federal responsibility for it.

Within the government the role of officers of the Department of Primary Industry was as understated as the government's involvement as a whole. The minister for primary industry was active in all policy matters affecting the department, and, at first, most government activity on wheat quotas took place at the political level. Indeed, when first asked for advice on the significance of trends in production, the department expressed doubts about the need for government intervention and production controls. However, as the

---

This chapter is reprinted with some revisions from Smith and Weller 1976. It is based on a detailed study of material supplied by the Department of Primary Industry and several grower organizations. Precise documentation can be found in the original.

process of formulating policy on quotas proceeded, departmental officers had increasingly important, if unobtrusive, roles to play.

This discussion of the case concentrates on the process by which the situation of the wheat industry in 1968 and 1969 was defined as one requiring the control of deliveries. In particular it concentrates on the ways in which the federal government interacted with the AWF to produce the quota scheme. This involved a lengthy chain of decisions which stimulated considerable tension within the AWF and its affiliated organizations. Wheat farmers became subject to an onerous set of administrative provisions which aroused anxiety and discontent. (For details see Hellier 1972; Rosenthal 1975; Campbell 1969, 1971; Rolfe 1970; Connors 1972.) To many farmers the commitment of their own organizations to the scheme provided little comfort. As the application of delivery quotas took place, the gap between the simplicity of the original conceptions of the scheme and the complexities of applying it equitably and expeditiously became wider. It is not the purpose of this chapter to give detailed attention to problems of implementation, or to the role of state governments, which carried the main legislative burden of the scheme. This would lead to a more complete study, but also to a much larger one. Nevertheless, in examining the processes of policy formulation in this case, some reference to these topics will be made.

EXISTING ARRANGEMENTS IN THE WHEAT INDUSTRY

The introduction of delivery quotas made an important adjustment to well-established price support and marketing arrangements which had first begun in the 1940s. Their main components were the Australian Wheat Board, which was responsible for the acquisition and disposal of each year's crop, and a system of price guarantees which involved the setting of a home consumption price and a guaranteed price for a specific volume of exports. Formally, the Wheat Board's responsibility was confined to its acquisition, marketing, and closely related functions, but the majority of its members were leading farmer politicians and its senior managerial staff were well informed about all aspects of wheat policy. Provisions of the wheat scheme ran for five years, and normally as one scheme was due to expire a new and similar one was negotiated. The main points at issue in each renegotiation concerned the level and method of calculation of guaranteed prices to growers, the extent of growers' contributions to a stabilization fund to be drawn on in times of reduced overseas prices, and the financial commitment to the scheme of the federal government (Connors 1972).

During each harvest, farmers delivered their wheat over a period of a few months while the board's selling activities took place throughout the year. To meet growers' requirements for payment, the board made a series of advances, beginning soon after delivery and concluding, sometimes several years later, when all grain from that season's pool had been sold. The first advance was a high proportion of the expected return and was financed by the board through an overdraft from the Reserve Bank. This overdraft was guaranteed by the federal government. The level of the first advance was set annually by the government, but for many years before the 1968/69 season the government had maintained it at $1.10 a bushel.

The Wheat Board was not itself responsible for handling grain as farmers delivered their crops. This was done by bulk-handling authorities in each major wheatgrowing state. These authorities had different histories and capabilities. In Western Australia and South Australia cooperative bulk-handling companies, owned by farmers themselves and directed by their elected representatives, handled the grain. Both companies operated under state legislation. In Victoria and New South Wales the handling was done by grain elevators boards, operated and financed by the state governments but with farmer representatives among the directors. In Queensland the handling authority was the State Wheat Board, constituted under state provisions for the statutory organization of primary producers. Of necessity, all of these bodies cooperated closely with the Australian Wheat Board.

The Wheat Board and the price-support arrangements were underpinned by a network of agreements between governments and growers' organizations. Complementary legislation by the federal and state governments was needed. Whenever the scheme was due for renewal, bargaining and consultation about the details of such legislation took place between governments and between the federal government and the AWF. Within the AWF, constituent organizations from the different states often took some time to reconcile their positions. State organizations also communicated freely with their state governments, and sometimes a state organization and government would make common cause against the federal government and other constituents of the AWF.

The complex relationships supporting the arrangements made adjustments difficult. Even marginal changes could provoke protracted disturbances and produce effects spilling over into other areas. Unless reasons for making changes were extremely pressing, the easiest course was to allow the arrangements to continue without change. No change was possible without the active support of the federal government. Although it had no constitutional responsibility for agricultural production, the federal government's financial strength made it the virtual entrepreneur of most changes in wheat policy. If it chose to deploy its resources towards the gaining of specific objectives, it could usually get its way. But the difficulties involved, and the risk of spreading disturbances, constrained it too to use its strength sparingly.

CENTRAL PARTICIPANTS

An understanding of the relationships between the central institutions described so far can be reinforced by a consideration of other relevant institutions and of the relationships between individuals within institutions. When wheat quotas were introduced, a member of the Country Party, J. D. Anthony, was minister for primary industry and Sir John McEwen was still leader of the party. Within the parliamentary Country Party the roles of the leader and ministers were not subject in any substantial way to the influence of party backbenchers. Nor were there any clear lines of control extending from the extraparliamentary organization of the party (Aitkin 1972, ch. 16). Country Party leaders and ministers used their own judgment about what was best for their party and for the interests it claimed to represent. This had important consequences for relations between the government and farm organizations. Under Sir John McEwen, the view most commonly publicized of the Country Party's role in the making of farm policy was of a party consulting farm bodies about their requirements and then ensuring that these requirements were met. But Country Party leaders tended to operate rather differently. When they had made up their minds on an emerging issue, they had little hesitation in suggesting to farm organizations what organization policy ought to be (Aitkin 1972, pp. 272-73; Connors 1972, pp. 90-91).

The AWF, like all other major farm organizations, was non-partisan. Indeed, for some of its founders in the 1930s, being non-partisan had meant being anti-Country Party. However, its constituent organizations arose from the same rural base as the Country Party, and to a great extent its leaders shared the party's orientation and style. Some of them were active in the party's organization, and a majority of them supported it. But it was not common for AWF leaders to transfer from industry politics to represent the Country Party in parliament. They tended to pursue specialized careers as industry officials. Here they had opportunities to acquire several different roles. The path to membership of the Australian Wheat Board lay through prominence in a state affiliate of the AWF (Smith 1974b). It was not uncommon for delegates to the AWF to hold senior positions in their own organizations and also be members of the Australian Wheat Board. Some were also directors of bulk-handling authorities. The ladders of opportunity for AWF delegates brought them into close contact with the minister for primary industry. If he wished, the minister could make use of many opportunities to let his views and preferences be known. This was especially the case with Country Party ministers who shared a common background with AWF leaders and often knew them personally. Moreover, the minister could deploy tangible benefits of value to industry leaders. He determined appointments to several official positions, including the chairmanship of the Wheat Board, and could influence the filling of other official positions, regulate the access that industry leaders had to himself as minister, and bind them to his interests by taking them into his confidence.

In terms of the resources available to it, the AWF was not a well-endowed organization. It drew its funds from the affiliation fees of constituent organizations and consequently had a very small budget. Its secretary in 1968, T. C. Stott, who had been secretary since its foundation, was also secretary of the United Farmers and Graziers of South Australia and a member of the South Australian parliament. His salary as secretary of the federation was negligible. The AWF's only other employee was an economic adviser, whose salary was drawn from funds levied on farmers for wheat research (Connors 1972, p. 72). While Stott worked from Adelaide, the economic adviser was based in the Wheat Board's head office in Melbourne. During his long career, Stott had achieved some remarkable political *tours de force*, but even he could not do this on the federation's behalf every time it was needed. Moreover, by 1968 his influence within the federation had declined considerably, he was enmeshed in a complex and time-consuming situation in the South Australian parliament and he was near the end of his career.

The AWF often found it hard to determine its response to policy proposals by the government. On matters of importance, delegates were often divided between two contradictory tendencies. On the one hand were those concerned to assert the independence of the AWF, its capacity for making its own decisions, and its determination to stand up to government proposals with which it disagreed. But on the other were those who emphasized that the federation did not have the resources with which to fight the government. They appeared to adopt a strategy of close contact with members of the government in the hope of gaining benefits for the federation by timely cooperation and acquiescence. Paradoxically, delegates with a strong Country Party background were often in a better position than others to stand up to a Country Party minister. They had their own political standing. This latter point emphasizes the extent to which AWF decisions were influenced by the inter-woven personal and political interests of its delegates. Whether deciding to agree with a government or to campaign against it, AWF delegates were a small group of farmers explicitly committed to advancing the interests of their fellows but, by their rise through the ranks of farm organizations, exposed to incentives and ambitions differentiating them from those they sought to represent.

Behind the many-stranded politics of the Country Party and the AWF stood the Department of Primary Industry. Since its creation in the 1950s, when the former Department of Commerce and Agriculture was divided to make way for the Department of Trade, the Department of Primary Industry had not been known as an assertive department. Between William McMahon, who was its first minister (and the only Liberal to intrude on Country Party control of this area during the Liberal-Country Party coalition govern-ment), and J. D. Anthony, it had had as minister C. F. Adermann, who was not assertive either. The department was organized largely on functional lines, and its areas of expertise tended to be concen-trated in, say, the marketing of specific products rather than in re-viewing general trends in farm policy. Thus its officers who dealt with wheat matters had had considerable specialized experience. They were very conscious of the federal government's responsibility, both formal and informal, for wheat policy. They were also familiar, as public servants whose work often had direct political consequences, with the political as well as the administrative aspects of primary industry issues. They knew that departmental advice to the minister, based on economic or other technical grounds, would on occasion be judged to be politically inappropriate. Departmental officers were thus skilled at formulating advice leading to one set of conclusions and then administering policies based on the different considerations regarded as important at the political level. In the course of their work they became familiar with the ways of farm organizations and exchanged information with them on matters of mutual concern. But farm leaders often preferred to deal directly with the minister, believing that he was more likely to be sympathetic to their position. When discussions between the minister and farm bodies were going badly, departmental advice to the minister was often blamed.

PROBLEM IDENTIFICATION

Awareness of problems about disposing of the expanding volume of wheat production came to prominence in the second half of 1968. At the same time, negotiations on provisions of the fifth five-year wheat scheme were coming to an end. The negotiations had not been easy. The minister, advised by his department, had sought successfully to break the link hitherto existing between the home-consumption price and the guaranteed export price (Connors 1972, ch. 6). These had been determined by a much criticized "cost of production" index. Although not a few farm leaders recognized that the final result of attempting to apply a formula based on production costs had been a negotiated price, the AWF was reluctant to accept a two-price scheme and the drastic revision of the costs approach also insisted on by the minister. Among farmers the notion that the wheat scheme guaranteed them the "costs of production" had a wide and often emotional appeal. Before negotiations came to an end, the AWF had split openly in its attitude and the Victorian Farmers' Union, supported by the state government, had tried to stand out against agreeing to the proposals. The AWF's resistance to the minister's proposals was widely criticized by agricultural economists and journalists. The system of guaranteed prices tended to encourage production when it was not needed and to discourage it when overseas prices were good, but at this particular time the federation's stand showed a singular lack of appreciation of trends in supply and demand.

During the late 1960s, wheat production in Australia had boomed. An important factor was poor prices for wool. As wool prices fell, producers, attracted by the guaranteed price and the level of the first advance, turned to growing wheat. Acreages under wheat rose dramatically, especially in Western Australia and New South Wales. In New South Wales, graziers who occupied much land never used for agriculture but eminently suited for it swallowed their pride and went into wheat. Often they did not buy a farming plant themselves but engaged sharefarmers. Mixed farmers who usually both grew grain and raised sheep also increased their production. While this was happening, prices in international markets were declining and competition between the major exporting countries was intensifying. The International Grains Arrangement, recently negotiated to succeed a series of International Wheat Agreements, proved to be a weak instrument. Its agreed minimum prices could not withstand any substantial shifts in supply.

After the event, many people claimed to have foreseen the problem of overproduction. These included some who had been predicting it, in season and out, for so many years that sooner or later they had to be right. Others argued that there was nothing wrong in taking advantage of the "wheat bonanza" while it lasted. The critical point was in signalling to growers when it came to an end. The price-support arrangements did not do this. Moreover, the concerns and past experience of the principal actors did not encourage them to focus on this point. Significant changes in overseas prices over short periods of time were normal and could remove a problem of oversupply as quickly as they could create it. Concern over the Wheat Board's capacity to dispose of its stocks had occurred before, but no action had been necessary. As a result, neither the board nor the government had a clear policy on what constituted an excessively large carry-over. Further, although it had often been pointed out that production controls were a corollary of pricing arrangements that did not transmit market signals effectively to growers, no attempt to work out a system of controls had been made. One of the reasons for this was that to farmers production controls were anathema. Primary producers tended to believe that if there were not a market for their produce at a price acceptable to them, then there ought to be. The acreage restrictions introduced during the 1939-45 war had been lifted before the war's end, and the machinery to enforce them had been dropped from the post-war wheat scheme. The wartime arrangements were cumbersome and inefficient, so discontinuing them was in itself no loss. But the consequence of pushing the problem of production control to one side was that in 1968 no one had much experience even in considering appropriate responses and institutional arrangements. Moreover, the considerations that led farmers to object to production controls applied with equal force to attempts to regulate supply by adjustments to the guaranteed price or the level of the first advance. Thus even if overproduction was seen as a definite prospect, the easiest course was to do nothing and to hope the problem would disappear. This was a risky but, given past experience, not unrealistic course. Finally, the prospect of a federal election in 1969, as deliveries from the 1969/70 crop were beginning, made the federal government cautious about accepting responsibility for any action.

Concern about levels of production was distributed unevenly and expressed in different ways. To begin with, the minister for primary industry followed the public course of issuing general warnings and keeping his options open. In April 1968, while reminding the conference of the Victorian Wheat and Woolgrowers' Association about the size of government contributions to the stabilization fund, he also expressed relief that marketing of the big crops of the 1960s had gone as smoothly as it had (Victorian *Wheat and Woolgrower*, 5 April 1968). More specifically he warned that in the past year prices had weakened and that there was not a ready market for all the grain that Australian farmers could produce. Later in the year he emphasized that, except under the defence power, the federal government had no power to control agricultural production. This, he observed, rested with the states (*CPD*, H of R 61: 3098). In May and October 1968 the chairman of the Wheat Board, A. R. Callaghan, also warned that the series of large crops was creating problems and that there was a need for restraint (Victorian *Wheat and Woolgrower*, 3 May 1968; *Victorian Farmer*, 23 October 1968). For farmers themselves the results of ever larger crops showed up most immediately as a delivery problem. The capacity of the bulk-handling authorities was stretched to the maximum. This meant long queues at silos and various measures designed to increase equity of access. The situation generated considerable anxiety and discontent.

The AWF took up the question for the first time in September 1968. According to the federation's minutes it was pointed out during a discussion of costs of production that the Wheat Board had a large amount of grain to sell and that the AWF should study the issue. It was decided that the president should make a statement to constituent organizations. It was also decided to hold a special meeting of the federation, but the stated reason for this was to discuss rising production costs. That the AWF recognized that the issue required examination contrasted with its efforts throughout negotiations on the fifth wheat scheme. The only concern shown then had been by delegates who thought that the government's proposals on price levels were part of a plan to discourage production. Their reaction was to resist this to the last. It has been suggested that the minister for primary industry stimulated the federation's interest by referring to the possibility of a cut in the level of the first advance (Connors 1972, p. 90). There is no direct evidence to support this, and subsequently the first advance for the 1968/69 crop was maintained at $1.10 a bushel. This was used by the minister to help quell resistance by the Victorians to the new stabilization scheme. However, the question of the first advance assumed a clear significance in later interaction between the minister and the federation.

STEPS TOWARDS PROBLEM DEFINITION

Although it was believed at the time that the special AWF meeting would take place within a month or so of being called, it was not held in the end until January 1969. In the meantime, several proposals for regulating production were canvassed among growers and their organizations. The first organization to suggest a specific scheme was the United Farmers and Graziers of South Australia. This followed discussion at a meeting of the Wheat and Grain Executive on 14 November 1968 of the difficulties expected by Cooperative Bulk Handling in handling the 1968/69 crop. The executive then discussed the rising rate of production and the case that the UFG should put forward at the forthcoming meeting of the AWF. One member set the tone of the discussion by declaring that any proposed measures should protect "the genuine wheatgrowers of Australia" and that no reduction should be contemplated in the amount of the first advance. The chairman of the wheat and grain section, T. M. Saint, who was also a member of the Wheat Board and the current president of the AWF, then read an outline of a delivery quotas scheme prepared by L. A. Simpson of Oaklands in New South Wales. Simpson was active in the United Farmers and Woolgrowers' Association of New South Wales, but was concerned more with meat and wool than with grain. How he came to draw up a scheme for delivery quotas is not known. Also not known is why his proposal was considered by the UFG but not by his own organization. However, his contribution marked an important step in the acceptance by growers' organizations of the delivery quotas scheme.

As outlined by Simpson, the scheme was designed to hold wheat production in Australia to 329 million bushels a year. This was estimated to be the amount that the handling authorities and the Wheat Board could deal with. The scheme would operate by setting national and state delivery quotas based on average deliveries over a seven-year period. It would enable the first advance to be maintained at $1.10 a bushel and would discourage production above the national quota by making surplus wheat the responsibility of individual growers. It envisaged that at all times in the handling and sale of wheat, quota grain would receive preference over non-quota production. Where space was available to receive non-quota wheat, growers would have the amount of their non-quota deliveries deducted from their next year's quota. However, where growers produced less than their quota they could carry forward an entitlement to make up the shortfall next year. New growers would be entitled to a quota related to average yields and property sizes in their districts.

The UFG wheat and grains executive agreed without fuss that the scheme had merit and should be forwarded for discussion by the AWF. Later the scheme was publicized by some as the "Stott plan", after the then secretary of the UFG and the AWF, but the person clearly responsible for introducing it to the executive was Max Saint. His standing within the UFG also contributed to its smooth acceptance. Whereas in some other affiliates of the AWF there were several competing wheatgrower leaders, in the UFG Saint had undisputed charge of affairs.

In other organizations there was less agreement either about whether there was a problem or about how it should be approached. The extent of the disagreement became plain at the special meeting of the AWF held in Melbourne on 17 January 1969. However, by deleting from the agenda the issue of rising costs of production, which was the originally stated reason for the meeting, delegates did show that the volume of production was the main issue before them. They received reports from the general manager of the Wheat Board, L. H. Dorman, who attended by invitation, and from the federation's economic adviser, T. S. Jilek. Dorman set out the situation faced by the Wheat Board: depending on the level of sales to China, the board would have a carry-over of between 200 million and 315 million bushels; given available facilities, it was possible for the board to export 340 million bushels in a year; and certain kinds of grain — prime hard and northern f.a.q. — could easily be sold. He discussed without optimism a number of factors which might lead to increased sales. Jilek's report was more contentious, as it recommmended the diversion of resources used for wheatgrowing to the production of coarse grains. Efforts were made to keep his report secret, and its proposals were not taken up.

During discussion a number of delegates were reluctant to accept the need for consideration of possible controls. For example, L. M. Ridd of the United Farmers and Woolgrowers' Association expressed the opinion that no state had firm views about whether there was overproduction, let alone about how it should be restricted. P. J. Meehan of the Victorian Farmers' Union described the dangers of overproduction as hypothetical. But the majority acknowledged the problem and eventually it was agreed unanimously that affiliates should submit their views to the next federation meeting. The scheme forwarded by the UFG received no specific attention. A proposal that the federation ask the federal government to call a conference of representatives of the AWF, Wheat Board, Department of Primary Industry, and state governments to consider appropriate action was soundly defeated. The view was put with considerable force that only after the federation had determined its own policy should it meet other bodies.

The meeting also received a letter from its secretary, T. C. Stott, who was prevented by illness from attending. The letter expressed his wish to retire. Delegates accepted his resignation with regret and appointed T. S. Jilek as acting secretary. This meant that later, during important contacts with the federal government, the federation had first an acting and then a newly appointed secretary in charge of its records and correspondence. However, even had Stott been able to continue, his health and other commitments would have prevented him from working at full effectiveness. From the federation's viewpoint the change in secretaries could hardly have come at a less opportune time.

ATTITUDES OF GOVERNMENT

During this period the government was also attempting to define its position. In November 1968 the minister asked the Department of Primary Industry to comment on a paper submitted to him by T. M. Saint. This was about the time that the UFG considered the letter from L. A. Simpson. Although not identical with Simpson's letter, the paper forwarded by Saint was similar in all important respects. The department presented its view on 29 November, a fortnight after the UFG had decided to send Simpson's proposals to the AWF. The department was not enthusiastic about the proposals, or indeed about any other suggestions for controlling production. After reviewing previous experience with large carry-overs, it concluded: "The need for production controls *at this time* is not established." However, it did not provide explicit reasons for this conclusion. The department then set out a number of alternative courses that could be taken if production controls were "deemed necessary", and commented point by point on the paper submitted by Saint. It identified a number of problems which, after delivery quotas were introduced, became painfully obvious to wheatgrowers. It pointed out that the administration of any form of quota scheme would be both difficult and costly and that it was "yet to be demonstrated that the end could be achieved by the means suggested". Further, it noted that quotas would tend to fix production patterns and could lead to an inefficient allocation of resources.

Of the other alternatives it identified, the department made specific comments on two — restricting acreages and reducing the first advance. It observed that controlling acreages without limiting total production could lead to intensive cultivation and large yields. It argued that reducing the first advance would be simpler than any quota scheme, but that a very sharp reduction would probably be needed to bring about measurable change. Although it did not put forward an extended argument in favour of reducing the first advance, it is likely that the department regarded this as the best course to follow. Such a course was supported by academic economists and had from time to time been studied in the department when the level of production was rising.

The government did not follow the department's advice. First, the department changed its mind soon afterwards on the need for introducing controls. Apparently officers of the department had formulated their advice at a time when estimates of the 1968/69 crop had fallen because of seasonal conditions. Although earlier in the year a large crop had been forecast, by November 1968 estimates had fallen to 435 million bushels. This was still big, but might possibly have been managed without drastic action. In 1966/67 the Wheat Board had disposed of a record delivery of 440 million bushels. This lower estimate was also a factor in the decision to maintain the first advance for the 1968/69 crop at $1.10 a bushel. However, once farmers began delivering the crop it was apparent that the estimate was too low. Final deliveries eventually totalled 515 million bushels. Moreover, at its meetings in January 1969 the Wheat Board, after estimating deliveries at 487 million bushels, reviewing the likelihood of a further large crop in 1969/70, and taking into account the reduced demand for wheat, concluded that a problem did exist. With existing storage capacity of 515 million bushels and a large carry-over from the 1968/69 crop (estimated this time at 185 million bushels), the board foresaw that another large crop would lead to storage difficulties and discontent among farmers. It concluded that these factors pointed to "the necessity for at least curbing the present rate of expansion of production in Australia".

Second, the government had already incurred the displeasure of many farmers by its stand in negotiations for the fifth stabilization plan. It did not wish to add to this by taking responsibility for action to curb production. Making a sharp cut in the first advance would have been both highly unpopular and clearly the responsibility of the federal government. Any minister, whether Country Party or not, with a significant number of rural seats contributing to the government's majority, would have been reluctant to do this. Farmer discontent would have been the greater because farmers had come to expect that the first advance would be maintained at $1.10 a bushel.

To growers, the first advance at this level was an assured and tangible benefit which made farm budgeting easier. For many growers it was sufficient to cover actual outlays in producing their crops. It also formed a basis on which to plan the following year's activities and could be used in approaching financial institutions for credit. Cutting the level of the advance would have meant that farmers would have had to wait for a greater proportion of their payment until shipments of grain from the pool concerned had been sold. This would have introduced more uncertainty into farm decision making, and uncertainty of this kind is bitterly resented by many farmers.

THE MINISTER AND THE AWF

Instead, the minister for primary industry adopted a strategy of inducing the AWF to accept a large part of the burden. This involved a carefully considered mixture of praise for the capacity and sense of responsibility of the federation, pointed references both to the powers of the federal government and to the extent of federal contributions to the industry's welfare, and a statement of the implications for wheat growers if production continued uncurbed. The minister did not put his views to a formal meeting of the federation. However, in the normal course of his work he had some contact, both formally and informally, with federation representatives. Also, a week before the federation met in March 1969 he made clear publicly his appreciation of the situation. This was in a speech opening the Wimmera Machinery Field Days at Longerenong Agricultural College in Victoria.

The appropriate sections of the speech were persuasively put, had a clear relevance for the issues due for discussion by the AWF, and indeed invited the AWF to recommend lines of action for the federal and state governments. The minister said:

> I believe it would be unfortunate if control of production was forced upon the industry by law. Control of production imposed by legislation against the industry's advice and wishes would be a policy of despair. I believe no one wants to see wheat production controlled in this way. I hope the industry itself will be able — in the meetings now being held in all wheat areas, and at the Australian Wheatgrowers' Federation meeting in Perth on 11th and 12th of this month — to work out some means of overcoming the problem the industry is now facing. I believe it

will, and I will be eagerly waiting to hear what decisions are made. Should the industry voluntarily put forward proposals that would require state legislative backing to curb production or control deliveries, I would be happy to make myself available at the request of the State Ministers to try to co-ordinate a uniform national policy. A uniform policy I would think essential.

The minister also made reference to the supply situation, the availability and expensiveness of storage space, the risk of providing too much storage in response to temporary circumstances, and the provision of the first advance. He posed the problems facing the industry in the following way.

> The wheat industry's problems lie in the fact that production has outstripped available outlets, and that the storage system will be unable to accommodate even a moderately large crop next season, let alone a crop of the dimensions of this season's. And the grower has reason to be very concerned about this. Even if it were possible to maintain the level of the first advance at $1.10 per bushel, you would get that $1.10 only when you delivered your wheat. If the storages were full you would not be able to deliver and you would not get paid. And if pool payments are delayed and the Wheat Board remains longer in debt, this in turn would mean heavier interest charges and lower returns. [Address by J. D. Anthony, 4 March 1969]

He stated that with an expected carry-over of more than 200 million bushels and storage space for 515 million bushels, growers could not expect to deliver more than about 300 million bushels from the next season's crop — unless more storage was provided or sales were unexpectedly good.

His discussion of the first advance was lengthy. He denied that he had advocated controlling production by manipulating the first advance but pointed out that the government could not guarantee that the advance would remain at $1.10 in future seasons. He outlined how the advance was financed and referred to the increase in the Wheat Board's indebtness to the Reserve Bank — from $509 million to approximately $600 million — because of the unexpected increase in deliveries during the 1968/69 season. He forecast that unless sales improved the board would not be able to repay the loan within twelve months and that, at the end of that period, up to $200 million could be outstanding. Further, he pointed out that the size of the debt outstanding would be a major factor when the government considered the level of the advance for the following year.

Thus while inviting the AWF to formulate a response for the

industry to its problems of production, and disavowing government preferences for alternative measures that had been canvassed, the minister in effect defined the federation's options for it. His argument turned on the value placed by farmers on the existing level of the first advance. By emphasizing the danger of a reduction, while denying that he intended to use such a reduction to control production, he transferred to the federation responsibility for making the first explicit movements towards controls. He reinforced this position by declining to consider proposals from state farm organizations, their branches, or individual farmers until the federation had met.

AWF PROPOSALS

The AWF met in Perth on 11 March 1969. Following its meeting in January, state organizations had sponsored meetings of farmers at which the issues before the industry were presented. Several state organizations had then prepared their own proposals. Except in Victoria, these followed principles similar to those outlined in the scheme discussed earlier by the UFG in South Australia. The VFU proposed that controls should be imposed on an acreage basis. This was put forward in an attempt to forestall problems of over-border trading outside the Wheat Board, which would arise as soon as there were plentiful supplies of over-quota grain. Because of the Constitution, the legislation setting out the Wheat Board's powers could not prevent over-border trading, although the board had developed a number of procedures which in normal times inhibited the practice.

Although most affiliates were moving towards similar policies, it was by no means certain that the AWF would be able to agree on a definite set of proposals. As soon as proposals were given a precise form, strong tensions emerged. These involved rivalries between states and between regions within states, differences in the kinds of wheat produced and in the ease with which they could be sold, and differences between kinds of producers. For example, soft wheat growers in South Australia, Victoria, and southern New South Wales, all mixed farming areas where wheat had long been established as a significant crop, feared the move into wheat in northern New South Wales and Queensland by graziers and large property holders who could produce large quantities of more easily sold hard wheat. In turn, producers in these areas, whether newcomers to the industry or not, did not see why their capacity for production should be curbed in order to assist growers producing grain in less demand. Further, producers had different histories of production, resulting from variations in seasonal conditions and past management decisions. The precise base period on which any controls were founded thus assumed great importance. Finally, some organizations and farm leaders were still unenthusiastic about the path they were taking. The Graziers' Association of New South Wales (recently admitted to membership of the AWF) was still formally committed to opposing production controls, the United Farmers and Woolgrowers' Association had no firm policy to take to Perth, and J. P. Cass, a member of the Wheat Board and UFWA delegate to the AWF, suggested publicly that the federal government could assist the industry by enabling the Wheat Board to offer more attractive terms to overseas buyers. Cass also suggested that the government ought to state more definitely its attitude towards the industry's future and whether it considered present production excessive.

Nevertheless, at the AWF meeting, delegates readily agreed that production control was necessary, that the federation should prepare a plan for recommendation to its affiliates, that any controls should be conditional on the first advance remaining at $1.10 a bushel, and that any plan should be ratified by federation affiliates by 30 May 1969. Resolutions on these points were carried without dissent. Victorian delegates found no support for acreage restrictions, and the meeting then decided, also without dissent, that production controls should be on a delivery quota basis and that any scheme should be flexible, protect traditional and small growers, and not restrict production of "readily saleable" grain. Further, delegates set a basic national delivery quota of 344 million bushels and expressed the view that a desirable carry-over in any year would be 50 per cent of the delivery quota for the year.

But once the discussion turned to state quotas, disagreements came to the fore. These involved the base period on which such quotas should be calculated and the means of providing for producers of "readily saleable" prime hard wheat. Much debate took place on the merits of three-, five- and seven-year averages of production and on the possibility of establishing a separate pool for prime hard wheat. Ultimately, delegates agreed on a five-year average and supplementary prime hard quotas for New South Wales and Queensland, the two states producing prime hard wheat. Agreement on the device of supplementary quotas came only after a separate meeting of the president, T. M. Saint, the general manager of the Wheat Board, L. H. Dorman, and delegates from New South Wales and Queensland. At this meeting Dorman suggested the means of meeting the problem. With these matters agreed upon, delegates then carried a resolution setting out the basic quotas for each state and arranged to present their proposals as soon as possible to the minister for primary industry.

MAKING THE SCHEME WORK

Once the AWF had accepted delivery quotas, the minister for primary industry initiated a series of further steps to formulate the scheme on workable lines and give it legislative backing. This was not a simple process; nor was it one over which the AWF could have control. It involved further consideration of the scheme by the federation but also action by the Departments of Primary Industry, the Wheat Board, state governments, and bulk-handling authorities. In Perth the AWF did not discuss the implementation of the scheme. Members of the federation executive had a brief discussion before meeting the minister for primary industry in Sydney on 28 March 1969, a fortnight after the Perth meeting. They were concerned mainly with processes for allocating quotas to individual growers. On receiving assurances from the AWF that the scheme would work, the minister called a meeting of the Agricultural Council. He expressed his concern to have the scheme in operation for the coming season. Indeed, he attempted to secure binding agreement to it well before the AWF's deadline at the end of May.

The Agricultural Council meeting on 10 April 1969, however, did not go smoothly. State ministers had differing ideas about the contents and implications of the AWF's proposals. Although the Department of Primary Industry had asked for as complete a statement as possible of the proposals, it found that it had to rely on the record in the federation's minutes. This set out the proposals but did not explain them. Moreover, state ministers had received different accounts of the federation meeting from their respective state organizations. In one case a state organization had warned a minister of the inadequacy of the AWF's statement of the scheme and urged him to defer making a decision on it until further studies had been made. Further, ministers were concerned at being asked to agree to introduce controversial legislation without having adequate information before them. They also wanted an assurance that if the scheme were adopted, the first advance would remain at its present level. This the minister for primary industry refused to give; he pointed out that if the scheme did not operate and the 1969/70 crop was as large as expected, the first advance could be as low as seventy-five cents a bushel. The result of the meeting was an acceptance in general terms of the need to curb production and a decision to call a meeting of federal and state legal representatives to examine necessary legislation. The meeting also requested that the AWF draw up a statement of its proposals in detailed form and send it to each minister.

The minister for primary industry promptly directed his departmental officers to arrange a meeting with the AWF and secure an appropriate statement. Accordingly, officers of the Department of Primary Industry, together for part of the time with officers from the Wheat Board, met the executive of the AWF in Melbourne on 16 April 1969. At this meeting an officer of the department specified the main problem areas. These included the means by which delivery quotas were to be implemented and the extent of state government responsibility for implementation; the right of growers to carry forward amounts of quotas not filled; and the meaning of "readily saleable" and the eligibility of such wheat for the first advance. Discussion of the question of implementation revealed that understanding of the legislative requirements of the scheme was both uncertain and unevenly distributed. A delegate from one state reported that the state minister did not want to introduce any legislation at all and was hoping that existing legislation covering the bulk handling of grain would provide the necessary legal support. A similar position was also reported from another state. Another delegate suggested that the Wheat Board could simply tell the handling authorities how much wheat they were to receive. In the end the federation agreed that such matters were beyond its reach and merely expressed the wish that, as the fiscal and legal implications of the scheme were worked through, the principles formulated by the federation should be retained. Of the other problems mentioned, the question of growers carrying forward entitlements to unfilled portions of quotas was settled fairly easily once Wheat Board officers said it was administratively possible, but defining "readily saleable" was difficult. This question raised again the tension existing between producers of different kinds of wheat. No one wanted to concede that their varieties could not be sold. Ultimately a formula was evolved for assessing the sales performance of non-quota wheat accepted by handling authorities and allocating proportions of such wheat that had been sold to individual growers. Following the meeting, the newly elected general secretary, G. E. Andrews, the economic adviser, T. S. Jilek, and officers of the Wheat Board prepared a working paper which, after confirmation by affiliates of the federation, was circulated to all ministers concerned.

DECISIONS ON LEGISLATION

The working paper was dispatched to the minister for primary industry on 25 April 1969. Anticipating that the quota scheme could proceed, the minister had secured cabinet approval for it on 23 April. With the working paper in hand he completed the process of securing commitments from the state ministers, called a meeting of federal and state legal officers, and on 30 April issued a public announcement that the scheme would be put into force. The meeting of legal officers took place on 13 May 1969. Federal representatives advocated as much uniformity of legislation as practicable while attempting to restrict the extent of federal legislative effort. Agreement on most points was reached without fuss. But on the question of which level of government should legislate to empower licensed receivers pursuant to the scheme to refuse to accept deliveries of wheat, disagreement took place. This provision was to form the centrepiece of the scheme's legislative authority. Federal representatives argued that only the states could enact appropriate provisions, but one state's representatives, speaking on instructions from their minister, argued that the Wheat Board could cover the point by exercising its power to direct bulk-handling authorities. Although the other states did not pursue the matter, the state bringing forward the argument maintained pressure on the federal government. Had the government accepted the point, it would also have had to accept the unpopularity arising from the operation of the scheme. In the end, some time after the meeting, the department sought a formal opinion from the Attorney-General's Department and, when this supported the federal view presented earlier, the recalcitrant state fell into line. Although the incident did not seriously threaten the federal government's position, it provided a further and pointed illustration of federal reluctance to accept public responsibility for the scheme.

Following the meeting of legal representatives, the department sent a summary of proceedings (omitting references to the disagreement on the issue above) to the AWF. The federation agreed with the legislative action proposed, and thereafter state organizations had close contact with their state authorities about necessary legislation. As passed, the legislation differed from state to state, but federal officers drafted model legislation to indicate what was needed. By the end of 1969 all states except Queensland had passed legislation, and quotas applied to deliveries from the 1969/70 harvest. In Queensland poor seasonal conditions meant that there was no urgency in introducing the scheme, and legislation was not passed until 1970.

Federal legislation was also not passed until 1970. Its contribution to the working of the scheme, although essential, was inconspicuous. Except in respect of the ACT, the legislation did not deal directly with quotas. It recognized that the administrative costs of working the scheme should be chargeable to the relevant pool, that is, that the industry itself should pay the costs. More significantly, it altered the definition of a pool to exclude non-quota wheat. Previously the stabilization legislation had provided that all wheat from a season would form one pool. The federal legislation also gave discretionary authority to the Wheat Board to sell wheat in Australia, for other than human consumption, at a price lower than the home-consumption price. This arose from concern about over-border trading outside the Wheat Board and represented an attempt to reduce the incentive for those trading in and using wheat for stock feed to participate in such sales. The AWF's endorsement of this step had been secured, but on this occasion the federation had been reluctant to cooperate. When the matter was first raised at a joint meeting in August 1969 attended by federation delegates and representatives from the Wheat Board and Department of Primary Industry, federation delegates rejected by thirteen votes to nine any change in the home-consumption price. At a further meeting in September the federation agreed to allow sales below the home-consumption price provided that these did not go below the ruling guaranteed price for export wheat and that the federal government made up the difference in price to the Wheat Board.

PROBLEMS AND CONCLUSIONS

Once the quota scheme began operation, many difficulties, ignored or only partly appreciated during the process of formulating the scheme, became obvious. Each state had its own particular problems and controversies. The state affiliates of the AWF had to explain and justify the scheme to puzzled and often angry growers. Frequently their stands involved them in internal troubles and the loss of members. Doubts were raised about the fairness, effectiveness, and actual necessity of the scheme. Alternatives were proposed and debated with ardour and intensity. In retrospect, formulating the scheme was nowhere near as difficult or bothersome as trying to make it work.

It is not the purpose of this discussion to examine specific problems of implementation or to assess the impact of the quota scheme. However, it is relevant in reviewing the process of formulation to sketch some of the problems encountered. These can be divided, although with overlaps, into two categories: problems of procedure and problems of impact. Procedural problems included difficulties in allocating quotas fairly, even in straightforward cases; questions of allocating quotas to new lands farmers, newcomers to the industry, partnerships, and sharefarmers; dealing with appeals; disputes between states over the allocation of state quotas, the filling of state shortfalls, the alleged delivery in one state of f.a.q. grain against a prime hard quota, and the declaration of wheat as "readily saleable"; overborder trading; and clerical problems — lack of qualified staff, arithmetical and other errors, and, in one state, the loss of essential documents. Although derived from the application of a federally inspired scheme, these problems were the responsibility of state governments and state farm organizations.

For individual farmers and many farm leaders, procedural problems had more salience than questions about the impact of the scheme: however, the latter had considerable significance for the trend of policy in the industry. The scheme put immediate welfare considerations ahead of a concern for the efficient allocation of rural resources. It put a further shield between farmers and the impact of overseas markets and risked the freezing of wheat-production patterns along the lines current at its introduction. As Tom Connors states, "In the long term fixed quotas inhibit a shift in production from high to low cost regions, from inefficient to efficient growers and from areas producing varieties in oversupply to those climatically suitable for producing wheats in demand" (Connors 1972, p. 108). Some of these problems could be alleviated by making individual quotas negotiable: a farmer who did not want to produce wheat could sell or lease his quota entitlement to a farmer who did. However, while negotiability was allowed only in Victoria and New South Wales and was not possible between states, it introduced a further element of complexity into an already cumbersome apparatus. On the other hand, the imposition of quotas also stimulated diversification into other crops, notably coarse grains and oilseeds. This had beneficial effects but also opened the way for the possible transference of wheat's problems of oversupply to other crops.

Although the scheme involved a conspicuous change in the organization of wheat deliveries, it was an initiative taken with reluctance. It represented an attempt to maintain existing policies which were under challenge. Essentially, neither governments nor growers' organizations wished problems of overproduction to threaten the marketing and guaranteed price arrangements long accepted in the industry and renegotiated arduously in 1968.

In the process of deciding to introduce delivery quotas, the participants traversed uncertain paths, concentrated on a limited number of key factors, and left many others out of consideration. In determining that a problem of oversupply existed, and in shaping the response to it, the critical interaction took place between the minister for primary industry and the AWF. The important factors in their definition of the problem were the minister's concern to avoid political difficulties, which would arise from visible federal action, and the federation's concern to maintain the level of the first advance. Once the federation had agreed to the quota approach, the state governments were induced to assume the legislative burden of the scheme. The federal government retained substantial control over the setting of the national quota by its control over the amount of money made available for the first advance. However, once the scheme was in operation both the federation and the state governments could win some points at issue by standing firm and raising the possibility that the federal government would be made responsible for the consequences of disagreement. This course was not possible, except at the risk of heavy costs, in the actual shaping of the scheme.

While the AWF took responsibility for formulating the scheme in outline, the federal government took the lead in organizing its practicable formulation. At this stage the department of Primary Industry and the Wheat Board both had important roles to play. In particular the department, despite its initial reservations about the whole enterprise, had responsibility for securing a revised statement of the scheme from the federation and ensuring that the state governments did indeed assume the required legislative burden.

For critics of the scheme the problem is to identify means by which the minister for primary industry and the AWF could have been induced to change their definition of the problem. At the outset the Department of Primary Industry had clearly and cogently expressed doubts about the scheme, and even more elaborate and sophisticated policy advice from the Department of Primary Industry would probably have had little effect on the ultimate direction of policy. In the field of agricultural policy the acceptance by political actors of professionally based advice is situational and incremental. For those who argue that political actors should take more notice of such advice, an appreciation of this state of affairs is the first step.

7

Bureaucratic Politics and the Department of Foreign Affairs

Conflict between departments has been a common but intermittent theme of previous chapters. Now we concentrate on how the Department of Foreign Affairs has managed its relations with other departments of the Australian Public Service, especially during 1972-75 when the Labor government gave a new attention to foreign policy and to the organizational requirements of the department. Foreign Affairs grew and attempted to enlarge its responsibilities, and we seek to explain how policy intentions were linked to organizational resources. This is not a simple success story. The department's encounters with other bureaucratic institutions had few or no decisive outcomes, for Foreign Affairs found it difficult to create and modify organizational forms and procedures to meet new opportunities. Here is a case of aggressive institutional maintenance with no distinct winners and losers: the struggle continues in conditions as ambiguous and intractable, and as captivating to the participants, as anything described below.

To describe this is a novel exercise. Published works on Australian foreign policy concentrate on substantive issues of international politics or on historical studies of relationships between countries in which Australia is one actor, and usually a rather rational actor. National self-interest is still the essence of the prevailing explanatory paradigm. The links between domestic and foreign policy have been little explored, and the emphasis has been upon electoral and interest groups in the community rather than upon activity within the bureaucracy. While the occasional writer has argued, in a glancing way, that "foreign policy is made essentially by a small group of cabinet ministers and senior departmental officers" (Altman 1973, p. 99), it has not been unknown for others to dismiss out of hand a concentration upon bureaucratic dynamics. T. B. Millar, for example, in playing down the influence of the press and military upon foreign policy decision making, adds that "nor is [the government] subject to pressures from . . . the department of External Affairs, or the public service generally" (Millar 1968, p. 34). A single chapter about the department cannot supply a missing dimension of such magnitude. This chapter is not a study of foreign policy or of any particular foreign policy. If such a study paid attention to bureaucratic dynamics, it would elaborate the processes within the department which interact with processes in wider structures beyond — in the wider public service, in the polity as a whole, and in the community. This pattern of interaction is not random: procedures for consulting extra-bureaucratic agencies at various stages of negotiations, for example, arise when other agencies have gradually established their right to be involved. Making plain the results of that pattern of interaction might then be our aim, but here we are more modest. We do not elaborate the links between particular bureaucratic activities and particular policy outcomes but rather suggest that they are important, and we show one approach to their description.

DEPARTMENTAL TASKS

The execution of foreign policy, like the collection of taxes and the enforcement of law and order, is thought to be a core function of government without which no state could survive. Countries similar to Australia thus established foreign offices, with a variety of titles, at very early stages of their development. So did Australia: the Department of External Affairs was one of the original seven departments of state at Federation in 1901, and it had the prime minister as its political head. But for many years it operated as a branch of the Prime Minister's Department and, because of Australia's long dependence on Britain for foreign policy guidance and for representation abroad, it did not emerge as a separate body with its own administrative head until 1935. It was retitled the Department of Foreign Affairs in 1971. Its history as an organization of any significance dates from the years of the Second World War, for as late as 1938 the attorney-general, R. G. Menzies, believed that Australia's views on international events should be conveyed, in private, to the

British government; the only overseas representation was of the liaison type (Foreign Affairs 1975*b*, pp. 544-47).

For most of its life this "late starter" on the bureaucratic stage, to use the department's own term (Foreign Affairs 1974*a*, p. 17), was a relatively weak actor. Its minister was always a cabinet minister, it is true, and it soon became a large department with a rapid growth rate and a large complement of second division officers (by 1975, the second division amounted to 3.4 per cent of its total second and third division staff, equal to Treasury and higher than any other agency except the PSB (6 per cent) and PMC (11.3 per cent). But the department never had its powers clearly defined, as Britain, the United States, and New Zealand attempted to do legislatively in the mid-1940s; it developed slowly its trained and capable personnel; its main concerns were closely limited by other departments and its pretensions to the traditions of older foreign offices were not easily accepted by them; and it was headed by ministers not enthusiastic about its claim to greater weight in the bureaucratic world. These problems arose from a fundamental uncertainty about the functions of the department. Unlike some foreign offices, the Australian department was supposedly responsible both for diplomacy abroad and for the formulation of foreign policy at home; the same officers carried out both sets of tasks. The often-made distinction between these tasks is not precise, and their careful and successful integration is the source of the greatest strength to a foreign office. But the Australian department was not very successful in this attempt. It established a more than reputable diplomatic service, but the department in Canberra was not seen as a major policy actor. The department was "always more engaged in the exercise of collecting other people's views than giving [its] own", as its permanent head during 1973-76 said (*Australian*, 4 May 1974). Its officers felt keenly "the difference in bureaucratic position between the foreign affairs officer drafting a cable in a chancery and his or her colleague preparing a submission in Canberra" (Collins 1977).

Events beyond the control of any person or institution in Australia made this separation increasingly difficult for Foreign Affairs to endure. Australia's adjustments to the international uncertainties of the last decade inevitably called its arrangements for foreign policy administration into question. The department found itself confronted with a host of new issues and tried positively, some said aggressively, to assert a new role for itself. In 1974 it claimed that it was "the only organization equipped to facilitate a harmonious interaction and accommodation between domestic and international policies and requirements" (Foreign Affairs 1974a , p. ii). The interaction had two faces. In its own view, Foreign Affairs was involved in "the central role of ensuring that sometimes competing and conflicting interests are coordinated and reconciled at home so that a single, coherent and united policy is presented to the world outside" (Foreign Affairs 1974a , p. ii). In addition, the international scene had its own problems and sources of problems which could not be viewed simply as a reflection of domestic concerns. "The subject matter of foreign policy", the department claimed, "is the impact of international considerations on national interests" (Foreign Affairs 1975e , p. 1). A specialist agency was required to deal with these unique problems, it was said, which necessarily involved Foreign Affairs in coordinating work on the domestic front.

The department faced many difficulties in attempting new tasks. One was the organizational demand of diplomacy itself. A high proportion of Foreign Affairs staff is always abroad, and the proportion has risen, if erratically, from under 50 per cent in the late 1940s to around 60 per cent in the late 1970s, compared with Overseas Trade 6.5 per cent, Defence 5.3 per cent, Treasury 1.4 per cent, and the PSB 0.07 per cent (Public Service Board 1977, p. 138). The department has a less visible presence in Australia than other departments have, and that presence is concentrated almost entirely in Canberra.

Foreign Affairs is not without its client groups in the business, artistic, charitable, and educational communities, but to an uncommon extent it must rely on its own resources of personnel and the strength of its argument in bureaucratic encounters. The department is acutely aware of the dangers of isolation. Isolation, of course, works both ways. One of the problems facing Foreign Affairs is that its colleague departments believe it spends a great deal of time dispatching messages into the void; other departments find it difficult to recognize, let alone welcome, the translation of those messages into activity overseas and are disposed to call Foreign Affairs unproductive. On the other hand, its officers stationed overseas often do not know what happens in distant Canberra to the reports they file: feedback is slight.

THE DIPLOMATS

Foreign Affairs' very success in creating a diplomatic service has contributed to its difficulties. The department claims that it has a very special need to ensure "the development of career foreign service officers with wide and diverse experience, and with skills both in dealing with other governments and international organizations, and in managing diplomatic missions and implementing policies and programs overseas" (Foreign Affairs 1974*a*, pp. 22-23). From such statements some very specific staffing consequences follow. The characteristic of Foreign Affairs most clearly separating it from the rest of the APS is, indeed, its staffing arrangements. The diplomatic career structure of the department is sharply separate from the rest of the APS. Trainees to the diplomatic stream are specially chosen to enter Foreign Affairs, and few transfer to other departments (though the number is rising, as is the number leaving the public service altogether); few lateral recruits join them. This has been traditionally a matter of pride for the department and for the great majority of its officers. It has shown that "apprenticeship diplomacy" is working. It has been a departmental strength. A sense of clarity of purpose, or even mission, has pervaded the whole department. But that sense is declining as uncertainty about the role of Foreign Affairs increases; it is less of a strength.

The department obtains its diplomatic staff (some five hundred were employed in Australia and in missions overseas in 1977) through a department-specific scheme of graduate recruitment. Successful entrants pass through a complex and often criticized series of tests operated, under increasing challenge, by the department itself and spend an initial year as trainees before entering the diplomatic service proper as Foreign Affairs Officers (FAOs). The part of the PSB in this selection process is "minimal" (RCAGA 1976: 3, pp. 276-79). The scheme was begun in 1961, and former trainees now occupy over 90 per cent of the senior (class 11 and above) positions in the department. Recruits to senior rank from outside the public service or from other departments are few, as are political appointees. FAOs have a distinctive view of themselves which is a product of their selection, training, organizational history, and substantive work. A survey in 1975 of the attitudes of public servants towards their work and prospects, for example. showed clearly how the institutional history of Foreign Affairs had its reflections in individual perceptions at that time (RCAGA 1976: 3, pp. 1-189, especially pp. 156-60; Cass and Hawker 1978). The job satisfaction of FAOs was very high. They found their tasks demanding and responsible; 94 per cent, the highest in the public service, said that they did not "have a dead-end job". These characteristics alone were sufficient to separate FAOs in spirit and in fact from other public servants, and they were different in other ways also. They saw their careers as almost inextricably tied to the department, and perhaps it is this which made them so unresponsive to a range of questions which agitated public servants generally; questions about union membership, political activity, the morality of public comment by public servants, and similar issues elicited a consistently higher proportion of "don't know/undecided" responses from FAOs than from other groups. This is not surprising: diplomats are necessarily receptive to viewpoints which arise outside the domestic structure, and this circumstance may distance them from the outlook of their fellow public servants as much as it may distance their department from other departments responsible for narrower matters of policy. So long as diplomatic staff spend, on average, about half to two-thirds of their careers abroad (and some spend as much as 80 per cent), that effect must persist.

Other people and other departments are less sanguine about what Australian diplomats do. They have attacked the social unrepresentativeness of recruits which produces an "elitist image . . . reinforced by the administration of a closed shop which inevitably gives rise to resentment by those who feel excluded" (Mediansky 1974, p. 315; see also Clark 1975). Foreign Affairs officers cannot, it is said, legitimately exercise wide coordinating powers when they have had so little experience of other departments. Critics have tried to break down the isolation and perceived separateness of the department at its public service root (at the recruitment point) and at its key positions of influence (through lateral appointments) and Foreign Affairs has responded over the years with an articulate, and partly successful, defence of its boundaries. It has conceded that recruits to the elite diplomatic ranks are unusually unrepresentative either of the community at large or of other public service recruits, and it could hardly do otherwise. FAOs surveyed in 1975 were predominantly male (91 per cent); Anglican (32 per cent) or agnostic (41 per cent) but not Catholic; educated at GPS schools (30 per cent); city-bred (84 per cent); and from professional or government-employed parents (RCAGA 1976: 3, pp. 79-81). But this situation has not been static, and the department has said that it seeks to make "certain that each year's intake represents a genuine cross-section of the community" (Renouf 1974, p. 116). There has indeed been a gradual "levelling-out" of recruitment patterns, exemplified by, for example, the decline in GPS-educated recruits from 61 per cent in 1962 (External Affairs 1968, p. 81) to some 30 per cent in 1975. The department is less willing to concede that its former trainees can be matched by outsiders without relevant experience. It emphasizes "the *length* of time and the kind of experience required to equip a person to carry out successfully the responsibilities of a Head of Mission". It may, the department says, take four or five years before recruits are "really beginning to acquire professional expertise as Foreign Affairs officers. . . . It may be another fifteen or twenty years, acquiring wider knowledge and experience in the service, developing long-range skills and extensive knowledge of a variety of foreign economies and cultures, before they become Heads of Mission" (Foreign Affairs 1975*d*, p. 2).

We will see that a new role in policy implies other staffing changes for Foreign Affairs. Here it need only be noted that the officials of the successful and apparently satisfied diplomatic service just described actively seek this new role. Indeed, the level of satisfaction revealed by the survey should be discounted somewhat: the survey was undertaken precisely at the time when departmental ambitions and success were at their height (as we shall see). Then 36.7 per cent of respondents saw their main work as "policy formulation"; 11.4 per cent saw it as "executive management", 10.8 per cent as "regulatory work" and 10.1 per cent as "negotiation" (but 29.7 per cent saw it as unspecified "other", the highest figure for any group surveyed and possibly a reflection of the changes under way in the department). The *esprit de corps* of officers was especially high as their legitimate expectations were expanding.

TIME AND TRADITION

The history of the department ran against those expectations, however. For twenty years, until the late 1960s, Foreign Affairs was involved in policies which were initiated by powerful allies, inhibiting its development in a more autonomous role, and the department was often headed by ministers who had only a limited conception of such a role. Frequently both restraints applied. The active department of Dr. H. V. Evatt (minister 1941–49) was regarded with suspicion by the Liberal-Country Party coalition government of the early 1950s. Recruitment and the opening of overseas missions were at a low level, and neither the Treasury nor the PSB took a helpful stand. When the department recovered its position somewhat, it came under the control of a minister (P. M. Hasluck 1964–69) who was often called "strong" and was at any rate remote from the department, often in a physical sense. Permanent heads (Watt 1951–54, Tange 1954–65, Plimsoll 1965–70) were content to develop the department slowly. The only review of the functions and top structure of the department took place in 1964. This did not result in substantial changes. As the department later said, its divisions "were simply numbered I to IV and the allocation of Branches within the Divisions sought to balance work-load rather than to bring together Branches and Sections dealing with related areas of functions" (Foreign Affairs 1972, p. 94). The work of the department certainly expanded in scope throughout the 1960s — new missions were opened and ever larger numbers of trainees were recruited — and after 1966 Foreign Affairs grew especially quickly. In the next decade, the number of missions nearly doubled and staff numbers more than trebled. Most of this growth took place at overseas posts, however. Diplomacy had primacy still. The years of the cold war provided many landmarks in Australian foreign policy — ANZUS, SEATO, and, at the end, the Vietnam war. But political leaders did not see the department as requiring any special attention, and so it was not subjected to any comprehensive review and probably the need for such a review was never raised. The reorganizations of the US State Department and British Foreign and Commonwealth Offices aroused no similar questioning in Australia, and the Boyer Committee (1958), which reviewed recruitment to the Australian Public Service generally, paid no special regard to Foreign Affairs. It could not be said that foreign policy was of little relevance to governments or the electorate generally. On the contrary, foreign policy was a vote-winner and loser of importance at election time. Political intentions were, however, capable of accommodation within the existing structure of the department. The role of Foreign Affairs was limited, and its organization reflected this position.

As we have noted, international events made this accommodation increasingly unsatisfying for Foreign Affairs. A minister more sensitive to the aspirations of the department was McMahon (minister 1969–71). He had been treasurer until forced to take the Foreign Affairs post by a hostile prime minister (Gorton) and it was widely reported that he intended to build up the department along the lines of the powerful Treasury and make it a strong bureaucratic base in his continuing intra-party struggle. McMahon's term, though brief, was indeed marked by substantial organizational change and a new departmental assertiveness. Three new divisions were created, and for the first time some were given functionally rather than geographically organized tasks; a second deputy secretary post was added; the proportion of senior positions increased markedly; and a policy-planning section, intended to give the department a forward-planning capacity, was established. McMahon claimed that the department would "approach the decade of the 70s with a new name and a new top structure. The reorganization is fundamental. The department will begin the decade with an organization specifically geared to handle those challenges and situations which seem likely to emerge in the field of foreign affairs in the years immediately ahead" (*Age,* 22 December 1970). But it was hard to effect reorganization "down the line", and McMahon's changes were far from complete when he left the portfolio. The succeeding two ministers (Leslie Bury 1971 and Nigel Bowen 1971–72) showed little interest. The department was able to claim, in retrospect, that even the reorganization of 1970 was "basically an elaboration of the then existing structure" (Renouf 1974, p. 111).

Certainly this incompleteness gave the department and some later ministers a reason to urge further reconstruction. Even McMahon's administrative intentions sprang more from personal and party-oriented motives than from any more general concern with policy issues, let alone a concern with administrative issues. Administrative reorganization has not usually been important to Australian politicians. It is a means to an end, and says very little about that end. Organizational change has its own driving force, however, since it may create new expectations within an institution.

That was certainly the case with Foreign Affairs. At the same time, the expansion of its capacity under McMahon coincided with a period of three to four years when officers of the department found themselves less and less in accord with the drift of government policy. With increasing frequency the department found its advice rejected or ignored. For example, the department had little to do with the celebrated speech by Gordon Freeth (minister 1969), which played down the significance of Russian naval interests in the Indian Ocean (and had even less to do with the successful attempt by the DLP to force a reversal of that emphasis); and it was unable to persuade the government to recognize China. The capacities of the department, it seemed to many within it, were not being used. This was unsurprising. A department responding to new international pressures, felt acutely through its rapidly growing number of overseas missions, was bound to feel uneasy with an inflexible government unable to move beyond increasingly falsified hopes. Some Foreign Affairs officers saw a Labor government as more likely to be in tune with the department's views and thus more likely to take notice of the department and to use its capacities fully, perhaps even to extend them. Before the election of 1972, consultations between the department and the then leader of the opposition took place on, for example, the recognition of China and on questions related to the United Nations.

FOREIGN AFFAIRS AND LABOR

On the whole, the department and its new minister, Whitlam, worked well together during the time he held office as foreign minister (December 1972 — November 1973). This was the period of Labor initiatives in foreign policy. Government and department meshed on policies where there was agreement between them, and cabinet was reasonably happy with its ability to bend the department to its will. Inasmuch as departments and ministers are able to agree that they are making progress, this was such a period. Of course the whole story of policy cannot be told so simply, and there were cases where the department opposed vigorously, and sometimes successfully, the government's intentions. Yet this period must be seen in perspective. It was not a time when a new government undertook radical action to meet the country's complex problems of foreign policy, and it did not call for radical new thinking from Foreign Affairs. To be sure, the government's opponents did not see it this way. They sometimes claimed that the Whitlam government was taking the country in revolutionary directions. "We have not even become neutral," said one well-known critic, B. A. Santamaria. "We have simply changed sides" (quoted in Solomon 1977). In retrospect it would, however, be difficult to argue that the Labor government undertook any fundamental questioning, let alone re-shaping, of Australian alliances and dependencies. This is not to deny that the new government gave a welcome legitimacy to views that had ripened gradually within the department; that such change would not otherwise have happened; and that new possibilities were opened up in a way that is still being worked out (Albinski 1977). In a more spectacular way, the government demonstrated some independence in foreign relations by recognizing China, by trying to implement a new treaty with Japan, and by supporting the idea of a new regional association. It would, however, be wrong to see the policies of the Labor government as some sort of base line from which explanation for bureaucratic behaviour can alone begin.

Even within the Labor government, questions about Foreign Affairs' resources were not very prominent. Whitlam found that the department responded quickly to him and he made no radical changes to it, a restraint in keeping with his general approach to the public service which we have noted before. He retained Sir Keith Waller as permanent head for a year, for example, and made only two ambassadorial appointments which could be called "political". The RCAGA did not include specific terms of reference concerning the department; this is a "missing instruction" which we will mention again in the chapter on the commission (chapter 8). Still, there were political inputs which had organizational outcomes. It was helpful to have the head of government in charge of the depart-ment, for example. Only once since the Second World War (under Menzies 1960–61) had Foreign Affairs been able to identify its co-ordinating role as potentially congruent with the coordinating role of the prime minister himself. When Whitlam surrendered the port-folio to Senator D. R. Willesee in November 1973, he continued to take a close interest; he continued to receive departmental sub-missions to cabinet in advance, for example, and was briefed by the department on foreign policy issues before parliamentary question time (Albinski 1977, p. 299).

Whitlam moved at a leisurely pace to place at the head of Foreign Affairs a man of his choice, but when he did so it was over protests from some senior officers of the department. His choice, A. P. Renouf, had been a career diplomat since 1943 but had spent most of his time abroad and had had limited experience of departmental management in Canberra. He was thought, however, to be sympathetic to the policies of the new government and was also identified with a desire to question, review, and reorganize the existing structure of the department. He was expected to initiate sweeping administrative reforms, which partly explained the reluctance with which his appointment was accepted by some. Both he and Whitlam tried to ensure that Foreign Affairs received more of the resources the department thought it needed to do its job. Whitlam intervened with the PSB, for example, to get rapid acceptance of Foreign Affairs' proposals for a major organizational restructuring of the department. A division was added, reorganization along functional rather than geographical lines was carried a considerable way forward, a more diverse system of support to the permanent head was created, including an executive secretariat and the new positions of legal and scientific advisers, and, most important, the department took on new functions in legal, information, and economic areas. The amount of money spent on the department also increased sharply. But perhaps the most obvious measure of the department's growth was simply the increase in the number of its staff. During 1973–75 Foreign Affairs was the fastest growing of all departments.

USING RESOURCES

Such a story of apparent success needs qualification. The burgeoning of the department was far from being an automatic outcome of the government's intentions, and some outcomes were not what the department had expected. In the first place, political support was not constant. The tenure of the prime minister as foreign minister could not last. Other ministers found that the prime minister spent too much time on "invisible" international affairs which brought no domestic returns, and they helped to persuade him to relinquish the foreign affairs portfolio to Senator Willesee. The Labor style of government brought disadvantages for the department as well. The ministerial officers of the prime minister appeared sometimes to usurp the department in offering advice, and negotiated for it at times, as when the principal private secretary to the prime minister had discussions with the United States secretary of state on a wide range of issues without the prior knowledge or briefing of the department. The permanent head of the department claimed that it had had "constant problems over the years with the minister's personal staff". He went on:

> The problem has been compounded by the fact that most of the individuals concerned have been officers of the department who, while supposedly liaison officers, have taken it upon themselves to be an alternative form of policy advice to the minister, in terms highly critical and even abusive of senior officers. . . . it should be specified that officers seconded to a minister's offices from the department of the minister should be liaison officers and nothing more. [Foreign Affairs 1975c, p. 2]

Foreign Affairs had to make the best use it could of the resources available to it in a fragmented situation. Some of its resources were simply the words of politicians — for example, Whitlam's statement of May 1973: "We now view the conduct of external relations as a task which involves a total evaluation of our interests abroad and at home. The effective management of these elements in our overseas relations will require a major effort of coordination at many levels within the Australian government. Foreign policies must now be integrated with domestic policy" (Whitlam 1973). It was on the necessary basis of this and similar statements that the department argued for augmentation. The department was able to complain, for example, that it was not "at present being consulted fully on many important matters affecting Australia's international relations. . . . this situation should be rectified" (Foreign Affairs 1975, p. 2), and that it found it difficult to get adequate consultation and co-ordination on "economic and financial matters, natural resources and energy questions and, to a lesser extent, overseas information, immigration and trade activities" (Foreign Affairs 1974a, p. 16); this did not leave much unsaid.

In seeking to create a more activist Department of Foreign Affairs, the Whitlam government did not seek to redefine the responsibilities of other departments in some reciprocal way. In any case, problems alter their nature over time and so pass confusingly from one jurisdiction to another; ministers change their minds about where responsibility for particular tasks should rest, and they do not always agree among themselves; their decisions may be ambiguously presented and variously interpreted; they may, as the secretary of the Department of Defence has said, "sometimes look to their department[s] to negotiate away conflicts with the policies of cabinet colleagues" (Defence 1974, p. 6); and so on. There are, in short, interstices as well as contradictions between the intentions of politicians, and there is accordingly plenty of space for departments to pursue their honest disagreements. In the case of Foreign Affairs, other ministers sometimes resented what they saw as an interfering department, and they resented it whether its head was the prime minister or not. A well-publicized instance erupted over energy policy in late 1974. The secretary of the Department of Foreign Affairs was reported to have claimed to journalists that his minister was disenchanted with the policies of the energy minister and that big changes, even at the price of big arguments, were shortly to be expected. The press headlined the story, and a round of apologies and half-apologies followed before the affair drifted from the front pages — but certainly not from the consciousness of those government departments vying for influence in the area of energy resources policy.

The department was aware of the dangers of isolation, as we have noted:

> There is a clear need to develop a much better informed public opinion in Australia about foreign relations and to a subsidiary degree a knowledge of what this department does. The government sees this need. . . . This defect, which extends in part from our isolation in Canberra, will have to be remedied. We have a good story to tell; it must not go by default. . . . the department [must] expand as much as possible public speaking engagements throughout the country and . . . expand its contacts with parliament and the press. [Foreign Affairs 1974, p. 28]

The department found some organizational answers to the problems in the creation and rapid expansion of its public affairs and cultural division. This division, the fastest growing within the department in recent years, not only presents Australia to the world through its cultural and information activities but seeks to publicize the activities of the department within Australia, both to the community generally and to selected and influential groups. Through a weekly newsletter which has restricted distribution, the department attempts to reach such opinion makers as journalists, academics, and the members of the Australian Institute of International Affairs; it gives regular briefings to newspaper editors; and it publishes its historical documents through a special section of the department. In general, Foreign Affairs follows a policy of openness unequalled by other departments; it sought successfully in 1973 to be added to the IDC that considered freedom of information legislation, proposed unsuccessfully to Senator Willesee that it introduce Green Papers on foreign policy, and was an influential member of the IDC on the co-ordination of government publicity during the Whitlam years. Because of its concentration in Canberra, contacts are not always easy to maintain throughout Australia, so in recent years the department has increased its representation in state capitals. There is a limit to how far this can go, however. For example, the department's tentative suggestion in 1973 that it might represent other Australian government departments in their relations with state government departments in the manner in which it represents Australian interests generally abroad was universally deplored, especially by DURD. Its organizational initiatives do not always work out, in other words.

DEPARTMENTAL DISAGREEMENTS

The most important battlegrounds for initiatives were within the Canberra-based bureaucracy. The claims the department made for itself seemed bland enough, though in fact they contained assertions unsettling to other departments. It is unusual for a department to be on the public record with such claims. We might expect such brief but broad aims to have counterparts in central departments like the Treasury, the PSB, and PMC, but in fact it is difficult to find departments willing to undertake such a definition. Some are not prepared explicitly to do so; others develop a vaguer description at greater length; in most cases, departments present their responsibilities in more diffuse and perhaps less provocative terms. There is a real though somewhat hidden conflict here. The conduct of foreign relations is never solely the concern of a single department. Even departments with, apparently, exclusively domestic tasks have a stake in external matters and may from time to time become actively involved in external administration. In Australia the Department of Overseas Trade, the Treasury, and Immigration and Ethnic Affairs are the main participants in external affairs apart from Foreign Affairs itself, but there are several others: Attorney-General's, Defence, Post and Telecommunications, Science, Transport, and PMC all have varingly large parts to play. Whatever their diffidence in committing to paper a succinct statement of their functions, these and other agencies are united in seeing their domestic functions paralleled on the international stage; and they claim the right to exercise these functions there. They therefore aim to reduce the tasks of Foreign Affairs to a residual capacity — to whatever is not elsewhere specified — and frequently label this the "political function". Sometimes it is called the "coordination function". In the economic field, for example, it has been argued that "because of the Department of Foreign Affairs' specific concern with the international political issues, it is not an appropriate coordinating department where economic as well as political issues are of major importance" (Economic Policy Task Force 1975, 11.105). Or, as the secretary of the Department of Defence put it, "International activity is in many respects an extension of our national life and the reconciliation of these interests to international practicalities. Ministers and departments necessarily have their own international responsibilities and their own foreign relationships" (Defence 1975, p. 6). The Department of Overseas Trade bluntly thought that "it appears more difficult to specify precisely the objectives of foreign policy than it is normally possible to do for trade policy" (Overseas Trade 1975, A34).

The departments of the Australian Public Service, as we have already remarked more than once, are jealous of their prerogatives and fight to maintain them with an intensity which has provoked international comment. Foreign Affairs' assertions were bound to be contested. But the "fury with which federal departments fight for their preserves", as Whitlam put it, is not based simply upon crude expediencies and jealousies. The different views departments have of their own proper functions, which lead them into conflicts with one another, are not misrepresented (at least not always misrepresented) by other departments: often they are simply misunderstood. Even when they are properly understood, a mutually satisfactory reconciliation may not be possible.

Conflicts between Foreign Affairs and other departments were essentially of two kinds. In one, Foreign Affairs sought to extend externally the control it exercised over its own internal resources, such as finance and manpower, and this brought the department into dispute especially with the PSB and Treasury. In the other kind, the department fought a sporadic series of battles with a large number of other departments on a wide range of policy issues. Although these two kinds of conflict took place concurrently and were connected in the minds of participants, it is convenient to illustrate them separately.

AN INTEGRATED FOREIGN SERVICE?

The department had long felt constricted in the management of its internal resources. There were two problems. The first concerned the roles of the Treasury and the PSB, which were claimed to be "disruptive of the internal management processes" of Foreign Affairs, whether at home or abroad. The department claimed that "the constant and detailed intrusion of outside elements that have no expertise in foreign policy matters and no responsibility for the achievement of the Department's objectives leads to an undesirable separation between the processes of the planning of policy implementation and the allocation of new resources" (Foreign Affairs 1974a, p. 36). The second problem concerned the way in which officers from other departments, while serving overseas, were in some fields outside the control of the heads of diplomatic missions. Here was fertile ground for jurisdictional disputes in which Foreign Affairs had by no means any natural advantage.

These were difficult problems because they were enmeshed in regulations, laws, and conventions which had grown up over a long period; they involved the powerful controlling departments and reflected the historical weakness of Foreign Affairs' position. A piecemeal approach to reform by Foreign Affairs was unlikely to have any effect because financial and personnel controls were spread widely and interconnectedly through a network of rules and procedures. The department had some success; in 1973 it was given control over the provision of common services, such as office and transport facilities, at missions. This was a significant issue, but the department sought more. It accordingly decided on a direct statement of its position and of the remedy it proposed. It argued in 1974 for the creation of an "integrated foreign service", in which staff of departments other than Foreign Affairs posted to a mission overseas would be under the sole control of the head of mission for the duration of their tour of duty; for the regular inspection of posts by an inspector-general based in Foreign Affairs, not in the PSB; for the establishment of a separate training institute for foreign affairs officers; and for the revision of methods for establishing conditions of service overseas, to the heavy cost of PSB and Treasury responsibility (Foreign Affairs 1974a). Though stopping short of proposing a totally separate foreign service, or so-called "mega-ministry", these were not popular proposals for the rest of the public service.

In making them, the department was seen distinctly as the attacker or aggressor. Other departments responded quickly with statements of their cases, some with detailed rebuttals (see, e.g., Treasury 1974; Public Service Board 1975a; Overseas Trade 1975; Defence 1975). The PSB produced a lengthy memorandum seeking to explain why it should maintain its existing controls over establishments, staffing procedures and the determination of conditions of service overseas (Public Service Board 1975a). The Department of Overseas Trade argued that its trade commissioners (officers with term appointments under statutory authority who carry out trade work overseas) should continue to report to it and, as a precautionary move parallel to Foreign Affairs' own preservation of the separateness of its officers, added that "a broadening of the role of Trade Commissioners would, among other things, probably hinder the continued development and the further accumulation of specialized skills and experience increasingly needed to perform their functions effectively" (Overseas Trade 1975, C31). The secretary of the Department of Defence thought it "to be unacceptable and politically impracticable for the Minister and Department of Foreign Affairs to be given the authority over other Ministers and Departments that [Foreign Affairs] appears to contemplate" (Defence 1975, p. 6).

Some counter-proposals were made. Overseas Trade, for example, thought that PMC might instead "operate as the coordinating agency where there are issues broader than, by way of example, trade, monetary or foreign policy. This suggestion benefits from the fact that, with one or two exceptions such as protection policy, that Department is likely to be free of specific functional responsibilities for the issues involved" (Overseas Trade 1975, B44). It also suggested "the creation of a Cabinet foreign policy coordination committee with Foreign Affairs, Overseas Trade and Treasury and Prime Minister's (probably also Defence) — ideally with the Prime Minister (as Prime Minister) as chairman and perhaps also an official committee with a rotating chairmanship at the officials' level" (Overseas Trade 1975, B43). Foreign Affairs' proposals were thus turned on their heads, but in general departments contented themselves with affirming the need to retain the existing structure of widely dispersed control. They were reluctant to propose an actual reduction in Foreign Affairs' powers, and no department was so rash as to criticize, for example, the overall cost of representation overseas though such criticisms had been directed at the British Foreign Office and would have been greeted enthusiastically by the Australian press. Departments wanted to contain their disputes as much as possible within the family, which meant that Foreign Affairs' case (as presented to the RCAGA) got an unimpeded run in the press. The department's leadership saw public presentation of its case as no mean achievement.

INSTITUTIONAL CONFLICTS

But in the longer term the department's widely publicized power play aroused suspicions which may have played a part in the outcomes of the second set of conflicts we have identified, between Foreign Affairs and a number of departments over a range of particular policy issues. Here Foreign Affairs' record was mixed. A department can seek to enlarge its area of functional responsibility in a number of ways. The most spectacular because it is the most visible involves the transfer to it of functions (and therefore of organizational capacity) which are part of some other section of the bureaucracy. There were a number of instances in the 1970s: Foreign Affairs gained responsibility for the Overseas Property Bureau (OPB) and for the Australian High Commission in London, and it attempted to assume some control over the Australian Information Service, Radio Australia, the ceremonial and hospitality branch of PMC, certain of the functions relating to passports of the then Department of Labour and Immigration, some of the legal responsibilities of Attorney-General's for offshore mining, and for the overseas aid functions of the government generally. Here we will consider briefly the cases of the OPB and the Australian Development Assistance Agency (ADAA).

Overseas Aid

The establishment of an independent ADAA was a loss to Foreign Affairs. Labor's commitment to expend more resources generally on foreign affairs strengthened the department, but the corollary to this commitment, to expend more resources also on foreign aid specifically, weakened it. The Labor government was attracted to the idea of a separate aid agency which would be seen to be independent of the political concerns of the Department of Foreign Affairs, and there were those within the department who supported that view. The majority in the department fought the proposal strongly but unsuccessfully, however; in December 1974 ADAA was established as a statutory authority with its own organization, budget, and administrative head reporting direct to the minister for foreign affairs, and with formal accountability to parliament through annual reports (Viviani and Wilenski 1977). If those who staffed the agency, principally from Foreign Affairs and from the disbanded Department of External Territories, expected a boost to their careers to coincide with its establishment, they were not disappointed. For a short period the agency promoted its officers to levels they could not have expected to reach in Foreign Affairs for many years. The department did not allow the change to pass unchallenged. It identified problems of coordination between itself and the agency and persuaded its minister to agree to a set of procedures which bound the agency closely to it; a section was established in the department to maintain "day-to-day consultation" and to present the department's views to ADAA; the staff of the agency overseas was to remain under the direction of the head of mission. These controls were stated clearly in the minister's second reading speech which introduced the bill for the establishment of the agency. Neither did the department easily accept the fact of the agency's organizational autonomy. Within a year of the cabinet decision to establish ADAA, the department called into question the desirability of having a separate agency. The agency responded that this was "a little surprising. . . . a decision so recently taken by the government, and in fact not fully implemented . . . should have been allowed to run a test of experience before representations were made to reverse it". In private, less gentle views were expressed. The agency maintained that "foreign policy considerations are not the only determinants in aid policy". Its staff members justified expansion in the terms used by Foreign Affairs itself by pointing to the need to develop the skills and experience that were missing in the department. They thus maintained that "a significant section of the Australian public . . . were not happy with the administration of aid by Foreign Affairs and we think relations with the public were much improved by the creation of the agency" (ADAA 1975, p. 1).

Overseas Property

The second case concerns the OPB, which had been established in late 1972 to concentrate in one agency the responsibility for the ownership, leasing, and maintenance of Australian property overseas. It had first been located in the Department of Services and Property (later Administrative Services) but was suddenly transferred in June 1974 to Foreign Affairs after an informal talk between the minister for foreign affairs and the minister for services and property. The permanent head of the Department of Services and Property learned of the prime ministerial decision to endorse this private arrangement some time after the event, and he responded angrily in a letter to a group of permanent heads. He claimed that the impartiality of the bureau would be called into question in its new location and that other departments with overseas interests, such as the Department of Overseas Trade, might wish to create their own bureaus and so come into conflict with the "competitor", Foreign Affairs. He was careful to distinguish the intentions of the department from the actions and "sterile arguments" of the minister for foreign affairs, but in fact the minister had justified the change by saying that his department had "overall operating responsibility" for property overseas.[1] The department had publicized its expertise in the area of property management only shortly beforehand in a departmental publication and later defended its control of the OPB to the RCAGA (Foreign Affairs 1974*b*).

Both these changes were short-lived, as the Fraser government abolished ADAA and placed its functions within Foreign Affairs, at the same time returning the OPB to Administrative Services. It is not evident that these changes had any effect on policy outputs, but it is clear that they involved a good deal of work for the departments and even for the ministers concerned. It is often unavoidable that

---

1. Based upon interdepartmental material of June-August 1974.

political intentions, whether clear (as in the case of ADAA) or not (as in the case of OPB), will be translated into administrative outcomes very different from those originally intended.

OTHER CONFLICTS

The operation of interdepartmental committees provides an enduring focus of disagreement between Foreign Affairs and other departments. In general, the department has a substantial presence on IDCs, as its claims to a coordinating role would seem to warrant. A survey in early 1975 showed that Foreign Affairs, then close to the peak of its influence, sat on 49 IDCs, behind only Manufacturing Industry (55), PMC (60), and Treasury (108). It was the convening department for 13 IDCs, equal to the PSB and behind only Defence (22). But such extended involvement stretched the department's resources very thin, and slowed down the operation of some IDCs to Foreign Affairs' disadvantage. The secretary of the department complained that IDCs were dominated "by entrenched attitudes which are . . . out of date and which create a situation tending to weaken the Government's effectiveness" (Albinski 1977).

The operations of the Japan IDC and the general problems of managing Japan-Australia relations illustrate these difficulties clearly (Matthews 1976). Until the late 1960s the Department of Trade and Industry under the strong leadership of McEwen occupied the leading position in supervising Australia's relationships with Japan. Two former diplomats, W. R. Crocker and Sir Alan Watt, have testified to Trade's domination of the then External Affairs. The Department of Trade, said Crocker, "judged by its functions or its performance has not been a major department . . . yet owing to the minister's special status the department was given a unique position. In effect it rated with Treasury well above Foreign Affairs. It was well known in Canberra that no cabinet minister would risk a dissension with or over the Trade department." Hence the trade commissioner service "was allowed for some time to carry on as a sort of rival to our diplomatic service" (Crocker 1971, p. 95). Although he was ambassador to Japan, Watt was not informed of details of the important trade agreement being negotiated there by trade officials in 1957 until, as he writes, "the text was suddenly telegraphed to me" (Watt 1972, pp. 263-64). An important change came with the creation in 1970 of an interdepartmental committee at permanent-head level to review relationships with Japan and to formulate and coordinate future policy. It was under the chairmanship of Foreign Affairs, and standing committees were eventually established on which the department took the leading role. This was not quickly done, and there were reverses. In 1975, for example, responsibility for the newly created Australia-Japan Foundation was placed within PMC rather than Foreign Affairs after Foreign Affairs had seemed less than enthusiastic about the idea.

Foreign Affairs had success also with the law of the sea. This was a subject of emerging importance where the expertise of other departments was not well established. The department's recruitment of an internationally recognized legal expert was as significant in Canberra as it doubtless was at the United Nations; it helped the department to take the lead in interdepartmental discussions and, incidentally, broke Attorney-General's claim to be the "legal counsel for all departments" (Hawker 1978a). It is possible that other staffing innovations at lower levels will follow.

But by no means was Foreign Affairs always successful. The department said, for example, of a committee set up to examine arrangements for recording international arrangements about scientific and technical services that it "should have made up its own mind on a new home for the registry. Involving other departments only complicated the matter" (Foreign Affairs 1975a). A more prolonged difficulty arose between Foreign Affairs and the Department of Minerals and Energy. "From minister and permanent head down", said D. M. Connolly, a former Foreign Affairs officer, and later a member of parliament —

> the Department of Minerals and Energy has refused appropriate co-operation with Foreign Affairs in the formulation of an Australian policy overview of countries such as Japan or members of the EEC. The dislocation of interdepartmental coordination has seriously affected the implementation of government policy and Foreign Affairs has not been kept informed of negotiations conducted overseas by officers of the Department of Minerals and Energy. [Connolly 1975, pp. 4-5]

In early 1974 Foreign Affairs tried to establish a foreign economic policy committee to coordinate and implement government policy involving Overseas Trade, Minerals and Energy, Treasury, and itself. The other departments and their ministers refused to cooperate.

SURVIVAL?

The day-to-day task of maintaining the functions, structure, and morale of an organization is one that forces outside the organization can sometimes overwhelm. In recent years the APS has been rearranged very substantially as new functions have been defined and as organizational forms have arisen and disappeared. The process of change has owed much to the sudden inclinations of ministers and their advisers, and the Labor government especially paid a heavy price in the public eye for its "bureau-shuffling". Less obvious was a lowering of staff morale in the more frequently rearranged sections of the bureaucracy, as, for instance, in Manufacturing Industry and in Urban and Regional Development. Foreign Affairs escaped from this flux relatively unscathed, though the cases of ADAA and OPB show that the department is by no means insulated from "bureau-shuffling". Its functions and structures are malleable and subject to change as sudden and uncomfortable as that visited upon other parts of the bureaucracy. If the integrity of its "core functions" has been tacitly accepted, by and large, this has not been achieved automatically. The work of the department has been explained, elaborated, and defended at length and with skill by its officers at all levels, and this has given Foreign Affairs a peculiar cohesion which has been reflected in its life and survival as an organization. Yet the department has not been able to do this easily. As A. P. Renouf conceded, "the rigidity of the vertical chain of command, frustration of up-and-coming junior officers, inadequate allowance for the contemporary expectations of women involved in the department's activities and the excessive compartmentalization and conservatism of many of its practices and outlooks combined to make the institution not as prepared as it might have been to meet the challenges which it was facing from all directions" (Renouf 1974, p. 113).

The rapid expansion of the department has made the filling of senior positions difficult, and Foreign Affairs has been forced to accept a certain level of recruitment from outside its normal career stream. The question always remains: What level? The answer has not been unanimous or, more accurately, the department has not pursued an unchanging policy. Many of the recruits of the 1940s entered laterally, and this policy found some favour again in the late 1960s. Recently, more traditional attitudes have been asserted

(Foreign Affairs Association 1975). There are also questions about what sort of people diplomats should be. Traditionally, diplomatic trainees have been recruits of high intellectual standard, able both to grasp the essential concerns of other departments in a general way and to manage those concerns in a specialized way, for example through negotiation, consultation, and intelligence gathering. These special skills retain their relevance for Foreign Affairs, as we have noted. But when the department sought a more active and a more comprehensive coordinating role, the general capabilities of its staff were thought to need strengthening with specialist skills in such areas as energy policy, international law, and aerospace. For many reasons this was an awkward transition to make: the organization was not prepared for it, other departments were resistant, skilled people were in short supply, and in any event the desirable skills were not very tightly articulated. Other difficulties lay within the organization itself, and most were beyond managerial manipulation. The age structure of the department was unusually youthful, which meant that it was not easy to promote with any rapidity those officers who possessed new and desirable skills. The alternative was to change the capacities of existing officers better to fit the new tasks of the department. The recruitment history of the department made this difficult also: to a greater extent than in other major departments, senior officers have humanities and literary backgrounds. There was little possibility (or intention) of retraining individual officers, but the structure of the department was already being altered to accommodate its desired new tasks. The functions of these new positions were to be "filled out" as officers developed relationships with departments with affiliated concerns. Another problem of balance concerned the mixing of diplomatic and non-diplomatic staff within the department both at home and abroad: could the functions of the two groups be separated, and to what extent should diplomats be drawn from non-diplomatic ranks? The department maintains distinct "diplomatic" and "clerical-administrative" (including consular) career streams but claims to favour transfer both ways between them. In fact, this does not happen often, and one result is that diplomatic officers fill most of the senior positions, even those which might seem pre-eminently suited to the clerical-administrative stream, as in the management services area. Transfers from that stream to other departments have accordingly become all too frequent, exacerbating the problem of balancing the recruitment of both streams.

These problems of personnel are crucial to the organization. The core of the department is its carefully trained diplomatic members. But there are not enough of them in enough places to do everything the department wants, and its instruments for action are therefore in a sense diluted, especially as new tasks arise. These are continuing problems; indeed, stories about bureaucratic politics seldom have neat endings. Some of the institutions mentioned above have ceased to exist or exist in different forms, but Foreign Affairs is stronger than some other, more recent, bureaucratic creations, which is to say that it has managed to maintain with relative success its organizational identity, morale, and capacity to function. We might nevertheless ask what differences the events we have described have made to the department and to its officers in the longer term.

Perhaps the period of Foreign Affairs' ambition was too brief to have had many discernible outcomes. Certainly its most recent history has been chastening. If the department had been until the mid-1970s a department on the way up, it has ever since been a department on the way down. Even before the fall of the Whitlam government the departmental counter-attack on its pretensions had begun to tell: for example, Foreign Affairs was hard hit during the financial stringencies of 1975, and its staff numbers stabilized quickly. So far the Fraser government has seen that tendency carried strongly forward. No longer does the department have a minister with the ear, or the identity, of the prime minister. Rather, the foreign minister is a party rival whose very qualities tempt this prime minister, like so many before him, to be his own foreign minister. The costs of the department have tempted an economy-minded government to make large cuts, the more tempting when the disadvantages of the cuts are hidden, at least for a time, from much of the domestic polity. The scope and painfulness of retrenchment has been anything but hidden, however. In sharp contrast to the placidity of the earlier years, the department was the subject of no less than four inquiries into its operations during 1976-78. The prime minister's inquisitor of government programmes, Sir Henry Bland, recommended reductions in staff numbers and functions in mid-1976, as did a commissioner of the PSB in a rolling review throughout 1976, and as did the parliamentary Committee on Expenditure, which reported in May 1977 on the "value for money" of Australia's overseas representation. In 1978, the Senate Standing Committee on Foreign Affairs and Defence also inquired into Australia's overseas representation. The RCAGA had in the meantime reported, but its brief and ambiguous endorsement of some of Foreign Affairs' earlier claims counted for little against this onslaught (Collins 1977).

Departmental retreat was no less spectacular than the advances of two or three years before had been. Recruitment of trainees stopped altogether in 1977; staff numbers fell by some 17 per cent in less than two years; some posts were closed; and departments, in their submissions to the Expenditure Committee, reasserted their traditional roles at length and more vigorously than they had to the RCAGA (Expenditure Committee 1977). Departmental morale stood in sharp contrast too. Because "expansion has painfully and suddenly given way to contraction", said the secretary, 1976 had been "an austere and rather embattled year"; the department had been required to "bear a disproportionate share of the various economy moves" (Foreign Affairs 1977, pp. 1-2). The PSB and Treasury, said the department's staff association, had been "intransigent and generally unsympathetic" (Foreign Affairs Association 1977, p. 2). This was emphasized in April 1978 both by the department and the Foreign Affairs Association in submissions to the Inquiry on Australia's Overseas Representation by the Senate Standing Committee on Foreign Affairs and Defence. The department's submission stressed that although the department had suffered greatly from the austerity measures, its workload had not diminished but increased (Foreign Affairs 1978, 5.8). The association's submission stressed the "deterioration in career prospects for Foreign Affairs Officers" (Foreign Affairs Association 1978, p. 24), and its president, in evidence to the inquiry, spoke of "the shattering of morale" of FAOs (17 May 1978). Industrial action in the department over certain conditions of employment revealed the strains. Publicly, Foreign Affairs has altered its self-portrait. It has, said its new permanent head, "neither the desire nor the expertise and capability to assume the responsibility of other departments when the subject matter at issue is largely an extension of domestic sectors" (Foreign Affairs 1977a, p. 6).

Yet he has also said that the department "must have officers with specialized skills able to hold their own in interdepartmental discussions". Recent developments have not nullified the experiences of the last decade, and the aspirations of the department remain. So does its capacity, which has indeed been augmented in some ways. Recent staff reductions have fallen disproportionately on locally-engaged staff at overseas posts, for example; a reduction in departmental strength has not prevented redeployment to growth areas. Even with reduced resources, the department does what it did before and can, perhaps, learn to do better: to write memoranda which explain its positions, jostle for staff and other resources, and try to outmanoeuvre its rival institutions.

Such activity may seem undesirable to some; so it was during 1973-75. A study of ADAA's history, for example, emphasized the "constant debilitating effect on the Agency of continuing bureaucratic politics in its role in the aid policy process" (Viviani and Wilenski 1977, p. 35). We might possibly extend such judgments if we examined comprehensively the other policy disputes involving Foreign Affairs mentioned above. But whatever judgments we make about particular outcomes, the struggle for institutional maintenance will be part of every case. Thus to introduce bureaucratic politics is not to introduce an unnecessary capriciousness. The bureaucratic politics we have described is inescapable in the mixed struggle over institutional maintenance and policy. Some institutions are clearly more capable than others: the contrast between the Department of Foreign Affairs of this chapter, even in victory, and the Treasury of chapter 9, even in defeat, will become clear. Bureaucratic institutions are no more autonomous than other policy participants: bureaucratic politics is not a bureaucratic conspiracy.

8

The Genesis of the Royal Commission on Australian Government Administration

An inquiry into the public service was on the agenda of the Labor Party the day it came to office. But little thought had been given to the purposes or scope of an inquiry, and as time passed, enthusiasm for one in any form lessened. Only with difficulty was an inquiry eventually established. This chapter is concerned not with its operations or outcomes but with its genesis (for those other matters see Hawker 1976*b*, 1976*c*, 1976*d*, 1977*a*, 1977*b*, 1977*c*, 1978; Parker 1976, 1978; Cass and Hawker 1978; Schaffer and Hawker 1978; Smith and Weller 1975, 1978; Weller and Smith 1976, 1977). Our themes are about the difficulties of defining problems and of keeping promises when other questions take on greater importance; about the politics of satisfying diverse groups with promises for the future; and about shelving problems through the creation of an investigatory body. We examine why public service reform was on the agenda, what reform meant to different groups, why they disagreed over the form, nature and membership of an inquiry, and finally what legacies were left to the royal commission by these conflicts.

There had been many calls for an inquiry into the public service since the mid-1960s, sufficient almost to be bipartisan. In 1967, for example, the leader of the Democratic Labor Party in the Senate had spoken in favour of an inquiry, and that party later supported motions by the Labor Party in 1970 and again in 1972 to establish a parliamentary investigation. In 1968 and 1971 the Associated Chambers of Commerce had added their support. Both

---

This case-study is based more upon interviews and official files than upon public sources, so citations are few.

major parties promised an inquiry in their election campaigns in 1972. Academic writers had argued in favour of an investigation since the mid-1960s. By the time of the 1974 campaign the Liberal Party was still calling for one, even though Labor had by then already announced the appointment of the chairman of the royal commission under review here.

At a general level it is not hard to see why the idea of a public service inquiry should have been popular. The idea was in the air because of similar activity in other countries. Major inquiries were held in Britain, federal Canada and Ontario, New Zealand, the United States, and some American state governments between 1965 and 1970. The bureaucracies of the Australian state governments were affected as the federal bureaucracy was to be, and inquiries were established in South Australia, New South Wales, and Victoria during 1970–73. It is not evident that any of these inquiries had a direct influence on Australian thinking at the commonwealth level, for such links are always hard to show. Those interested in public service reform in Australia were indeed largely ignorant of the details of overseas experience, as some incidents showed during the establishment of the RCAGA. But the factors underlying the creation of those inquiries existed also in Australia, perhaps especially in Australia.

The federal public service had grown almost unexamined. There had been some fifteen inquiries into particular aspects of the bureaucracy since 1901, such as machinery of government (for example the royal commissions or inquiries on the Post Office in 1908 and 1973, and defence organization in 1915 and 1973), the effectiveness of procedures and priorities (for example the Economies Commission in 1918 and the Coombs Review of Government Expenditure in 1973) and personnel policies (e.g., the Bailey Committee on Promotion in 1943 and the Boyer Committee on Recruitment in 1958), but the only broad-ranging inquiry had been the McLachlan Royal Commission of 1918. The public service had trebled in size between 1945 and 1972 and had assumed new functions in finance, social welfare, defence, urban planning, and legal control. The unsettled policies of party and parliament that followed the resignation of Menzies had their effect on the bureaucracy, and the performance of the very large, powerful, and complex organization of the late 1960s did not satisfy everyone, as we have already noted. The public service was not an institution exempt from criticism as political leaders changed and as the range of public policy concerns expanded rapidly. At this general level it is possible also to see why the Labor Party especially should have harboured some dissatisfaction and reformist thoughts about the bureaucracy. Labor had been long out of office, it was suspicious of what the senior bureaucrats might do to its programmes, and it was under pressure from its supporters in the unions to improve industrial conditions in the service.

These were the reasons, then, why a variety of groups, but especially the Labor Party, might have been favourably disposed to the idea of public service reform. Yet such a general disposition implied very little about what the content of reform should be, and nothing at all about the instrument to achieve it. When questions about the scope, purpose, and methods of an inquiry were raised, there was no general agreement. Different viewpoints emerged and came into conflict. The Chambers of Commerce, for example, had been concerned to cut the costs of government, to reduce its functions if possible, and generally to raise its efficiency. The Labor Party in its Senate motions of 1970 and 1972 had touched upon a broad range of disparate concerns, including the roles of the Public Service Board and the Post Office, the applications of ADP techniques in the service, and the impropriety of public servants doing political work for politicians. The public service unions, as represented especially by their peak council CCPSÖ,[1] wanted a review of the Public Service Act and of the powers and functions of the PSB, greater authority for the Joint Council (a staff-management consultative body with statutory basis), and changes to provisions affecting leave and the rights of public servants to undertake community work. The Liberal governments of the late 1960s were willing to undertake reviews of some legal issues associated with public administration, such as the discretions entrusted to public servants.

---

1. For Council of Commonwealth Public Service Organizations; it later became the Council of Australian Government Employee Organizations, but we have used the earlier acronym throughout.

LABOR IN OFFICE

These different views took new shape after the election of December 1972. The views of opposition groups were then largely ignored by the new government, which had, however, to come to terms with its own contradictory intentions. Within caucus, especially within its left wing, commitment to an inquiry was expressed early and often repeated. The reform of such a major institution as the public service was seen as a necessary task for any social-democratic government. Similar views were held by the personal staff of the prime minister. Young and capable former public servants were prominent in both places; sensitive to the problems of the public service through recent contact, they reminded the government powerfully in its early days of its promises. Most ministers were, however, reluctant to make any precise statements about their intentions for public service reform. The prime minister especially displayed a growing coolness to the very notion of an inquiry, whatever the intensity of his original views. It had been useful for electoral purposes, but once in office he found the case for public service reform less pressing. Other chapters in this book describe the new problems that forced themselves on the Labor government; but its difficulties, at least in those early days, seemed not to rest with the public service departments, which proved more responsive than some ministers had expected.

The prime minister's views were reinforced by sections of the union movement, which feared that any comprehensive inquiry might injure them. CCPSO preferred the PSB to undertake internal reviews of problems if the board would definitely take its views into active account; this seemed likely to be a more stable arrangement than reliance on the emerging views of other participants, especially those of a volatile caucus. As CCPSO said:

> The Public Service is apprehensive about the tenor of some political or industrial attitudes which could be reflected in any inquiry held. . . . the press has launched what could be described as a campaign against the public service. . . . Individual public servants find it difficult to dissociate at least some elements of the Labor government from the vilification . . . which is occurring.

Neither did the senior management of departments generally welcome the idea of an inquiry. Departments were being pushed hard by the new government, and they had enough to do without coping with an inquiry as well.

The PSB especially appreciated the risks of an inquiry. It was experiencing difficulties with its own role, as we have noted in chapter 4, and it could not expect that an inquiry that it did not conduct would solve its problems. Yet its very problems were evidence to justify inquiry into the public service. The board recognized this. In its report for 1973, for example, the PSB raised the question of how well public servants had responded to the advent of a new government, and its reply was optimistic. But the board did not rule out the possibility of an inquiry being needed, and it promised full support (Public Service Board 1973, p. 1; 1974, pp. 1-2). The board had little choice. It had no desire to be seen to oppose an inquiry which, if established, would involve it centrally. It wanted to be a partner in any involvement, not a discredited antagonist.

The participants could not all have had their own way. It was not even clear in some cases just what this would have been. Those who wanted an inquiry were not of one mind, and they could not in any case have imposed their intentions on other participants. It was possible rather for them to keep the issue alive, at the necessary cost of involving others with quite different ideas about what an inquiry might become. The accommodation of imprecise interests marked the inquiry from its earliest moments.

The prime minister was crucial in promoting that accommodation. He had ministerial responsibility for the PSB, the main instrument of public service control, and an inquiry could not be established without at least his formal concurrence; he had in fact a personal though changing interst in the matter. His declining enthusiasm brought him under pressure from caucus and his private office. A motion for an inquiry was moved in caucus in March 1973 and deferred, but it was proposed to move the motion again, and some members of the parliamentary Public Accounts Committee began to canvass the possibility that the committee might take responsibility. The prime minister reluctantly came to regard the issue as a persistent one unlikely to disappear. It could be fought, but only if there were not more important battles. Indifference was a less good ground on which to fight than outright hostility. In August 1973, anticipating further caucus pressure, he informed cabinet that an inquiry might be conceded but that the pressure on members was such that another major inquiry should not be undertaken by the parliament. He therefore favoured an outside inquiry and would not himself baulk at a royal commission, but it should not be set up until the Vernon Royal Commission on the Post Office had reported. His proposal was communicated by the permanent head of his department to the heads of Treasury and the PSB. This was not a cabinet decision, it should be noted; it was rather a promise by the prime minister that action would follow.

In clearing the ground like this with cabinet colleagues and with senior officials, the prime minister cut across caucus' thought. Caucus had preferred a parliamentary inquiry, or at any rate an inquiry of which one member would be a parliamentarian. The line adopted by the prime minister followed advice given by his private office, which thought a royal commission better than no inquiry at all. It had the advantage of keeping possibly troublesome back-benchers from membership. Once the prime minister had made his proposal, others adopted it with little argument. The price the prime minister paid for this desirable result was to commit himself firmly to having an inquiry and to selecting members who would be acceptable to caucus. This last cost was moderate, however, for caucus had no formal way of intervening in the process of selection once it had begun. Caucus informally set limits beyond which the prime minister would be unwise to go, but his room for the excercise of discretion was considerable, especially since the time-table for establishing the inquiry was vague.

A ROYAL COMMISSION

Thus was the existence of the inquiry and the choice of the instrument determined. It was not the only instrument possible, but it came to seem inevitable. A royal commission had done a related task on the Post Office, and the other choices were limited in their appeal. Caucus, for example, did not find much attraction in the idea advanced by CCPSO that the PSB might do the bulk of the work in consultation with such bodies as the unions. Not only did a royal commission satisfy the prime minister in his relations with his back-benchers, but it seemed a respectable and big enough instrument for the subject, a sign that public service reform was being taken seriously after so long a period of neglect. A commission had prestige and legal powers not possessed by, say, a parliamentary inquiry or expert task force. In this case, however, the royal commission form proved not to be sufficient to allay all suspicions within the opposition. Although committed to instituting an inquiry itself, the opposition was by no means committed to a Labor-established inquiry.

Just what the inquiry would become was not clear. The instrument had been chosen, but neither the terms of reference nor the membership had been decided, and the prime minister was, at this point, not in a hurry. Although debate over these questions had begun with the caucus motion of March 1973, the decision to have an inquiry was not made public until the appointment of the chairman in May 1974; the terms of reference and full membership were not announced until the next month. The intervention of the prime minister in August 1973, however, altered the capacity of participants in the debate. Once the interests of the head of government were clear, the departments of the public service had a large part to play: they could confidently offer advice to the government and could consult formally between themselves in proffering it. While the PSB was especially important, other institutions such as the Priorities Review Staff (or PRS, described in chapter 3) were able also to develop their views. The prime minister's adviser on economic affairs, Dr H. C. Coombs, who eventually led the inquiry, also began to offer advice. The interest and capacity of the prime minister's private office remained high, especially because it monitored correspondence between the prime minister and government officials and agencies on this as on other issues. Caucus and the unions, however, had reduced parts to play when they had no such assured access to the relevant documents, meetings, and telephone conversations. In late 1973, for example, a caucus committee drew up draft terms of reference which were circulated to public service departments and the prime minister's private office; but later drafts from other participants were not widely circulated. Suggestions also came unsolicited from academics, or informally from sections within the bodies just mentioned. Overseas examples did not appear relevant. In January 1974 the prime minister's private office, for example, was requesting copies of the terms of reference of other inquiries, but by then the debate over the terms was well advanced within the limits set by the Australian participants.

The debate was, however, slow to begin. For several months after the August decision or promise, little happened. Other issues preoccupied the government. But after some promptings from his private office and economic adviser, the prime minister asked the PSB for its views in late 1973, and the tempo quickly increased in the new year as the possibility of an early election became clearer. Then the electoral usefulness of having established an inquiry became clearer also.

THE TERMS

The draft terms of reference which the participants suggested had certain elements: for example, an inquiry should set out the desirable relations which should exist between ministers, parliament, and the public service; it should also review ways of creating and modifying the establishment and the efficiency of the service, and examine a number of related personnel issues such as wage fixing, recruitment, appointment, promotion, and job satisfaction. These common elements were expressed with several shades of meaning. The staff unions, for example, called explicitly for an investigation of ministerial control of the service and of the role of permanent heads. The PSB emphasized the importance of relations between public service and parliament and of mobility of personnel into, out of, and within the public service. It also supported an examination of policy development, forward planning, decentralization, and the determination of the functions of government, all questions raised originally by the PRS. Subtle nuances of wording could of course convey quite different views of the main tasks of the inquiry. The PRS, for instance thought that "efforts should be made to make the Australian public service representative of Australian society as a whole". It accordingly referred in its suggested terms to "the special problems of women in the public service", but the PSB rephrased this to "matters affecting particular groups including . . . women" and ignored the call for representativeness. Agreements, and such subtle disagreements as these, took time to crystallize yet had to be quickly resolved.

The PSB's first formal contribution to the inquiry, prepared in consultation with the departmental heads of Treasury, PMC, and the Attorney-General's Department, was put to the prime minister in December 1973 in the shape of a rewording of the caucus committee terms. A few weeks later, after further consultation with these bodies, the board offered a more considered view. It argued that there was need for a fundamental review of the public service and it supported the establishment of a royal commission, preferably with a judge as head. Some possible members were suggested. But the board said little more. The submission of the PRS, made in response to the PSB document and with informal advice from the prime minister's private office, was more detailed. It spoke of a need to base the commission firmly on research, to give it an adequate time scale within which to work, and to staff it at all levels with the best people obtainable. The PRS later drafted a parliamentary speech for the prime minister to deliver in introducing the commission. It described the growth of the service and its increasing specialization of functions and pointed to some of the criticisms that had been made of its lethargy and cost. It offered reassurances that an inquiry was not associated with an attempt further to enlarge commonwealth functions and that it should not be seen as indicating want of confidence in the public service. But it was a "political" speech: "there were important areas of public activity", it would have had the prime minister say of the pre-1972 period,

> which were left starved of senior officers in policy fields because responsible ministers were content to stick to stale and tired policies which were increasingly irrelevant to Australia's needs . . . . My government has had to engage in an urgent task of bolstering [the levels] of public service at which most advice to ministers is generated and assessed . . . . we do need to have the political role of public servants examined in depth.

The PSB, in commenting on the PRS draft, objected to this emphasis. Any speech the prime minister might give, it said, should be "shorter, non-partisan, stress the wide degree of support from various quarters for the inquiry, and avoid prejudging particular issues". The speech was not in fact delivered, and neither was any other parliamentary statement. The board thus reduced the likelihood that the terms of reference could be interpreted as the "witch-hunt" some public servants feared, but in other ways it was forced to concede ground. The way in which the inquiry might approach the role of the board itself was an example. Caucus had once proposed, mildly, to examine "the role of the PSB in relation to (i) the administration of the Public Service Act [and] (ii) service responsiveness to government policy", and CCPSO later repeated this emphasis. The private office wanted to go further. It wanted to examine "the capacity for forward planning, analysis of public expenditure programs and co-ordination of policies and programs by departments and Government instrumentalities and especially the principal co-ordinating authorities to achieve the objectives of Australian Government". It also queried "the need for a central management authority such as the Public Service Board". The board's own suggested terms of reference did not include corresponding items, and the final terms were a compromise: the inquiry was asked to examine "(f) the extent to which central management of the Australian Public Service is necessary, and internal control and co-ordination in that Service, especially the functions of the Public Service Board, the Auditor-General and the Treasury".

In short, each group had its own particular interests to pursue, and this made quick agreement on brief or precise terms of reference impossible to achieve. The draft terms of reference were never detailed. Rather, they were both wide and ambiguous in scope. In the end, only certain matters relating to superannuation and questions covered by the Post Office inquiry were excluded, though the specific issues were notable by their absence: patronage, the administration of section 96 grants, and the selection of Foreign Affairs trainees might have been such issues, for they had been raised in parliamentary debate over the years. There were some specific possible instructions missing from the commission's terms. The final terms were wide ranging yet very general; the language was neutral. The Office of Parliamentary Counsel, which did the final drafting, washed out the nuances which had existed before. All groups found their concerns catered for, and none could say that a pejorative tone inimical to them had crept in or been retained. There were no complaints, public or private, when the terms of reference were announced. The terms gave no indication of where the commission might go, and this suited participants who had been careful not to put their wishes, which were difficult to formulate or later might read badly, on paper in any detail. This caution of course helped to give the terms their lack of direction. Participants did have preferences, but a muted compromise proved acceptable.

Do these issues matter? From the point of view of the commission which was eventually appointed, it might seem not. Even questions that were especially hard though not impossible to deduce from the terms of reference became part of the commission's work as it found expedient. The relations between the public service and the community, for example, received only oblique recognition in the terms but became of central concern to the commission. At the same time the commission could not escape the consequences of the width of the terms. The terms did matter to it. If the commission felt an obligation to cover them all, this would mean some diversion of investigatory resources away from topics that might otherwise have been treated more intensively. If the commission were to take the opposite course of emphasizing some terms to the exclusion of others, it might come into conflict with those who had shown their particular interests in the commission. This was not an equal choice. To ignore some concerns was to risk slighting those individuals and organizations upon which the commission would rely for advice, information, and, ultimately, implementation. The first way was safer and coincided with the conventional view that an inquiry should try to do what it was told to do no matter how difficult this might be. But even the easier way showed the difficulty inherent in any choice. To take either a comprehensive or a restricted view involved the commission in guessing about what its own concerns would be in the future. The dispute over the terms of reference did matter, then, to the extent that the compromise arrived at gave the commission scope for choice and indeed demanded choice. More specific terms would have directed the commission to a greater degree at least towards some concerns and away from others. But by no means would this necessarily have made life easier for the commission.

The terms of reference were wide precisely because a sense of specificity was missing from the policy mixture. Participants had their viewpoints on particular issues, but the issues themselves were not congruent. They could support compromise at a level of generality high enough to encompass their various concerns; but between those concerns lay gaps the commission would have to think about. It is not enough to say that the conflict over the terms of reference was of symbolic importance. We have implied that the terms were a compromise because no group was strong enough to impose its concerns exclusively upon the inquiry. Terms of reference that emerge from a process of negotiation and compromise reveal the positions of the negotiators even if some deciphering is required. The inquiry itself must certainly make this deciphering; in doing so it receives an imprint of the policy forces at the time of its creation. A compromise agreement which had been struck at a general level necessarily revealed by inference some quite specific exclusions. It meant that no agreement could be reached that certain specific questions were of importance, and so the inquiry was given no precise agenda for reform. It was cast loose to devise its own, a demanding task. This prospect in turn raised problems for the sponsors of the inquiry, since they could not foretell where the inquiry would lead. Their uncertainty reflected well the prevailing lack of agreement about exactly what reform of the public service should involve.

THE INQUIRERS

Once the instrument of inquiry and its terms of reference were settled, members had to be selected. This was a further direct influence of the participants on the course the commission would take. But the members, once chosen, would have a capacity to go their own ways. There were many questions about membership. How many members should there be? How many should be full time? Should the commission have a judge as its head? Should the members be representative of those with a stake in the inquiry? Would that mean sacrificing the best people for the job? How much attention should be paid to their likely patterns of interaction as a group?

There was little agreement about the criteria for choosing members. The caucus motion of March 1973 had made the first firm proposal and had been specific. It had suggested an inquiry led by a judge with two other members, one an experienced public servant and the other a government supporter, preferably a Labor member of parliament. CCPSO did not follow caucus and omitted any reference to a judge as member or to anyone overtly connected with politics. It instead suggested a representative commission drawn from businessmen, academics, unionists, and public servants. The PSB included all these groups as well as judges and politicians in its listing. Like the private office, the PRS queried the idea of having a representative commission at all. It urged that the best people should be chosen, but in fact it also mentioned the need to have representatives from business, academic, and judicial circles, and from state public services and parliament. The chairman of the commission also sought a business, academic, judicial, public service, and parliamentary representative. Other groups were mentioned at various times, including critics and defenders of the service, women, representatives of minority ethnic groups, those from overseas with relevant experience, former ministers and other less easily classified eminent citizens. In all, just under a hundred names were put in writing to the prime minister, and his private office suggested numerous other names informally to him, as representatives of groups or simply as individuals.

The PRS stated explicitly and other actors implicitly that members should be chosen above all for their capacity or quality, but this exhortation was in practice restricted by the need to have a representative commission, however this was eventually defined, and by the availability of potential members. There was not necessarily conflict between quality and representativeness, since representation was never defined so closely as to restrict choice. Apart from the necessity to have at least one member acceptable to the PSB and to the unions respectively, which called for an experienced public servant and a unionist, no other restrictions were really made. Still, the very number of names and categories made questions of balance difficult. The only agreement reached by the participants was that membership should be as broadly based as possible; and the range of suggestions pushed the inquiry towards a larger and larger membership. Caucus had suggested three and the PRS suggested eleven, some of whom would be part-time. The PSB thought this too many, but the prime minister was considering a commission of seven or nine members up to the last moment. Five members were eventually selected after the chairman at a very late stage had put a choice between three and five to the prime minister.

The type and number of commissioners was limited naturally enough by the availability of people. Availability meant not only that likely candidates had to be ready for appointment at a particular time; they had also to be reasonably confident that they would continue to be available for the whole life of the commission, which was expected to take about eighteen months to do its work. The last condition was especially difficult to meet, and in the end one commissioner was appointed on a part-time basis and another acted part-time for the six months the commission ran beyond its expected span. Both conditions combined to rule out any members from abroad and any with a background in the private sector.

Time was a crucial factor in another way, too. Members were suggested and approved at different times, and earlier choices influenced those who might be chosen later. These restrictions were intensified by the speed of the selection process. In the end only a few days could be allocated to determining finally the availability of those on the short list. The prime minister wanted to choose the chairman quickly, certainly well before the election of 1974. Being available at a particular time came to mean being available immediately. The chairman, Dr Coombs, was chosen first. He was then the sixty-eight-year-old adviser to the prime minister on the economy, as we have noted, and had been a governor of the Reserve Bank, a member of government boards on Aborigines and the arts, and the permanent head of the Department of Post-War Reconstruction. He thus had an unusually long and diverse acquaintance with the Australian bureaucracy, but he had long been reluctant to take a direct role in the commission, though pressed to do so by an admiring Whitlam. His willingness grew only as his difficulties as economic adviser also grew during the confusion leading up the 1974 budget, discussed in chapter 9. The combination of opportunity, need, and the reluctant and perhaps revocable availability of Coombs coincided to give the inquiry a distinctive stamp.

His appointment meant that the inquiry would not be along the lines of a judicial model. It did not seem likely that a judge could be appointed to subordinate membership. Yet these considerations were not necessarily paramount in the mind of the prime minister. They followed rather from his desire to appoint this particular chairman. It was an appointment welcomed by the media and accepted, though less enthusiastically, by senior public servants. Coombs had a political history acceptable to the Labor Party, though not to all sections of the then parliamentary opposition, despite his having been an adviser to previous Liberal prime ministers. The Liberal–Country Party opposition had no wish to endorse any Labor initiative during an election campaign, and its response was guarded. It continued to promise an inquiry in any event if it were elected. The subsequent Labor victory indicated that other members had to be appointed quickly. It seemed obvious that the commission could not be left half-begun for long.

At that time, however, only one other person was clearly in the minds of Whitlam and Coombs for appointment. He was P. H. Bailey, a deputy secretary of PMC who had become involved in drafting the terms of reference in March, when the PRS terms were circulated. He had a broad interest in the problems of the service and had been a member of the Bland Committee on administrative discretions (and, significant in the eyes of many public servants, his father had been on another public service inquiry thirty years before). His name had been suggested with other senior public servants by the PSB in January. The desire of the prime minister to appoint neither a retired public servant nor one at the very top of the service ruled out all permanent heads and former permanent heads and made Bailey's qualifications obviously suitable. The private office and caucus were less impressed with a public servant whom they regarded as too much part of the "establishment" of the service, but to find another of similar seniority and experience was very difficult, especially when the private office and the unions indicated that they would be unhappy with any member drawn from the PSB, the most likely recruiting ground.

The other three commissioners were all appointed in a hurry, though for different reasons. The possibility of Bailey's appointment seemed to call for a member with a "balancing" union background. But uncertainty grew about the need to have a public servant and a union representative at all. Perhaps the question could be resolved by including neither. This seemed daring, but a middle way was possible: the appointment of a judicial figure who had the respect of both management and unions. The prime minister was attracted to the idea especially because one suitable candidate was also a woman. Here were a number of constituencies in one person. The fact that she was not available left no other candidate with the same characteristics, but this did not call into doubt the need, once it had been expressed, for a judicial figure, even if male. With the appointment of J. E. Isaac, a deputy president of the Conciliation and Arbitration Commission, the need was met. The inquiry thus took on something of the judicial flavour which the appointment of the chairman had seemed to rule out. The need for a capable woman member, which all participants supported or at least conceded, was then met with the appointment of E. M. Campbell, a law professor with experience in the study of public administration.

Those two appointments were made with great speed. Only a few days elapsed between the chairman's approach to the candidates, the prime minister's approach to their employers, and their acceptance. But the appointment of the last member was even more hasty. Indecision about whether to have both a "public service" and a "union" member was partly the cause. As well, the chairman and the prime minister were reluctant themselves to explore possibilities within the unions for fear of causing offence, though they did not want to rely entirely on the suggestions of the PSB. They could not approach a possible union member individually, as they could the members already selected or tentatively selected. One of the commissioners commented that "when the prime minister makes the invitation, it is virtually a royal command", but for the last member clearance by union organizations had first to be obtained. CCPSO was also in a difficult position. It had put names forward to the prime minister as early as September 1973, but the attitude of CCPSO changed when it saw that its constituent unions wished to approach the inquiry individually, rather than collectively through itself. In order for CCPSO to retain its direct influence on the commission, it became necessary to propose one of its own members for inclusion. The secretary of CCPSO, P. R. Munro, was accordingly appointed at the last moment after informal exchanges of which he was unaware between the chairman, the prime minister, and party and trade union activists within the Victorian branch of the Labor Party.

The five members chosen combined a number of representative characteristics, but the mixture was not the product of an open choice and it was generally conceded not to be ideal. The press, for example, considered the commission "unrepresentative" because it included three members with legal qualifications but no one from the business community (as the chairman and others had sought). As a team, however, the commission was thought to be well balanced internally. It had imputed to it no strong views about the nature of public service reform. The parliamentary opposition was by no means enthusiastic — the leader of the opposition privately said that the commission "at least appeared to be political" — but in the aftermath of electoral defeat the inquiry was not given much attention. It was almost a neutral or a non-political instrument.

This moderately satisfactory result, it scarcely needs emphasizing, did not arise in a tidy way. The hundred or so names submitted formally to the prime minister were certainly not scrutinized by him and his staff with equal care. The speed with which they worked meant that suitable choices were therefore unavoidably excluded. Fluctuating considerations of representativeness helped to make this so. The pool of names from which members were drawn was not unlimited. Names came from the networks of the participants which were necessarily restricted. This reinforced the tendency to appoint the first available suitable people. The fact that a name appeared on a list was almost a sufficient guarantee of its respectability. Yet it remains the case that two of the commissioners eventually appointed did not figure on any of the early lists. Their availability was the necessary, if not sufficient, cause which won them their place. There was nothing irrational about this, though it might perhaps have been done better. But a better process of selection would not have been very different: the restraints of time would simply have been relaxed a little, with consequent costs to other issues. Once it had been decided to have an inquiry, the business of establishing it had to be fitted in somehow.

PEOPLE, MONEY, AND TIME

The last direct influence exerted by the participants on the shape of the commission was in determining the staff and financial resources available to it. These were not important issues until it was clear that the inquiry would go ahead. In its submissions to the prime minister of late 1973 – early 1974, the PSB made no mention of staff or costs, which drew critical comment from the prime minister's private office. The PRS, on the other hand, went to some lengths in February 1974 to emphasize the importance of staff, money, and time. It drew explicitly upon Canadian experience with the Glassco inquiry to argue for the creation of a "high-powered" research unit in addition to the usual secretariat, for the possible employment of a commissioner as research director, for a budget of $2 million, and for two years' life for the inquiry. The board responded only by noting that task forces might be a way of tapping expertise not otherwise available, but the chairman in May 1974 went further. He emphasized that a high-quality staff would be needed and suggested a further senior position of adviser on community relations. The specifications which the then Department of the Special Minister of State (responsible for royal commissions) had drawn up did not meet the views that were being urged in the case of this particular inquiry. Its standard briefing notes for chairmen of inquiries mentioned that the department normally chose the secretary; that it normally approached the PSB for staff; that the staff usually consisted of five or six clerks or research officers; and that the employment of additional research workers would be taken to indicate that consultants would not be required. The outcome was a compromise: the suggested senior positions were included on the inquiry's establishment, support staff was roughly doubled from the departmental estimate, and the total budget pencilled-in at about $1 million. But this was not a rigid compromise. The commission did not at the outset know what it might want; if later it wanted more dollars and bodies (as it did), this would have to be negotiated with the PSB and Treasury, two of the agencies certain to be under scrutiny by the inquiry. Staffing was no more a settled issue than the interpretation of the terms of reference or the dispositions of the commissioners.

CONCLUSIONS

We have discussed decisions about the instruments of the inquiry, its terms of reference, its membership, and its staff as though they were difficulties of choice confronting certain participants. And so they were, but the outcomes of these choices can also be regarded as resources posing further choices for the commission that was eventually established. The choice of the royal commission instrument, for example, gave the inquiry status and legal powers. Its terms of reference gave it an almost unrestricted field for investigation. Its membership gave it a particular strength of personal resources consisting of the members themselves and the knowledge and staff they were able to recruit to the inquiry. It had other resources also of money, intelligence, and purpose. It began work against a background of general interest and considerable goodwill from the media and the public service. A widespread belief that public service reform was a worthwhile activity, a low level of agreement on the particular issues to be investigated, a pressing need for the government to give more attention to other emerging issues, and the need not to offend a powerful public service all combined to produce a "respectable" commission with a wide but vague brief. It was not an inquiry fuelled by particular political purposes. It had no (or at least insignificant) axes to grind. It had no single dominating constituency to which to report. The commission was left to make what it could of the resources it had been born with. An early suggestion by the PRS, for example, that the commission should be required to submit an interim report and so test ministerial reactions at an early stage was not adopted by the government.

All this might be taken as the prescription for an ideal inquiry. But that would be a retrospective judgment and certainly could not be made on the basis of evidence presented here. The commission had begun as an instrument to resolve questions which bothered politicians, but politicians did not have a clear idea of what they wanted the commission to do: they changed their minds, discovered other concerns, and in the end agreed that the chief thing about the inquiry was simply to get it going. Yet this inquiry, like so many others, was represented by nearly all participants in terms which conformed to a rational model of sequential decision making. The government or parliament was represented as its initiator, as the definer of problems to be solved or of issues to be explicated. The inquiry was represented as the expert instrument which would assess issues, marshall evidence, and present choices or recommendations for action. The public service was subsequently represented as the implementer of the choices or recommendations accepted by the government, and the outcomes of public service activity were presented as responses to the problems that had originally bothered the government. This was not necessarily an unhelpful orthodoxy for the commission, but its genesis was not like this and neither could be its later life.

9

The Politics of Advice and the Making of the 1974 Budget

The annual budget is one occasion when a government must make choices. It must not only decide in broad terms how the economy will be run, but also decide on what items expenditure will be increased, maintained, or reduced. The budgetary process thus provides a good example of government in action on a wide-ranging front.

This case-study describes how the budget was made in 1974. It was not a typical year. Procedures that had come to be regarded as normal proved incapable of dealing with competing pressures, and the advice of the Treasury, traditionally the core of the budget strategy, was not acceptable to cabinet. Political considerations made things worse. The Liberal-Country Party opposition had forced one election in May and were already, a mere three months later, talking about forcing another. The three-year horizon on which most new governments are able to focus was reduced to four months. Nevertheless, the 1974 budget does illustrate the interaction between various parts of the polity.

The case-study concentrates on three main points. First, it shows that the "how" and the "why" of advice are important factors in determining what a cabinet decides. The tensions of the budgetary discussions show the importance of the way in which advice is presented. They illustrate the significance of a monopoly over advice where "wicked" problems exist; that is, areas of policy for which there is no simple or permanent solution and where the definition of what has to be solved will determine the range of possible answers. The management of the economy is obviously one such area of policy. The economy needs constant adjustment, although it is always affected by forces not wholly subject to the control of a single government. As one economic problem is temporarily alleviated, another emerges. One year's solution may create the next year's problem. Further, there is seldom unanimity about the choice of the best policy; different actors may have perspectives that are so diverse that a variety of proposals can be presented, each of which can be legitimately defended, with reconciliation between them almost impossible. In attempting to present appealing alternatives to cabinet, information is a major resource.

Second, and obviously related to the first theme, the advice that is provided is part of the constant struggle for influence between departments. Whether or not the best available advice may be presented to cabinet, it is certain that the advice will be couched in such a way that it will have the best chance of being accepted. As a result, a submission must not only explain why its proposals are necessary; it must also discredit the alternative suggestions. Such a tactic is the inevitable outcome of the adversarial nature of the budgetary process.

Third, this chapter explores the appreciative system of cabinet, that is, its mechanism for obtaining and understanding the information it needs if it is to operate effectively and act as arbiter between the alternatives presented to it (Vickers 1965). This means that it is necessary to examine the factors that limit the availability of alternatives, the cabinet's capacity to find and assimilate advice from alternative sources when the accepted procedures do not work, and its relationship with caucus and other institutions. It also means that cabinet's responsiveness to change must be examined. The budget process occurs in an environment that is far from static. Economic conditions and bureaucratic influences change, and cabinet should be able to take account of the changes in the formulation of its proposals. The question is whether it can.

Since the budget process is secret and documentary evidence is at best partial, the analysis is bound to be tentative. For example, the distinction between a minister and his department is difficult to draw; yet in a close analysis the distinction must be made. A minister formally signs all submissions from his department before they are presented to cabinet and is constitutionally responsible for them, but whether or not he personally influences the form and content of those submissions is another matter. He may disagree and yet find that the department argues that options can only be presented within a limited range because any other policy is likely to be unsuccessful. In such a case it becomes difficult for the minister as an individual to devise any alternatives. Nevertheless, the 1974 budget does give a clear sense of the importance of the character of the advice offered, of the appreciative system of cabinet, and of the interdepartmental struggles for influence in the general budgetary process.

EARLY DEVELOPMENTS

During the long Liberal period of office, a budgetary routine had been established which was widely regarded as a "normal" pattern (see Weller and Cutt 1976, pp. 55-75). From April to early July the departments and the Treasury negotiated what levels of expenditure would be required for existing programmes. Submissions for new policies were also prepared. At a week-long budget meeting, usually held in July, cabinet discussed the budget strategy, all the new proposals for expenditure and the "disagreed bids", that is, those items of recurrent expenditure on which Treasury and departments could not agree. During budget cabinet, the main background papers were presented by the treasurer, who was briefed by his department on the implications and acceptability of the disagreed bids and new proposals. Four weeks later the budget itself was presented to parliament. This detailed cabinet involvement is unique to Australia; in Britain and Canada the cabinet is not fully involved until the budget is almost completely formulated. Nevertheless, the treasurer and his department played the central role in the preparation of the budget. In 1973, the Labor Government's first budget for twenty-three years, the traditional procedure was followed. In 1974 it broke down.

Budgeting is usually incremental. Any budget must be shaped largely by the decisions of previous years. The greater part of public expenditure at any given time is predetermined by existing commitments that are politically or legally irrevocable. The economy in 1974 was severely affected by the decisions made two or more years before. The 1972 budget had tried to stimulate the economy in the hope of ensuring a Liberal win at the elections; the consequences of the boom that it created were among the causes of the recession that developed in 1974.

However, for convenience, this case-study starts with the 1974 election. During the campaign, the opposition leader, B. M. Snedden, concentrated on the rising inflation rate and made it the central topic of the campaign. Whitlam was forced to respond and discuss the problems of economic management. Using the consumer price index figures for the March quarter, which showed a decline in the rate of inflation (although they were recognized as being false indicators), Whitlam argued that the Labor government had defeated inflation. In another move designed to show the economic responsibility of his government, Whitlam promised that the next budget would provide for a domestic surplus.

Labor won the election, but narrowly. Directly the results were known, the Treasury, some of whose senior officers believed that the electoral economic proposals of both parties were unworkable, repeated a warning made several times in the previous six months. It argued that inflation was in danger of increasing rapidly and that a "short sharp shock" was required. Its advice was at first accepted. At the Premiers' Conference early in June, the prime minister demanded in a tough speech that the states play their part in re-straining public expenditure. Then in two meetings of an *ad hoc* kitchen cabinet at the beginning of July, the Treasury's package of harsh measures, which included rises in taxation and interest rates, was accepted, mainly because of the support it received from Whitlam. Frank Crean, the treasurer, did not support his officers strongly when they put their arguments to the kitchen cabinet meeting. It was decided to introduce a mini-budget in late July as an immediate response to inflationary pressures, since the election had forced the postponement of the normal budget until September (for details, see John Edwards, *National Times*, 9—14 September, 18—23 November 1974, and P. P. McGuinness, *Financial Review*, 5 November 1975).

But at these meetings opposition began to emerge. Two major premises in the Treasury's analysis were disputed. Several commentators, both inside and outside parliament, were arguing that the problem was no longer demand inflation. They argued that demand had declined, as illustrated especially by the downturn in the building industry, that the growth in the money supply had slowed, and that, as a downturn had already occurred, a recession was inevitable. Whether the Treasury had failed to monitor the change, or had interpreted it differently, or whether the knowledge did not get through to the higher levels of the department and

thence to ministers is impossible to discover, but as late as 11 July
the Treasury was claiming "that overall activity appears to be continuing at a very high level" (*Financial Review*, 11 July 1974).

The second point of dispute was the level of unemployment that
would be created by the Treasury's proposals. The Treasury
accepted that unemployment would follow, but could not accurately
predict the level, although its officers agreed that it might reach
180,000. As a result, even if the Treasury's diagnosis were correct,
the solutions that it proposed would lie uneasily on a government
committed to a policy of full employment to keep its supporters in
work.

In late July the Treasury's proposals were discussed by the full
cabinet. Whitlam was alone in giving them full support. The
treasurer was quiet and several other leading ministers were now
directly opposed to them. Cabinet refused to accept any increase in
direct or indirect taxes or any rise in petrol excise. It did accept the
imposition of higher postal charges and a postponement of the child
care programme, but offset any savings on expenditure by accepting
a rise in the pension rate.

The following day, caucus was given notice of the details of the
proposals an hour before they were to be presented to the House.
Uproar followed as members declared that they should have been
consulted. The castrated mini-budget was accepted, but primarily
because there was no time to change it. The measures were
announced by Crean in strong terms that had been written before
the harsh measures were cut out by cabinet; he himself appeared to
be out of touch.

By August, the month in which the week-long budget cabinet
meeting was to be held, several forces had emerged to disrupt the
procedures that had been adopted in previous years. Caucus was
demanding a voice in the determination of the budget strategy, and
Crean had in principle accepted that the economic committee of
caucus would be consulted. The treasurer himself was known
publicly to be out of sympathy with the advice being presented by
his department. The prime minister, annoyed by his own defeat in
cabinet on 22 July and by the lack of support he had received there,
took little interest in the shaping of the budget, leaving the running
more and more to his deputy, Dr Cairns. At the same time the
economic situation was deteriorating. The growth in the money
supply had become negative. In July unemployment rose sharply by

a further 14 per cent, a figure that was unacceptable to many members of the Labor government. Inflation continued.

But perhaps the most important change concerned the Treasury. Its basic advice was under challenge. Some ministers and other departments now challenged its strategy; they denied that demand inflation was the problem. They rejected the view of the Treasury that the situation would continue to deteriorate unless more restrictive policies were adopted and that increasing unemployment was an unfortunate product of any cure for inflation. The Treasury was neither supported nor directed by its minister. When its advice was unacceptable, no alternative source of advice was immediately available. Ministers had to look elsewhere for possible solutions and were forced to rely for advice on ministerial advisers and other sources. Other departments like the Department of Urban and Regional Development (DURD), which had the capacity to tender alternative advice, also took advantage of the situation to try to fill the gap. A number of individuals and institutions were thus able to become involved in bureaucratic areas which previously had belonged almost exclusively to the Treasury, and they inevitably used the situation to their own advantage.

LABOR AND POLICY ALTERNATIVES

The Labor government did not enter office without preconceptions about the type of strategy that would or would not be acceptable. Unemployment especially was anathema to Labor politicians, for whom the experiences of the Depression were part of the party's communal memory. Departmental advice which was inconsistent with the party's ideology and policy preconceptions was bound to have a rough passage, and given Labor's procedural rules, it could not be pushed through by the leader or by cabinet without the approval of caucus.

Some of these political constraints were emphasized in the paper circulated by Hayden, the minister for social security, in July. Caucus, he argued, would not accept an unemployment rate higher than 2 per cent.

> It is essential to recognise and respect the role of Caucus in future economic policies. Measures taken which lead the economy in a direction unacceptable to Caucus are certain to be rescinded by Caucus.

From now on there will be little time for lengthy decision making processes involving Caucus Committees, so the upshot of economic measures unacceptable to Caucus is that they will be rescinded and quite likely replaced with unsuitable, even disastrous substitutes. Caucus is likely, that is, to find itself substituting policies on the basis of inadequate information.

The first parameter we must acknowledge then, in assessing future measures, is that Caucus will not tolerate significant unemployment and that it may very well be disastrous to the Government, but more importantly, to the nation if there is any effort to short-circuit Caucus by ignoring its basic attitudes.

Hayden then proposed an alternative course of action. His strategy recommended an easing of the credit squeeze, the pruning of expenditure, a deal with the unions which included reductions in the income tax for lower income earners, a capital gains tax and improved social security payments, including a guaranteed income. The package was designed to reduce the demands for wage increases by showing that the burden of taxation was more evenly distributed.

Hayden's proposals recognized the restrictions imposed by the political situation. The deliberate creation of unemployment was not acceptable to the party as a means of combating inflation, nor after the July fiasco could caucus be ignored. Hayden did not support the Treasury's hard line but did argue for some restraint. His paper indicated how far party pressures limited the debate and restricted the alternatives that could be adopted. Further, the discussion was still based on the Treasury's submissions. Whether or not they were acceptable, they were the starting point for debate because they alone provided a focus. This was probably inevitable, given the Treasury's monopoly at the time on the provision of advice.

Caucus was duly consulted. The secretary of its economic committee circulated a paper listing the main questions that had to be discussed. It began:

Budget strategy generally, including whether the reported view of Treasury that there should be considerable unemployment as an anti-inflationary move, should be accepted or rejected.

Also, whether Australia is now suffering from Demand and/or Cost Inflation and whether the alleged policy advice advocated by Treasury as outlined above would lead to Stagflation.

It was a loaded way of putting the question, but it was indicative of the general mood of caucus — suspicious, worried, and torn between the various interpretations of the economic climate.

Several other members circulated papers to caucus, with varying interpretations of the economy and what could be done to solve it. A sense of political urgency, indeed of crisis, ran through them all. One paper started: "The September 1974 Budget should be an Election Budget with an election expected either in December 1974 or in May 1975." And this was written less than three months after the former election. A policy to dampen demand had no supporters. One member commented that because of the imprecision of economic knowledge, measures to reduce demand were difficult to apply effectively, since they took time to work and it would "necessarily involve some increase in unemployment since that is what demand reduction is about". He then went on:

> Of course there is no doubt, that if we are prepared to depress demand sufficiently, we will eventually create the economic environment in which inflation is considerably reduced. Demand for labour will slacken, profit margins will be reduced as demand dries up and employers will no longer be able to raise prices without losing further sales. Eventually — and no economist can say with any certainty at what level, or even at what approximate level of unemployment this would occur — through reduced demand for labour and reduced ability of employers to absorb or pass on wage increases, the crazy spiral will come to an end. Meanwhile we'll probably be watching the state of play from the opposition benches — those of us who are left, that is.

In this atmosphere it was not surprising that the Treasury's proposals, explained to caucus by the first assistant secretary in charge of the general financial and economic policy division of the Treasury, were unwelcome. Nor were the more moderate proposals of Hayden better received. Electorally nervous and ideologically opposed to unemployment, caucus was not prepared to accept the "blood, sweat, and tears" strategy of the economic managers in the Treasury; indeed, there were even unsuccessful attempts to censure the Treasury.

Cairns and Hayden independently had talked to a few non-Treasury economists around Australia. The economic committee of caucus now adopted the general strategy presented by Cairns in a paper that was widely circulated. It claimed that the main objective was to cure inflation without creating unemployment. Cairns dismissed the Treasury's strategy: "There is but one justification now for demand restriction policies — to create a sufficiently high level of unemployment to break the bargaining strength of the unions." He suggested that an increase in unemployment would not solve the problem of inflation. Inflation started in the private sector and therefore, he argued, reductions in the public sector would have no effect. Besides, he believed that the public sector needed further resources. Cairns rejected the conventional solution of squeezing credit, demand, and wages both because he believed it was unjust and, on a practical note, because the opposition-controlled Senate might reject it. In its place, he preferred a neutral or mildly inflationary budget, with a policy of wage restraint, a restructured income tax, and an increased if graduated company tax. He proposed direct subsidies of employment-creating activities and a penalty tax on wage increases that were above an acceptable level. Cairns's paper talked about inflation, but did not really suggest any positive anti-inflationary measures. It expressed the unease of members of caucus and sounded as though it promised more than it did.

Caucus endorsed Cairns's paper. It did not suggest how the plan should be implemented, but its acceptance of the strategy in the paper made clear that caucus members believed that cost-push inflation was now the problem and that the creation of unemployment was an unacceptable weapon to defeat it. Crean had attended the meeting, but it was now clear that he disagreed with his department's advice, even though he appeared to make no effort to change it, to force the department at this stage to provide alternatives or even to request a detailed analysis of the Cairns package of proposals.

The 12 August meeting illustrated some of the limitations of caucas. Caucus did not spell out detailed proposals for implementation, because it had neither the time nor the information to present an overall view. The papers circulated by backbenchers show with one exception the problems caused by a lack of time and access to information. The *Financial Review* (13 August 1974) headlined the report of this meeting "Caucus Calls the Tune". In fact the meeting illustrated how dependent caucus was on alternatives presented by ministers; it was Cairns, not caucus, who called the tune. Whatever the cause, the result was that cabinet was certain to examine seriously the proposals in the Cairns paper. Caucus could not be ignored; its veto power was still great.

OUTSIDE INFLUENCES

The fact that economic strategy was being widely debated within the political system meant that much of the debate was publicized. And from both sides. Opponents of the Treasury line attacked it publicly and privately; Clyde Cameron carefully leaked unemployment figures in an attempt to discredit the Treasury. On the other side, some senior Treasury officers reputedly held "background briefings" for selected journalists who could discuss the government's economic proposals critically with a better appreciation of the economic situation as it was seen from within the Treasury.

Every year, delegates from industry and the unions confer with the treasurer about the directions in which they consider the budget should go. These interviews are scarcely ever influential, although they can indicate a general mood. With a Labor government in power, the union attitudes were especially important, particularly as the government was discussing the possibility of a reduction of income tax in exchange for wage restraint. But any discussion of a "social contract" or similar agreement was limited by the constitutional inability of the federal government to control wages, prices and many areas of non-company profit and also by the multiplicity of unions.

The unions' attitudes were best expressed by R. J. Hawke. He argued that a Labor government had not been elected to preside over a high level of unemployment, particularly on the advice of "those comfortably situated non-removable economists" in the Treasury (*Sydney Morning Herald*, 13 August 1974). Hawke campaigned vigorously to ensure that the Treasury's advice was rejected.

Other commentators were equally outspoken. An editorial in the *Australian* attacked the Treasury's demands for a harsh budget and asked: "Will the federal treasurer realise in time before a potentially disastrous September budget that the Treasury view of Australian economic prospects, on which he apparently depends entirely, is now totally discredited among non-Treasury economists and contradicted by events in the real world" (*Australian*, 10 August 1974). A wide variety of commentators were therefore arguing that the Treasury was wrong, that a recession had begun, and that a tough budget would only lead to stagflation and unnecessary unemployment.

THE TREASURY'S ADVICE

When budget discussions began, it was obvious that cabinet would receive a wide range of advice which differed from that of the Treasury. As usual, ministers wanted to expand their programmes; the Treasury wanted to restrain expenditure. Although few departments had the capacity to debate the forecasts of the general economic conditions, most were prepared to discuss the details of their new proposals. With this general background in mind, the Treasury's advice and the strategy or tactics behind it require detailed attention.

The Treasury was, and remains, the main adviser of the federal government on economic affairs. It has always tried to maintain a monopoly of economic advice, which attempt becomes especially important when, as in 1974, its formulation of the situation is challenged. By the time budget cabinet met on 19 August 1974, it was common knowledge that the Treasury's strategy of a "short sharp shock" had been rejected by most cabinet ministers and by caucus and that caucus had endorsed a prices and incomes policy which did not limit public expenditure dramatically. In the circumstances, as one journalists argued: "Surely Treasury's obligation as a professional economic adviser to Government was not to go on pressing its own preferred policy but to present the Government with an alternative along the broad price and income lines the majority of Cabinet and Caucus so clearly favoured" (*National Times*, 23-28 August 1974).

Treasury provided three main submissions for budget cabinet. Two, *The Economic Situation and Prospects* and *The Balance of Payments*, described the general situation; the third, *Budget Parameters*, suggested the broad approach to be adopted. Naturally, each of the papers went through several drafts, and the changes that can be found in these drafts might be expected to reflect sensitivity to the changing political climate.

In the case of two of these papers, *The Economic Situation and Prospects* and *Budget Parameters*, the drafts written on 12 August and the submissions finally presented to budget cabinet differ in several places. Comments suggesting that the cabinet should take a tough line were often left out or changed. For instance, the phrase "tough decision-making" was replaced by "restraint", while the comment that the budget parameters "rest on the premise that we want to grasp the nettle now" was excised completely.

References to unemployment were also rephrased. The new phrases were invariably more oblique. For instance, the draft of *Budget Parameters* declared that costs and prices were accelerating rapidly and that "this will be combined with a gradually rising unemployment trend over the year ahead". The quoted sentence was left out of the final draft. The comment that "the general picture . . . reflects an outlook in which *both* inflation and unemployment would be rising" was changed to read: "if we were to accept the Budget picture . . . it would mean that the rate of inflation would be rising and the growth of activity declining". In another place "some unemployment will emerge" was changed to "we will experience difficulties in the labour market". Unemployment indeed was scarcely mentioned, even though from the first meeting of the kitchen cabinet on 1 July Treasury officers had argued that it was impossible to cure inflation without an increase in unemployment, and had then suggested that unemployment might rise to about 180,000.

All these changes were simply tactical; they were designed to reduce the salience of the unemployment that would be caused by their strategy because cabinet was opposed to it. There was no change in the Treasury's strategy. The drafting of these papers provides a lesson in how a submission is written for maximum effect; there was no attempt to argue the case, to try to educate ministers or to explain all the implications of a policy. It was a bland attempt to put the one case as if it were the only possible alternative. Yet in a couple of instances the Treasury failed to change sections which could be guaranteed to annoy Labor ministers. The most obvious case was paragraph 17 in *The Economic Situation* which read: "Again, let me [Crean, since he presented it] be stark about it. If inflation now is to be mastered, there will have to be a situation in which, for a time, employees value their jobs and hesitate to put them at risk by attempting to push up wage rates further, and in which on the employers' side there is a buyer's, not a seller's, market, for their output." Such a comment, written by those "comfortably-situated non-removable" officers, and whether or not countersigned by the treasurer, lacked any semblance of political sensitivity. Whether or not it was correct, it was the Treasury whose credibility was undermined, for by this time the treasurer had little of his own left. This paragraph was later used by those ministers who opposed the Treasury line to persuade their more nervous (or cautious) colleagues to reject it entirely. After all, such a strategy could be guaranteed to infuriate Labor ministers.

In the submissions there was no attempt to discuss the issues that had been debated in the previous months. Treasury's only concession to the idea that demand inflation might no longer be the main problem was to suggest that an increase in expenditure would "restimulate demand pressures"; in the draft it suggested an increase would "sustain" them. Otherwise it treated alternative economic strategies with contempt and dismissed them in a line. For instance, *Economic Situation and Prospects* declared that inflation was the major problem and then stated: "There is another viewpoint. That is that over-full employment must be maintained all of the time." There was little recognition of the fact that alternative strategies might have some value; the submissions provided a blanket dismissal of ideas which, after all, had the support of caucus and of a substantial section of cabinet.

Generally, the submissions repeated the demands for harsh measures. They claimed that cures for unemployment were easy to apply if inflation was low, but that inflation must be regarded as the main enemy. The submissions demanded cuts in spending and increases in taxation; they recognized obliquely that the result would be an increase in unemployment, but did not specify its amount.

The broad figures are worth quoting. On the expenditure side the budget proposed outlays of $15,350 million in agreed bids for existing programmes (although the treasurer announced his intention of reopening items accounting for $45 million in that category), $173 million in disagreed bids for existing programmes and $672 million for new expenditure proposals being brought to cabinet by ministers for the first time. If all outlays were agreed, the total would have been $16,195 million, an increase in expenditure of 32 per cent. The Treasury proposed that the total should be cut by $600 million. Revenue was estimated to increase by 32.9 per cent, but mainly as a result of inflation. The Treasury recommended that taxes be imposed to raise a further $400 million.

These figures are interesting. First the majority of bids for existing programmes were agreed at official level; they were seldom considered or even reviewed by ministers. In this case only 1.4 per cent of the total for existing programmes was to be considered as a disagreed bid by cabinet. In other words, despite the fact that 1974 was a year in which departments were more likely to take disagreed bids to cabinet, because of the greater chances of success there, most bids were settled to the Treasury's satisfaction. (In 1977, when the Department of Finance had reasserted central authority, the total amount included as disagreed bids was $8 million — or 0.04 per cent of expenditure on existing programmes.)

The preparation of the submissions and the tactics behind them raise important questions about the provisions of advice. The treasurer is responsible; he cannot be absolved from blame. But if, as in this case, he does not support the department, where can he go for alternatives? He can request that references to unemployment be deleted, but he can scarcely develop a coherent and constructive alternative. Nor, in the face of an insistent department, can he reasonably challenge its arguments. He does not have the information or forecasts on which its advice is based. That indeed appeared to be the case in 1974. It is true that "yes-men" officials can lead to great problems; but so too can intransigent "no-men" who will consistently argue the case they believe must be accepted, for they as much as ministers can lead to a breakdown in relations between a minister and his department. Further, the minister was seldom provided with alternatives even when they were being discussed in his own department. Reputedly there was considerable debate within the Treasury about the wisdom of the "short sharp shock". But it never reached the minister. Once the department had reached a decision on what advice should be tendered, all officers were expected to support and argue for that line.

Such a situation creates problems. The public servants in the Treasury were placed in a difficult situation; they had to work without directions from their minister. They had to present unpalatable advice to a cabinet that was out of sympathy with their views. Since they were apparently not directed to develop alternatives along the lines of the Cairns paper, they dismissed it with contempt. In the resulting vacuum created by lack of direction, the role of the Treasury as a lobby for a certain economic viewpoint became dominant. Treasury officials argued, and intransigently maintained, a definite stand which they claimed was the only economically responsible one. The adherence to that view was as much an ideological stand as were those of other departments with whom they disagreed.

The tactics of advice are instructive. The submissions carefully avoided most comments that might reduce their attractiveness.

Although the three submissions, as their titles suggest, were in theory designed to assist cabinet in making decisions of fundamental importance, in fact they were presented in such a way as to minimize informed discussion of a subject that is notoriously difficult. There were no policy options presented to cabinet, merely the one recommendation.

For an Australian bureaucrat, such behaviour is the norm. The Treasury is by no means the only department that adopts such tactics. To show alternatives is to invite debate; to admit weaknesses encourages rejection; to highlight the less welcome alternatives is tactically unwise. Information is a resource to be carefully husbanded; it should be carefully collected and when presented it should be timely, clear, reliable, and wide-ranging; but the fact that it is collected does not mean that it will be available to ministers or other departments. The amount of information that is used seems to depend more on tactical necessity, on what must be released to persuade ministers, than on the evidence ministers might need to make their decisions. The sieving and manipulation of information is obviously a function of the bureaucracy that can be used or abused. The decisions made by cabinet and the allocation of resources they entail are as much a result of the existing distribution of influence as of any intrinsic force in the arguments offered to support the choices made.

BUDGET CABINET

In theory all major allocative decisions are made during budget cabinet. Expenditure decisions on existing programmes and new proposals should be considered then. In fact, new proposals are often presented to cabinet throughout the year while, especially in inflationary times, departments may apply for more funds for existing programmes when additional estimates are considered. Indeed, so many programmes now have important consequences that stretch far beyond any one budgetary year that many economists consider that the annual budgetary cycle is already in-appropriate. Nevertheless, despite these shortcomings, the budget cabinet meeting is generally considered the most important meeting of the year (see Weller and Cutt 1976, pp. 65-68).

The procedures adopted by cabinet are themselves significant.

Submissions from the departments are circulated in advance to ministers in the week before the meeting; there were about 180 submissions in 1974, creating piles of paper behind each minister in the cabinet room. During the weekend before budget cabinet (which starts on a Monday and lasts for five days) the two background Treasury papers were delivered. As the cabinet meeting started, ministers were given the crucial *Budget Parameters* paper and the copies were collected at the end of each session. Ministers were therefore not only faced with a large pile of submissions, the economic implications of which they usually had no means of calculating, but they had to absorb the *Budget Parameters* paper even while the treasurer was speaking to it, for only the treasurer and the prime minister had seen the proposal before the meeting. The accuracy and clarity of the proposal therefore are important; if it is ambiguous, it has a greater chance of being misunderstood.

The potential influence of the treasurer is further strengthened by the fact that he is briefed on every submission, with details of how the case can be argued and what the broader implications are. The prime minister is usually given wide-ranging briefs as well, by his department and, in 1974, by the special economic advisers that he had appointed.

But what of other ministers? Hayden employed an economist on his personal staff; so did Cairns. But most of their colleagues had few contacts on whom they could rely for advice on macro-economic matters. Most departments comment on the submissions of other departments only insofar as they may affect their own programmes; they do not, as one former treasurer to his chagrin admitted, give recommendations to the minister. Cabinet members are often ill-equipped to challenge the assumptions and proposals of the Treasury.

In 1974 there was one major exception. DURD had established an economic division in the hope of challenging the Treasury's monopoly on economic advice. Obviously it had to make some comments on the central submissions of the Treasury, besides providing its minister with a brief on each proposal of other ministers. In a briefing note to its minister before cabinet began, the department calculated likely figures for income and expenditure (since it had not yet seen the *Budget Parameters* paper), provided an estimate of possible levels of unemployment, and challenged Treasury's view that there were no policy options and that a short burst of unemployment would break the inflationary expectations. The paper suggested that unemployment would have to be maintained for some time before it had any effect. It proposed that the minister should advocate a domestic surplus of $50 million, that he should join the treasurer in opposing the proposals of some other departments, and that any excess domestic surplus should be used to finance tax cuts. Finally, it listed the main recommendations that should be supported.

There is a similarity in tone between the papers prepared by DURD and Treasury, although not in content. DURD suggested that the Treasury proposals were "fanciful" and provided a quotation from an earlier Treasury paper to support its case. Both departments were preparing for a contest — and that is what budget cabinet always is.

In 1974, ministers began with a suspicion of the Treasury's advice that was based on its espousal of the "short sharp shock" strategy and its advocacy of increased unemployment as a means of fighting inflation. As we have seen, *Budget Parameters* argued the need for restraint, recommending a cut in proposed expenditure of $600 million and an increase in taxation of $400 million. In the summary, under the heading "Budget Outcome", the submission then read: "The expenditures presently being proposed, taken in conjunction with these *conditional* revenue estimates, show for 1974-75 the Budget in deficit approaching $250 million, with a domestic surplus of about $320 million." It was not immediately clear whether the conditional revenue estimates were made before or after the expenditure cuts and increased tax totalling $1,000 million was included. With no table setting out the calculations clearly, ministers initially read the paper to mean that the $320 million domestic surplus was the final figure after all the treasurer's proposals had been included. But if read accurately, it can be seen to include only the expenditures proposed by ministers. If the Treasury's proposals were accepted, the domestic surplus would have been $1,320 million.

That interpretation only gradually sank in. A few ministers, most notably Hayden, and an economist from DURD realized the figures seemed strange, and soon worked out what the proper interpretation was. The ministers were furious, claiming that the Treasury had deliberately sought to mislead. The next day, after a specific order from cabinet, the Treasury provided a table giving details of the possible budget outcomes before and after the Treasury's additional proposals were taken into account. It claimed the figures were:

	$ millions
Treasury's estimate of receipt (no tax change)	15,951
Estimates for total outlays bid (all bids agreed to)	16,195
Overall deficit	−244
Less overseas deficit	−570
	+326
Increased tax recommended by Treasury	400
Reduce expenditure as recommended by Treasury	600
Domestic surplus	+1,326

If the table had been provided with the original submission in the interests of clarity, much of the dispute might have been avoided. As the submission stood, it did not clearly explain what the treasurer proposed. It obscured the situation.

This incident added to the mistrust that already existed. It led to a widespread rejection of Treasury's advice and at least initially to a search for alternative proposals, since they could not be obtained from Treasury. DURD had provided some alternatives, but the general picture that emerged was of a policy vacuum. Spending decisions were taken without much appreciation of a general framework, precisely because there was no one who was recognized as legitimate to brief cabinet. The corollary to a monopoly of advice was a total lack of advice when that monopoly was discredited. At the same time Crean reputedly became even less willing to argue his department's case, claiming that the views he presented were the department's and not his own.

Much of the time the spending proposals of ministers were passed without cuts. Notably, in the light of the role DURD had played in undermining the Treasury, there were massive increases in urban and regional development (172 per cent); education expenditure was also increased by 78 per cent without challenge. The final result was a small domestic surplus (as promised in the election) of $23 million.

On the revenue side, cabinet also found the Treasury's proposals unsatisfactory and sought alternative advice. It established a committee which was chaired by Dr Coombs and included the head of the Treasury, Sir Frederick Wheeler, the commissioner of taxation, Sir Edward Cain, two advisers, Professor Fred Gruen and

Brian Brogan, and the "doyen" of the economics profession, Professor T. W. Swan. The committee was required to report within three days on what could be "done through the taxation system" —

(a) to restrain cost inflation
(b) to encourage saving and investment
(c) to prepare for a possible balance of payments crisis.

It was instructed to give attention to the possibilities of

(a) exclusion of wage and salary increases beyond an established norm from acceptable costs for the assessment of company income;
(b) imposition of a tax on income for which a rebate is given for saving as a means of countering the tendency in inflationary conditions for savings to be reduced to support previous expenditure patterns.

The committee met on each of the ensuing four days. Much of the time was spent examining the probable inconsistencies and shortcomings of any penalty tax on large wage rises. During its deliberations one senior public servant asked why ministers always wanted contradictory things. Another produced the politically unacceptable comment that the easiest way to increase investment was to abolish the Prices Justification Tribunal.

The committee's report pointed out all the problems inherent in a system of penalty taxes and emphasized that it was bound to be a rough and ready short-term proposal. But it did suggest that, administratively difficult as it might be, the penalty tax scheme could be applied by the commissioner of taxation. The recommendation was full of caveats, but it was signed by all members of the committee, including Wheeler and Cain. In principle, it was then accepted by cabinet, who asked for the administrative details to be worked out.

AFTERMATH

During the week of budget cabinet, articles appeared frequently in the press arguing both sides of the case. Cairns publicly announced that the credit squeeze would be eased and that the time for a harsh budget had passed. After budget cabinet ended, Whitlam went on television to address the nation on the problems of economic management. In the three weeks between the end of the cabinet meeting and the formal announcement of the budget in parliament, leaks were so frequent that Crean had little new to announce. For example, on 3 September the level of grants to the arts was published (*Sydney Morning Herald*, 3 September 1974), on 11 September the cuts in income tax were leaked, and on 16 September details of a proposed tax on unearned income were broadcast widely. Taken with the leaks in budget cabinet week and the "jawboning" of senior ministers trying to get the message across to the people, it was probably the most public preparation an Australian budget had ever had.

The Treasury was also keen to get its message across. Perhaps the view held by some of its senior officers was most neatly expressed in an article in the *Age* by Ken Davidson, described by one of his journalist colleagues as a spokesman for the Treasury (see Andrew Clark, *National Times*, 16-21 September 1974). Entitled "Labor Budget on Way to Disaster", it argued:

> Is it a greater total burden for the whole community if 97 per cent of the workforce is required to make generous provision for the remaining 3 per cent out of work? Or is it less costly for the whole community to put up with a 20 per cent — and accelerating — inflation rate.
> It is a murderous choice.
> The first may cause grievous, but short term, damage to the electoral standing of the Labor Party, but the second could well put the existing social structure and institutions at risk. [*Age*, 21 August 1974]

After budget cabinet the Treasury did not release the annual White Paper on the economy; it blamed the election and claimed, "We had a disruptive seven or eight weeks because of the election" (*Age*, 28 August 1974). But it was also clear that any such paper would be at variance with the government's accepted policy. It was, according to one commentator, a deliberate piece of self-censorship. The Treasury blamed its defeat especially on the ministerial staff who had the last word to ministers. They argued that they were not able to discover what advice was given or to comment on it (*Financial Review*, 27 August 1974). It is a revealing comment from a department that traditionally has had the last word on all sub-missions and had ensured that no department knew what advice it would give to the treasurer. Success in the battle for influence often depends on the capacity to give ministers advice on the proposals of others and hence to retain control over the necessary information. Like many other observers, the Treasury probably exaggerated the role of ministerial staff; but its view is interesting more for what it reveals about the Treasury's appreciation of the tactics of advice and for the comment on the normal unavailability of such sources of advice for ministers.

But it was far from true that the Treasury or its allies were powerless. The administrative arrangements for any penalty tax still had to be settled, and that itself gave the taxation office and the Treasury potential power. As P. P. McGuinness argued: "The arguments of the mandarins are likely to prevail. After all, if they say that a new tax is administratively impractical, they must be right — because they can prove themselves right by refusing to make it work" (*Financial Review*, 27 August 1974). Whitlam had mentioned the penalty tax in his address to the nation on 26 August, and it was widely expected to be introduced. However, the proposal was dropped and one observer argued that the committee had been "stymied" by the Treasury, even though it would have been the taxation office that had to administer it. Of course it is impossible to prove whether this was simply because it would not have worked or because the mandarins did not want it to work. That in itself is indicative of bureaucratic power when, as usually happens, only one department is working on an issue's feasibility.

The budget itself met with a mixed reception. The *Financial Review*'s editorial the following day summed up the two main lines which had earlier been presented. It began: "The Labour Government has invested all on its political instincts, ignored the contradictory suggestions of its permanent, self-selected and self-promoted economic advisers and drawn up a Budget that is aimed at securing some form of social contract from the trade union movement." It then argued: "Essentially, what the Treasury view represents is a fundamentalist dislike of public sector spending, a doctrinaire opposition to government involvement in economic activity and government intervention and the belief that government spending is the engine of inflation. . . . In other words, the only policy which it recommends is the now well publicised "short sharp shock" (*Financial Review*, 18 September 1974).

Caucus reacted in a variety of ways. It accepted the general strategy but criticized some of the details. It opposed especially the tax on unearned income which had been introduced at a late stage on the suggestion of Whitlam's principal private secretary, arguing that it would hit especially those with incomes of under $5,000 a year. A caucus committee amended the tax, but an attempt to abolish it entirely failed. Then, in a tactless display of arrogance, the secretary of the economic committee of caucus announced the change in parliament, long before amending legislation was introduced. It cannot often have happened that a backbencher announces a change to the budget, a mere ten days after it has been introduced. In mid-October caucus again tried to amend the budget when it sought to reverse the reduction of the tax-deductible allowance for educational expenditure. On this occasion it failed to do so.

Then, as the seriousness of the recession and unemployment became more evident, the government changed direction. In late September a devaluation of the dollar was suddenly announced. Then in mid-November, another mini-budget reversed some of the earlier strategies in a further attempt to reduce unemployment and stimulate the economy. The main advisers of this package were Ian Castles, a deputy secretary in PMC, and Professor Gruen — not the Treasury. One commentator claimed: "In seven months the Government moved from single minded concern with inflation in May to single minded concern with employment in November" (*National Times*, 18-23 November 1974). In fact, the new situation required new solutions. Nevertheless, the proposals to stimulate the economy that were accepted in November were argued by others earlier that year. The redirection of policy was caused as much by the change in the advisers to whom ministers listened and to their redefinition of the problem as to any other single cause.

CONCLUSION

The preparation of the 1974 budget exemplified many of Labor's worst problems. It was a case of continuous misunderstanding, mistrust, and misconceptions, allied to the temporary collapse of established relationships between the cabinet and the Treasury. It illustrates the frailty of policy making at the centre.

Cabinet relies on an adequate supply of information on which it can base its decisions. But it does not always receive that information. In part, this is because the bureaucratic ambitions or institutional ideologies of departments may screen out alternative information and strategies that challenge basic assumptions. In part it is because single departments monopolize advice on particular issues. If the system is working smoothly, the main result is that cabinet receives advice from only one perspective; if the situation is turbulent and uncertain, it means that cabinet may be cut off from the possibility of receiving alternative strategies. Further, it is difficult for cabinet to search for these alternatives because there are no procedures it can adopt. It is limited by its institutional framework, and the advice it receives is partisan. Departments are adept at presenting only the best sides of their cases, of trying to persuade and not to inform. As long as the existing structures determine what advice reaches cabinet, the budgetary system will remain adversarial and the politics of advice will help determine what courses governments take.

Conclusions

10

Understanding Policy Processes

At its simplest, policy making is regarded as the more or less rational activity of specifying objectives and devising means for attaining them. Reform of policy making then consists primarily of making the processes of decision more rational than they are believed to be, according to some standard of rationality.

There are many examples of this in political life. The Menzies government in 1963, for instance, set terms of reference for the Committee of Inquiry into Economic Policy (the Vernon Committee) which began: "Having in mind that the objectives of the government's economic policy are a high rate of economic and population growth with full employment, increasing productivity, rising standards of living, external viability, and stability of costs and prices . . . " The terms then went on to ask the committee to report, under fourteen heads, on a variety of different factors thought likely to affect the attainment of the objectives. The factors, all economic, included productivity, wages, population growth, availability of raw materials, the effect of tariffs, and trends in standards of living. The underlying supposition was that these matters could be subjected to scientific, that is rational, analysis which would help the government make decisions about the means best suited to achieve the ends it had chosen. Economic policy was regarded as a body of interconnected decisions about ends and means; the more internally consistent the means and the more skilfully adapted to environment, to the available resources, and to the desired ends, the more rational would be the policy as a whole.

Policy making can then be understood as a sequential problem-solving process, one in which, as H. D. Lasswell has said, "five intellectual tasks are performed at varying levels of insight and understanding: clarification of goals; description of trends; analysis of conditions; projection of future developments; and invention, evaluation and selection of alternatives" (Lasswell 1968, pp. 181-82). It is not difficult to find all of these tasks carried out to some degree in the work of the Vernon Committee. Other writers have broken the process of policy making down into different components and sequences, but that is not the focus of our interest now. We want to emphasize that just as policy itself cannot be thought to be rational, so the processes by which it is made cannot be regarded as composed of ordered, sequential steps, each linked in some way with the ones preceding it and the whole insulated against the intrusion of extraneous forces irrelevant to the solving of the given problem.

Further, when the Australian government is described as a variant of the Westminster model, underlying assumptions about the rationality of the policy processes and the centrality of policy are made more or less automatically. The main function of the system of parliamentary government is seen in the production of "policies". Other processes, such as the struggle for power, are regarded as subordinate to the policy processes in a properly functioning system; if they become dominant, then something is thought to be wrong. Problems should be solved, according to this view, by the use of objective evidence and expertise, not by political prejudice.

Rationalistic assumptions about policy making are not, of course, confined to the Westminster system. Similar assumptions are made about the American system of government, as much of the critical literature reviewed in chapter 1 shows. The institutions and procedures of government may be very different, but analysis indicating the non-rationality of the processes of American government is just as applicable to British and Australian government.

We have focused on policy-making processes, not on policy conceived of as an outcome in the form of a more or less complex set of connected decisions. We have emphasized the muddle, complexity, and disjointedness of the processes. It cannot be assumed, however, that because policy making is muddled, the outcome will necessarily be muddled or appear non-rational. The RCAGA study, for instance, shows how the establishment of the inquiry was achieved in a muddled way but still came close to meeting the wishes of its proponents.

We have argued that the processes of government are not simply about the creation of policy. Nor is policy necessarily the outcome of activity. In the first place, policy cannot be identified apart from the processes themselves. It serves a wide variety of purposes — as a means or an end to different actors. Often it is not even given a high priority; the gaining of office, for example, can be more important. Second, the term *policy* suggests that there is something final about a decision, that it has been decided beyond dispute, at least for a while. But in fact everything that looks like an agreed or fixed policy is for some a source of disagreement or the starting point for new efforts to alter the decision. The process is continuous. Policy is part of, not separate from, the policy-making processes.

The case-studies were chosen over the widest possible range to reveal the extent of muddle and complexity. We have not concentrated exclusively on problems of public policy that are regarded as especially difficult. We have not looked only at turbulence but at times of political and economic calm. The studies show that, whatever the kind of problem and its context, the processes are muddled and complex. Just as it is mistaken to seek some hills of order or rationality in a landscape of confusion, so it is mistaken to see confusion as a deviation from some more ordered and rational state. Explanations in terms of muddle and complexity will always enter into rounded accounts of the policy processes.

It is true that people (and institutions) are influenced by the expectations that others have of them. Although it is inadequate to say that policy is made rationally or sequentially, the fact that people expect it to be so made facilitates intervention at some points and inhibits it at others. Caucus, for example, found it difficult to pursue its interest in public service reform after cabinet had made a decision on it. Expectations of normality and acceptance of the rules buttress established procedures and make changes to them difficult. The 1974 budget was criticized partly because the government did not seem to be making it along the "proper" lines.

The case-studies show how a number of "extraneous" factors intrude into policy to bring about what might be regarded as deviations from a proper process. The institutions through which policy making takes place are subject to a range of pressures which evoke a range of responses. Institutions may accept and respond to pressures from a changing environment, as educational institutions did slowly and Foreign Affairs did more rapidly. But institutions are not merely the passive recipients of environmental pressure. They may seek to manipulate and mould the environment to make it more comfortable for themselves, as the Department of Primary Industry did.

The resources available to institutions and individuals are uneven and so policy is seen from different perspectives. Knowledge, time, motivation and access to influence are unequal and changing. One person's policy or opportunity is another's weapon. The 1974 budget fight, for example was about economic policy but it was also about the capacity of bodies like DURD to extend their influence; Foreign Affairs used the policies of a new government to give legitimacy to its organizational strivings; and the politically motivated expansion of federal involvement in education was necessary to explain the expansion of the Department of Education. Even the tools of policy analysis — ranging from techniques like PPB to evaluation studies and to planning strategies — can become resources in conflict about policy, if not the determinants of policy. And success in developing policy enhances reputation and power in the bureaucratic-political arena.

Furthermore, linkages between the steps of policy are not always clear or direct. Incrementalism is certainly common: the education case-study shows how a whole field of policy can be explained in this way, and the wheat quotas case-study also shows how a department builds on past experience. Alongside incrementalism, however, is the decoupling of problems and solutions. While a new education aid scheme was likely in 1968 for electoral reasons, the choice of libraries was far from inevitable; it was made because it was administratively convenient. The RCAGA study concerns a conscious (if unsuccessful) attempt to go beyond incremental solutions.

Policies are by no means always designed on sequential lines. The Department of Primary Industry, for example, prompted activity by interest groups to facilitate the solution of its problems; here problem solving might be said to precede its definition. In the 1974 budget the discussions of definition and solutions were inextricably intertwined. In the RCAGA case, actors came in and out of the process of defining the problem to be solved, and the distinguishing of means and ends was part of the problem. The activities of individuals and institutions thus were often linked in a discontinuous, fragmented way. Efforts were typically made to keep options open in the search for the most viable, but the tempo of activity changed markedly from time to time and from case to case.

Problems may be steadily worked upon, as with wheat quotas; or they may be delayed for the advantage of some participants; or they may arise, be ignored and then have to be dealt with swiftly, as with the RCAGA. Policy participants are not then equally well placed to make timely or orderly contributions to the handling of issues that concern them. Individuals and institutions operate with some knowledge of past experience, thought it may only be partial, learning does take place. The Department of Education, acting incrementally, learnt to avoid the problems of past programmes, while Foreign Affairs drew useful lessons from its mixed experiences. Despite their diversity, our case-studies may seem to lead to optimistic conclusions about the Australian policy processes in general, for the capacity of institutions to learn seems high. After all, a 1974 budget was formulated; wheat quotas were introduced and the RCAGA was appointed and reported. The case-studies do show outcomes, brought by hurried and confused, but not insensitive or stupid, activity.

But the definition of problems can be a matter of differing opinions and dispute, and sometimes problems cannot be defined at all. Intentions do not always have their desired effects, though bureaucrats and politicians may not realize this until too late. Policy is part of the relationship between certain individuals and institutions, but it may not be the key part. The removal of a potential problem (as in wheat quotas), the winning of an election (as in education), or the postponement of an issue (as in the RCAGA) are instances where "policy" itself is of secondary importance. Policy making is part, but only part, of the political processes. Institutional maintenance, the motivation of individuals, and the influence of past habits of thought and action all enter into policy making and must be accounted for.

There is another side to everything we have said so far. It would be possible to agree that policy making, as revealed by the case-studies, is indeed muddled and complex and far from rational, while yet arguing that this is a regrettable state of affairs. The authors of the Vernon Report, for example, commented on the general objectives which the Menzies government had prescribed for it, that —

the attainment or near attainment of any one of the seven objectives of economic policy may make the attainment of others more difficult. Thus, the nearer an economy is to full employment, the more difficult it is to achieve stability of costs and prices. . . . In short, all objectives cannot be "maximised" simultaneously. It may be necessary to "give" a little on one, so that another may be more nearly approached. This means that the design of economic policy depends on priorities or weights being attached, at least implicitly, to the objectives. . . . Although the weighting of the objectives is essentially a political matter and one for governments . . . [Vernon Report, vol. 1, p. 46]

This statement was the nearest Vernon came to saying that the objectives were not all susceptible of rational attainment — rational, that is, by economists' standards. The last line enshrines the whole of Westminster: that is, if there is to be any irrationality it must be regarded as "political", an unwanted intrusion from outside which ought to be minimized at the level of cabinet in the interests of coherent policy.

But the second part of our argument is to point out that it is simply not true. It follows from our demonstration, in chapters 3 and 4, that cabinet and the central coordinating agencies have great difficulty in drawing together the threads of policy and in doing much about the muddle and confusion of policy making.

In part the reasons are institutional. Regardless of the ability of the ministers themselves, cabinet often has difficulty in ordering its resources to effective use. The information that reaches it is often partisan and presented with the intention of persuading, not of enlightening, ministers. The structures of cabinet have made communication difficult, and its committees have seldom worked. Ministers must rely heavily on their departments, as they have little time and often less expertise to do otherwise. The difficulty that cabinet has in operating in conditions when its supporting structures temporarily disintegrate was shown in the budget case-study. But even in more routine cases, such as the decision to establish the RCAGA, cabinet was able to become involved only occasionally; that decision was made in the environs of the prime minister's office rather than in cabinet. Cabinet can become isolated at the centre of government. As the education and RCAGA studies show, a skilful prime minister is essential to make cabinet work at all. He sets the agenda of cabinet, and his wishes, personality, and style are central. The prime minister can dominate cabinet; at times he may become involved in the details of a colleague's portfolio. But he cannot do it all. Cabinet may only operate effectively if the prime minister chooses to allow it to do so, but there are still limitations on a prime minister's capacity. To emphasize the centrality of the prime minister, even with an enhanced and powerful PMC, is not to say that we have prime ministerial government.

Cabinet appears never to enunciate priorities in anything but general and rhetorical terms; the detailed allocation of resources following a "rational" set of views or choices does not take place. This is often regretted. Reports like that of the RCAGA, for example, urge that cabinet should provide coherence in policy and should indicate measures to achieve it. But that is to allocate a heroic and cohesive role to cabinet which it can seldom fulfil. Cabinet is a battleground for competing resources, not a judicial body. It is, as one senior Country Party minister put it, "a bullring — everyone has their position and makes sure they aren't knocked off too much". Neither cohesion nor the careful choice between alternatives is the central objective of cabinet. It is a political arena where political standards, not a set of rational concepts, are applied. As a result, while cabinet may be able to maintain a broad drive against inflation, for example, it is unlikely to be able to develop a coherent, or even compatible, set of criteria about inflation to guide its examination of all policy proposals. Cabinet's potential power is immense, but only in a limited number of areas at a time.

Nor can the central agencies — Treasury, Finance, PMC and the PSB — do the job for cabinet. The agencies have continuing strength, but their application of influence is still intermittent. It may be possible to predict that a central agency will usually prevail in situations of conflict; it is not possible to be sure what will happen on any given occasion.

The central agencies have their own interests to fight and their own policy preferences. Their organizational strength is not always dedicated to the pursuit of cabinet's objectives. The Treasury was always concerned to maintain its own monopoly of economic advice to cabinet, and the disputes in the 1974 budget were partly about this. The PSB opposed the RCAGA's initial terms of reference but was only partly successful in getting them changed. On the other hand, it did succeed in thwarting the attempts of Foreign Affairs to shake itself free from the restraints imposed by the central agencies. Established procedures, coupled with the institutional ideologies, define what should be done.

At the same time the perspectives of the central agencies differ and the commodities in which they deal vary. Coordination is achieved from different if connected assumptions; there is no consistent overview of how policy is made. The Treasury is concerned to ensure that public expenditure trends fit its proposals for economic management; the PSB maintains a control over the use of manpower; PMC, at least until recently, tried to ensure consistency of policy but had inadequate resources to do it. Clashes between the agencies are not uncommon; advice from PMC was, for example, primarily responsible for Fraser's decision to split the Treasury. The central agencies may appear to be monolithic from the departmental viewpoint, but there is no reason to expect them to unite to ensure total coherence in public policy. The expectation is bound to be disappointed.

We have shown that one way of tying together these uneven strands is through the explanatory notions of bureaucratic politics. One case-study, on Foreign Affairs, shows how an institution operated to expand its function and influence; the budget study illustrates the Treasury and its rivals in a similar role. Within institutions, the roles of strategic individuals are often important. The prime minister, whether Menzies in the education case or Whitlam in the RCAGA, can be a central actor. But individual ministers, as in the budget study, or senior public servants, as in Foreign Affairs and the budget, can also become involved at crucial moments; their intervention is clearly influential. There is always a problem in distinguishing between personal and institutional roles. It is possible to state that cabinet and such departments as the Treasury are always likely to be influential for — and to be limited by — institutional reasons. The individuals within those key bodies, especially the prime minister, ministers, and permanent heads, will have a large part to play in determining how resources are arranged within those institutional frameworks. Yet the individuals in influential positions change the use of resources only within the restrictions that procedures and institutional forms place on them. To change those procedures is possible, but the consequences are often unpredictable.

Bureaucratic politics is important. To disregard the crucial roles that institutions play in transforming ideas into policy or in manipulating the environment to their own advantage would be as foolish as to disregard the importance of individuals as they jostle for advantage. But bureaucratic politics is only part of the story. No matter how clever or lucky, how tricky or pedestrian, individuals and institutions are bound by their past records, by the expectations others have of them, and by their available resources; and they are constrained by such wider forces in the environment as the federal system, the state governments, and the demands of supporting groups or parties. No one and no institution can act in isolation and with a free hand.

Where does this take us? Three points should be clear. First, the Westminster assumptions about the way that policy processes work have only limited value in describing or explaining them in practice. Assumptions may direct activity by the expectations they create, but they neither determine the structure of influence nor account for the muddled fragmentation that exists. Second, reformers intent on improving the system invariably try to direct attention to the way that the Westminster system ought to work (but does not). They then try to make policy "better" or more rational, or to restructure existing institutions so that they can play their "proper" role more effectively. And, third, since reformers start with incorrect assumptions and understandings of the existing situation, we can expect such reforms to fail.

This has not been a hortatory study. We have not, for instance, asked whether institutions of government are overloaded or if public expectations of public policy are too high. We suggest no comprehensive remedies for restructuring the institutions of government, for improving the system, or for making better policy through changes which are essentially technical or institutional in nature; nor do we offer criteria for deciding what might be better or be an improvement. Proposals on these lines are not necessarily to be decried; they may change some of the structures of power. But their limitations should by now be evident. They have not, in any event, been our concern.

Rather do we suggest that realistic descriptions of the fragmentation and muddle of the policy processes have their uses. At a minimum they correct over-simple notions of rationality and sequence. They may also make us sensitive to policy-related activities which other individuals in the policy processes should take into account. At a more general level, such a description suggests that reform proposals should be based, not on any mythical view of how policy should be made, but on the realities. Bureaucratic failings, departmental ideologies, internal incentive systems, political pressures, and individual ambitions must all be accepted as proper and unavoidable parts of the policy processes, not as obstacles to rational policy. If reforms or changes are to work, they must accept these ideas and be based on the behaviour of the real world, not on the Westminster norms. To help create an appreciation of that reality has been our purpose; so perhaps, to that extent, it has been a hortatory study.

References/Select Bibliography

ADAA. 1975. Reply and attachments of Australian Development Assistance Agency to statutory inquiry questionnaire of RCAGA, February 1975.

Aimer, P. 1974. *Politics, Power and Persuasion: The Liberals in Victoria.* Melbourne: James Bennett.

Aitkin, D. 1972. *The Country Party in New South Wales.* Canberra: ANU Press.

Aitkin, D. 1977. *Stability and Change in Australian Politics.* Canberra: ANU Press.

Albinski, H. S. 1977. *Australian External Policy Under Labor.* St Lucia: University of Queensland Press.

Allison, G. T. 1971. *Essence of Decision: Explaining the Cuban Missile Crisis.* Boston: Little Brown.

Allwood, L. M., ed. 1975. *Australian Schools: The Impact of the Australian Schools Commission.* Drouin, Victoria: Australia International Press and Publications.

Altman, D. 1973. Internal Political Pressures on Australian Policy. In McCarthy, G., ed. *Foreign Policy for Australia: Choices for the Seventies.* Sydney: Angus & Robertson.

Anthony, J. M. 1975. The Politics of the Bureaucracy and the Role of Ministerial Staff. In Wettenhall, R. and Painter, M., eds. *The First Thousand Days of Labor,* vol. 2. Canberra: CCAE.

Art, R. J. 1973. Bureaucratic Politics and American Foreign Policy: A Critique. *Policy Sciences* 4:467-90.

Bailey, F. G. 1970. *Stratagems and Spoils: A Social Anthropology of Politics.* Oxford: Basil Blackwell.

Barnard, C. I. 1938. *The Functions of the Executive.* Thirtieth anniversary edition 1968. Cambridge, Mass: Harvard University Press.

Benveniste, G. 1972. *The Politics of Expertise.* Berkeley, Calif.: Glendessary Press.

Bessant, B. and Spaull, A. D. 1976. *Politics of Schooling.* Melbourne: Pitman.

Birch, I. K. F. 1975. *Constitutional Responsibility for Education in Australia.* Canberra: ANU Press.

Birch, I. K. F. and Smart, D. , eds. 1977. *The Commonwealth Government and Education 1964-1976: Political Initiatives and Developments.* Melbourne: Drummond.

Bland, H. 1975. Public Administration Whither? Garran Oration, Canberra.

Braybrooke, D. and Lindblom, C. E. 1970. *A Strategy of Decision: Policy Evaluation as a Social Process.* New York: Free Press.

Brogden, S. 1968. *Australia's Two-Airline Policy.* Melbourne: Melbourne University Press.

Brown, R. G. and Whyte, H. M. , eds. 1970. *Medical Practice and the Community.* Canberra: ANU Press.

Buchanan, J. M. and Tullock, G. 1962. *The Calculus of Consent.* Ann Arbor: University of Michigan Press.

Burns, T. and Stalker, G. M. 1961. *The Management of Innovation.* London: Tavistock.

Butler, D. 1973. *The Canberra Model: Essays on Australian Government.* Melbourne: Cheshire.

Caiden, G. E. 1967. *The Commonwealth Bureaucracy.* Melbourne: Melbourne University Press.

Cameron, S. H. and Hofferbert, R. I. 1976. The Dynamics of Education Finance in Federal Systems: Cross-time Analyses. *Policy and Politics* 5:129-57.

Campbell, K. O. 1969. Wheat. *Current Affairs Bulletin* 45(1): 2-16

Campbell, K. O. 1971. A Wheat Policy for the Seventies. *Australian Journal of Agricultural Economics* 15(1):51-56.

Cass, M. and Hawker, G. 1978. Information about Government Personnel: Reflections on a Survey Source. *Politics* 13(1):175-81.

Catley, R. and McFarlane, B. 1974. *From Tweedledum to Tweedledee: The New Labor Government in Australia.* Sydney: ANZ Book Co.

Clark, G. 1975. The Australian Department of Foreign Affairs: What's Wrong with Our Diplomats. *Australian Quarterly* 47(2):21-35.

Clarke, R. 1971. *New Trends in Government.* London: HMSO.

Collins, H. 1977. The "Coombs Report": Bureaucracy, Diplomacy and Australian Foreign Policy. *Australian Outlook* 30(3): 387-413.

Connell, R. W. 1977. *Ruling Class, Ruling Culture: Studies of Conflict, Power and Hegemony in Australian Life.* Cambridge: Cambridge University Press.

Connolly, D. M. 1975. Submission No. 536 to RCAGA.

Connors, T. 1972. *The Australian Wheat Industry, Its Economics and Politics.* Armidale, NSW: Gill Publications.

Cooley, A. S. 1974. The Permanent Head. *Public Administration* (Sydney) 33(3):193-205.

Crawford, J. G. 1960. Relations between Civil Servants and Ministers in Policy Making. *Public Administration* (Sydney) 19(2):99-112.

Crisp, L. F. 1955. *The Australian Federal Labor Party 1901-1951.* Melbourne: Longmans.

Crisp, L. F. 1961. The Commonwealth Treasury's Changed Role and Its

Organisational Consequences. *Public Administration* (Sydney) 20(4):315-30.

Crisp, L. F. 1961a. *Ben Chifley: A Biography.* Melbourne: Longmans.

Crisp, L. F. 1967. Central Co-ordination of Commonwealth Policy-Making: Roles and Dilemmas of the Prime Minister's Department. *Public Administration* (Sydney) 26(1):28-54.

Crisp, L. F. 1972. Politics and the Commonwealth Public Service. *Public Administration* (Sydney) 31(4):287-319.

Crisp, L. F. 1973. *Australian National Government.* 3rd ed. Melbourne: Longmans.

Crocker, W. R. 1971. Foreign Policy for Australia. *IPA Review* 25(4):91-96.

Crossman, R. H. S. 1963. Introduction to Bagehot, Walter. *The English Constitution.* London: Fontana.

Crossman, R. H. S. 1972. *Inside View: Three Lectures on Prime Ministerial Government.* London: Jonathan Cape.

Crossman, R. H. S. 1975. *Diaries of a Cabinet Minister.* Vol.1. London: Hamish Hamilton and Jonathan Cape.

Crossman, R. H. S. 1976. *Diaries of a Cabinet Minister.* Vol.2. London: Hamish Hamilton and Jonathan Cape.

Crossman, R. H. S. 1977. *Diaries of a Cabinet Minister.* Vol.3. London: Hamish Hamilton and Jonathan Cape.

Daly, F. 1977. *From Curtin to Kerr.* Melbourne: Sun Books.

Davies, A. F. 1964. *Australian Democracy.* 2nd ed. Melbourne: Longmans.

D'Cruz, J. V. and Sheehan, P. J. , eds. 1975. *The Renewal of Australian Schools: Essays on Educational Planning in Australia after the Karmel Report.* Melbourne: Primary Education.

Deane, R. P. 1963. *The Establishment of the Department of Trade: A Case Study in Administrative Reorganisation.* Canberra: ANU Press.

Dearlove, J. 1973. *The Politics of Policy in Local Government.* Cambridge: Cambridge University Press.

Defence, Department of. 1974. Letter of 24 December 1974 to RCAGA.

Defence, Department of. 1975. Letter of 17 January 1975 to RCAGA.

Defence, Department of. 1975a. Letter of 20 December 1975 to RCAGA.

Diamond, Lord. 1975. *Public Expenditure in Practice.* London: Allen and Unwin.

Dillon, G. M. 1976. Policy and Dramaturgy: A Critique of Current Conceptions of Policy Making. *Policy and Politics* 5:47-62.

Doern, G. B. 1971. The Development of Policy Organizations in the Executive Arena. In Doern, G. B. and Aucoin, P. , eds. *The Structures of Policy-Making in Canada.* Toronto: Macmillan of Canada.

Doern, G. B. and Aucoin, P. , eds. 1971. *The Structures of Policy-Making in Canada.* Toronto: Macmillan of Canada.

Doern, G. B. and Wilson V. S. , eds. 1974. *Issues in Canadian Public Policy.* Toronto: Macmillan of Canada.

Dogan, M. , ed. 1975. *The Mandarins of Western Europe: The Political Role of Top Civil Servants.* New York: Halstead Press.

Downs, A. 1967. *Inside Bureaucracy.* Boston: Little Brown.

Dror, Y. 1968. *Public Making Re-Examined.* San Francisco: Chandler.
Dror, Y. 1969. Muddling Through — "Science" or Inertia? In Etzioni, A. , ed. *Readings on Modern Organizations.* Englewood Cliffs, N. J. : Prentice-Hall.
Dunk, W. E. 1961. The Role of the Public Servant in Policy Formulation. *Public Administration* (Sydney) 20 (2):99-113.
Dunsire, A. 1973. *Administration: The Word and the Science.* London: Martin Robertson.
Dye, T. R. 1976. *Policy Analysis.* University, Ala.: University of Alabama Press.
Economic Policy Task Force. 1975. *The Process of Economic Policy Making in Australia.* Canberra: Australian Government Publishing Service.
Edwards, J. 1975. The Economy Game: Treasury and Its Rivals. *Current Affairs Bulletin* 51(12):4-11.
Edwards, J. 1977. *Life Wasn't Meant to be Easy.* Sydney: Mayhem.
Elkin, S. L. 1974. Political Science and the Analysis of Public Policy. *Public Policy* 22(3):399-422.
Emy, H. V. 1974. *The Politics of Australian Democracy.* Melbourne: Macmillan.
Emy, H. V. 1976. *Public Policy: Problems and Paradoxes.* Melbourne: Macmillan.
Encel, S. 1970. *Equality and Authority: A Study of Class, Status and Power in Australia.* Melbourne: Cheshire.
Encel, S. 1974. *Cabinet Government in Australia.* 2nd ed. Melbourne: Melbourne University Press.
Evans, G. , ed. 1977. *Labor and the Constitution.* Melbourne: Heinemann.
Expenditure Committee. 1977. House of Representatives Standing Committee on Expenditure, Sub-Committee on Australia's Overseas Representation. *Report.*
External Affairs, Department of. 1968. *Annual Report.* Canberra: Government Printer.
Foreign Affairs Association. 1975. Submission No. 703 to RCAGA.
Foreign Affairs Association 1977. Letter of 19 April 1977 to secretary, Department of Foreign Affairs.
Foreign Affairs Association 1978. Submission April 1978 to Senate Standing Committee on Foreign Affairs and Defence Inquiry into Australia's Overseas Representation.
Foreign Affairs, Department of. 1972. Organisation of the Department of Foreign Affairs. *Current Notes on International Affairs* 43(3):93-98.
Foreign Affairs, Department of. 1974. Renouf, A. P. Foreign Affairs and the Challenge of the Seventies. *Australian Foreign Affairs Record* 45(1):24-31.
Foreign Affairs, Department of. 1974a. Submission No. 214 to RCAGA.
Foreign Affairs, Department of. 1974b. Australia's Property Overseas *Australian Foreign Affairs Record* 45(7):426-30.
Foreign Affairs, Department of. 1975. Letter of 31 January 1975 to RCAGA.

Foreign Affairs, Department of. 1975a. Letter of 21 February 1975 to RCAGA.

Foreign Affairs, Department of. 1975b. *Documents on Australian Foreign Policy 1937-1949, 1, 1937-1938.* Canberra: Australian Government Publishing Service.

Foreign Affairs, Department of. 1975c. Letter of 10 November 1975 to RCAGA.

Foreign Affairs, Department of. 1975d. Letter of 21 November 1975 to RCAGA.

Foreign Affairs, Department of. 1975e. Comments on Report of RCAGA Task Force on Economic Policy.

Foreign Affairs, Department of. 1977. Letter of March 1977 to Foreign Affairs Association.

Foreign Affairs, Department of. 1977a. Speech by secretary, Department of Foreign Affairs to Australian Institute of International Affairs, Sydney, 22 August 1977.

Foreign Affairs, Department of. 1978. Submission April 1978 to Senate Standing Committee on Foreign Affairs and Defence Inquiry into Australia's Overseas Representation.

Forward, R. , ed. 1974. *Public Policy in Australia.* Melbourne: Cheshire.

Fraser, M. 1974. A National View. In Aitchison, R. , ed. *Looking at the Liberals.* Melbourne: Cheshire.

Fraser, M. 1977. Responsibility in Government. Garran Oration, Canberra.

Freedman L. 1976. Logic, Politics and Foreign Policy Processes: A Critique of the Bureaucratic Politics Model. *International Affairs* 52:434-49.

Freudenberg, G. 1977. *A Certain Grandeur.* Melbourne: Macmillan.

Goldman, S. 1973. *The Developing System of Public Expenditure Management and Control.* London: HMSO.

Gordon Walker, P. 1970. *The Cabinet.* London: Jonathan Cape.

Graham, B. D. 1966. *The Formation of the Australian Country Parties.* Canberra: ANU Press.

Harman, G. S. and Selby-Smith, C. , eds. 1976. *Readings in the Economics and Politics of Australian Education.* Sydney: Pergamon Press.

Hartle, D. G. 1976. *A Theory of the Expenditure Budgetary Process.* Toronto: University of Toronto Press.

Hasluck, P. M. C. 1976. *A Time for Building: Australian Administration in Papua and New Guinea 1951-1963.* Melbourne: Melbourne University Press.

Hawker, G. 1975. The Bureaucracy Under the Whitlam Government — and Vice Versa. *Politics* 10(1):15-23.

Hawker, G. 1976. Behavioural Scientists: The Role of the Researcher. *Australian Journal of Public Administration* 25(1):1-8.

Hawker, G. 1976a. The Coombs Report and Freedom of Information: Some Questions about Administration. *Rupert* 4:6-8.

Hawker, G. 1976b. The Royal Commission on Australian Government Administration: A Progress Report. *Public Policy Paper No. 2.* Hobart: Department of Political Science, University of Tasmania.

Hawker, G. 1976c. Review of Work. In RCAGA *Appendix 1*, 1-14.

Hawker, G. 1976d. The Royal Commission on Australian Government Administration: Prospects for Reform. RIPA — ACT Group *Newsletter* 3(3):9-14.

Hawker, G. 1977. The Use of Social Scientists in the Inquiries of the Labor Government 1972-75. ANZAAS paper given at University of Melbourne.

Hawker, G. 1977a. Public Service Reforms in Australia. In Hazlehurst, C. and Nethercote, J. R. , eds. *Reforming Australian Government: The Coombs Report and Beyond.* Canberra: ANU Press.

Hawker, G. 1977b. The Implementation of RCAGA: What Happened to the Coombs Report. *Australian Quarterly* 49(1):17-28.

Hawker, G. 1977c. Research Use: Some Recent Australian Experience. *Political Science* (New Zealand) 29(1):57-65.

Hawker, G. 1978. Inside the Coombs Commission. In Smith, R. F. I. and Weller, P. , eds. *Public Service Inquiries in Australia.* St Lucia: University of Queensland Press.

Hawker, G. 1978a. Lawyers in Government. In Tomasic, R. , ed. *Perspectives on the Legal Profession in Australia.* Sydney: Law Foundation of NSW.

Hawker, G. and Carey, B. 1975. Machinery of Government: What to Do? In Wettenhall, R. L. and Painter, M. , eds. *The First Thousand Days of Labor* 2. Canberra: CCAE.

Hawker, G. and Weller, P. 1974. Pre-Election Consultations: A Proposal and Its Problems. *Australian Quarterly* 46(2):100-104.

Hayward, J. and Watson, M. , eds. 1975. *Planning, Politics and Public Policy: The British, French and Italian Experience.* Cambridge: Cambridge University Press.

Hazlehurst, C. and Nethercote, J. R. , eds. 1977. *Reforming Australian Government: The Coombs Report and Beyond.* Canberra: ANU Press.

Headey, B. 1974. *British Cabinet Ministers.* London: Allen and Unwin.

Heclo, H. 1972. Review Article: Policy Analysis. *British Journal of Political Science* 2(1):83-108.

Heclo, H. 1974. *Modern Social Politics in Britain and Sweden.* New Haven, Conn.: Yale University Press.

Heclo, H. 1977. *A Government of Strangers: Executive Politics in Washington.* Washington, D. C. : Brookings Insitution.

Heclo, H. and Wildavsky, A. 1974. *The Private Government of Public Money.* London: Macmillan.

Heidenheimer, A. J. , Heclo, H. and Adams, C. T. 1976. *Comparative Public Policy: The Politics of Social Choice in Europe and America.* London: Macmillan.

Hellier, W. L. 1972. Australian Wheat Delivery Quotas. *The Wheat Situation* 35:38-44. Canberra: Bureau of Agricultural Economics.

Hirschman, A. O. 1970. *Exit, Voice and Loyalty.* Cambridge, Mass.: Harvard University Press.

Hockin, T. A. 1971. *Apex of Power: The Prime Minister and Political Leadership in Canada.* Scarborough, Ont.: Prentice-Hall of Canada.

Hodgetts, J. E. 1974. *The Canadian Public Service: A Physiology of Government 1867-1970*. Toronto: University of Toronto Press.

Jackson, R. J. and Atkinson, M. M. 1974. *The Canadian Legislative System*. Toronto: Macmillan of Canada.

Jecks, D. A., ed. 1974 *Influences in Australian Education*. Perth: Carroll's.

Johnson, A. W. 1971. The Treasury Board of Canada and the Machinery of Government of the 1970s. *Canadian Journal of Political Science* 4(3):346-66.

Johnson, A. W. 1971a. Management Theory and Cabinet Government. *Canadian Public Administration* 14(1):73-81.

Jones, G. W. 1975. Development of the Cabinet. In Thornhill, W., ed. *The Modernization of British Government*. London: Pitman.

Kelly, P. 1976. *The Unmaking of Gough*. Sydney: Angus & Robertson.

King, A. 1973. Ideas, Institutions and the Policies of Government. *British Journal of Political Science* 3(3):291-314 and 3(4):409-24.

Knight, K. W. and Wiltshire, K. W. 1977. *Formulating Government Budgets: Aspects of Australian and North American Experience*. St Lucia: University of Queensland Press.

Kristianson, G. L. 1966. *The Politics of Patriotism: The Pressure Group Activities of the Returned Servicemen's League*. Canberra: ANU Press.

Lasswell, H. D. 1963. The Decision Process: Seven Categories of Functional Analysis. In Polsby, N. W., Deutler, R. A. and Smith, P. A., eds. *Politics and Social Life*. Boston: Houghton Mifflin.

Lasswell, H. D. 1968. Policy Sciences. In *International Encyclopaedia of the Social Sciences* 12; pp. 181-89. New York: Macmillan and Free Press.

Lasswell, H. D. 1975. Research in Policy Analysis: The Intelligence and Appraisal Functions. In Greenstein, F. I. and Polsby, N. W., eds. *Handbook of Political Science* 6. Reading, Mass.: Addison-Wesley.

Lindblom, C. E. 1965. *The Intelligence of Democracy: Decision Making Through Mutual Adjustment*. New York: Free Press.

Lindblom, C. E. 1968. *The Policy-Making Process*. Englewood Cliffs, N. J.: Prentice-Hall.

Lloyd, C. J. and Clark, A. 1976. *Kerr's King Hit!* Melbourne: Cassell.

Lloyd, C. J. and Reid, G. S. 1974. *Out of the Wilderness: The Return of Labor*. Melbourne: Cassell.

Loveday, P. 1970. Pressure Groups. In Venturini, V. G., ed. *Australia: A Survey*. Wiesbaden: Otto Harrasowitz.

Mackintosh, J. P. 1968. *The British Cabinet*. London: Methuen.

March, J. G. and Olsen, J. P. 1976. *Ambiguity and Choice in Organizations*. Bergen: Universitat.

Matheson, W. A. 1976. *The Prime Minister and the Cabinet*. Toronto: Methuen.

Mathews, R. L., ed. 1974. *Intergovernmental Relations in Australia*. Sydney: Angus & Robertson.

Mathews, R. L. ed. 1976. *Making Federalism Work*. Canberra: Centre for Research on Federal Financial Relations.

Matthews, T. V. 1976. IDC Case Studies in RCAGA, *Appendix 4*, 293-308.

Matthews, T. V.   1976a. Interest Group Access to the Australian Government Bureaucracy. RCAGA, *Appendix 2.* 332-65.

Matthews, T. V. 1976b. Australian Pressure Groups. In Mayer, H. and Nelson, H. , eds. *Australian Politics: A Fourth Reader.* Melbourne: Cheshire.

Mayer, H. and Nelson, H. , eds. 1976. *Australian Politics: A Fourth Reader.* Melbourne: Cheshire.

Mediansky, F. A. 1974. "New Challenges in Foreign Policy Administration": A Comment. *Australian Outlook* 28(3):313-17.

Mediansky, F. A. and Nockels, J. A. 1975. The Prime Minister's Bureaucracy. *Public Administration* (Sydney) 34(3):202-18.

Meltsner, A. 1976. *Policy Analysts in the Bureaucracy.* Berkeley: University of California Press.

Menzies, R. G. 1967. *Afternoon Light, Some Memories of Men and Events.* Melbourne: Cassell.

Menzies, R. G. 1970. *The Measure of the Years.* Melbourne: Cassell.

Meyerson, M. and Banfield, E. C. 1955. *Politics, Planning and the Public Interest.* New York: Free Press.

Miliband, R. 1973. *The State in Capitalist Society: The Analysis of the Western System of Power.* London: Quartet Books.

Millar, T. B. 1968. *Australia's Foreign Policy.* Sydney: Angus & Robertson.

Millar, T. B. 1972. *Foreign Policy: Some Australian Reflections.* Melbourne: Melbourne University Press.

Miller, J. D. B. and Jinks, B. 1971. *Australian Government and Politics.* 4th ed. London: Duckworth.

Nieuwenhuysen, J. P. and Daly, A. E. 1977. *The Australian Prices Justification Tribunal.* Melbourne: Melbourne University Press.

Nieuwenhuysen, J. P. and Norman, N. R. 1976. *Australian Competition and Prices Policy.* London: Croom Helm.

Niskanen, W. A. 1971. *Bureaucracy and Representative Government.* Chicago: Aldine.

Oakes, L. 1973. *Whitlam, P. M.* Sydney: Angus & Robertson.

Oakes, L. 1976. *Crash Through or Crash: The Unmaking of a Prime Minister.* Melbourne: Drummond.

Oakes, L. and Solomon, D. 1973. *The Making of An Australian Prime Minister.* Melbourne: Cheshire.

Oakes, L. and Solomon, D. 1974. *Grab for Power: Election '74.* Melbourne: Cheshire.

Olsen, M. 1965. *The Logic of Collective Action.* Cambridge, Mass.: Harvard University Press.

Overseas Trade, Department of. 1975. Submission No. 467 to RCAGA.

Parker, R. S. 1960. Policy and Administration. *Public Administration* (Sydney) 19(2):113-20.

Parker, R. S. 1976. The Coombs Inquiry and the Prospects for Action. *Australian Journal of Public Administration* 35(4):311-19.

Parker, R. S. 1978. The Inquiries and Responsible Government. In Smith, R. F. I. and Weller, P. , eds. *Public Service Inquiries in Australia.* St Lucia: University of Queensland Press.

Playford, J. and Kirsner, D. , eds. 1972. *Australian Capitalism: Towards a Socialist Critique.* Melbourne: Penguin.

Plowden, W. 1973. The Role and Limits of a Central Planning Staff in Government: A Note on the Central Policy Review Staff. Paper presented to the Conference on the Study of Public Policy, September 1973.

Pollitt, C. 1974. The Central Policy Review Staff, 1970-1974. *Public Administration* 52(4):375-92.

Pollitt, C. 1977. The Public Fxpenditure Survey. *Public Administration* 55(2):127-42.

Postal Commission. 1975. Letter of December 1975 to RCAGA.

Pressman, J. L. and Wildavsky, A. 1973. *Implementation.* Berkeley: University of California Press.

Public Service Board. 1971. *Annual Report.* Canberra: Australian Government Publishing Service.

Public Service Board. 1973. *Annual Report.* Canberra: Australian Government Publishing Service.

Public Service Board. 1974. *Annual Report.* Canberra: Australian Government Publishing Service.

Public Service Board. 1974a. First Public Service Board Submission to RCAGA, October 1974.

Public Service Board. 1975. *Annual Report.* Canberra: Australian Government Publishing Service.

Public Service Board. 1975a. Memorandum No. 6 to RCAGA.

Public Service Board. 1977. *Annual Report.* Canberra: Australian Government Publishing Service.

RCAGA. 1975. Transcripts of hearings, 18 February 1975.

RCAGA. 1976. *Report of the Royal Commission on Australian Government Administration* (including four appendix volumes). Canberra: Australian Government Publishing Service. (Numbers after the citation refer to appendix volumes.)

Reid, A. 1969. *The Power Struggle.* Sydney: Tartan.

Reid, G. S. 1966. Parliament and the Executive: The Suppression of Politics. In Mayer, H. , ed. *Australian Politics: A Reader.* Melbourne: Cheshire.

Renouf, A. P. 1974. New Challenges in Foreign Policy Administration. *Australian Outlook* 28(2):109-17.

RIPA. 1955. Commonwealth Policy Coordination. *Public Administration* (Sydney) 14(4):193-213.

RIPA. 1977. Appointments of Permanent Heads: RCAGA and The New Bill. RIPA-ACT *Newsletter 3(4):13-14.*

RIPA. 1977a. Dent, H. R. Comment on "Appointment of Departmental Heads". RIPA-ACT Group *Newsletter 4(1):6-9.*

Rittel, H. W. J. and Webber, M. W. 1973. Dilemmas in a General Theory of Planning. *Policy Sciences* 4:155-69.

Robertson, G. 1971. The Changing Role of the Privy Council Office. *Canadian Public Administration* 14(4):487-508.

Rolfe, H. 1970. The Australian Wheatgrowers' Federation: Quest for Consensus. *Farm Policy* 10(1):29-36.

Rose, R. 1969. The Variability of Party Government: A Theoretical and Empirical Critique. *Political Studies* 17(4):413-45.

Rose, R. ed. 1969. *Policy Making in Britain.* London: Macmillan.

Rose, R. 1973. Comparing Public Policy: An Overview. *European Journal of Political Research* 1(1):67-93.

Rose, R. 1974. *The Problem of Party Government.* London: Macmillan.

Rose, R. 1976. Models of Change. In Rose, R. , ed. *The Dynamics of Public Policy: A Comparative Analysis.* London: Sage Publications.

Rosenthal, B. 1975. *Wheat Quotas in Australia.* Brisbane: Department of Primary Industries.

Sax, S. 1972. *Medical Care in the Melting Pot: An Australian Review.* Sydney: Angus & Robertson.

Schaffer, B. 1976. Spatial Factors and Institutional Performance. Paper delivered to 10th IPSA Conference in Edinburgh 1976.

Schaffer, B. 1977. On the Politics of Policy. *Australian Journal of Politics and History* 23(1):146-55.

Schaffer, B. and Hawker, G. 1978. The Rise and Fall of the Royal Commission on Australian Government Administration. In Smith, R. F. I. and Weller, P. , eds. *Public Service Inquiries in Australia.* St Lucia: University of Queensland Press.

Schultze, C. 1968. *The Politics and Economics of Public Spending.* Washington, D. C. : Brookings Institution.

Scotton, R. B. 1974. *Medical Care in Australia: An Economic Diagnosis.* Melbourne: Sun Books.

Self, P. 1972. *Administrative Theories and Politics.* London: Allen and Unwin.

Self, P. 1975. *Econocrats and the Policy Process: The Politics and Philosophy of Cost-Benefit Analysis.* London: Macmillan.

Self, P. 1978. The Coombs Commission: An Overview. In Smith, R. F. I. and Weller, P. , eds. *Public Service Inquiries in Australia.* St Lucia: University of Queensland Press.

Shann, K. C. O. 1978. Scrutiny of the Administration. Address to RIPA (ACT Group) Autumn Seminar, Bateman's Bay, 29 April 1978.

Sharman, C. 1977. *The Premiers' Conference: An Essay in Federal State Interaction.* Canberra: Department of Political Science, RSSS, ANU.

Simeon, R. 1972. *Federal-Provincial Diplomacy: The Making of Recent Policy in Canada.* Toronto: University of Toronto Press.

Simeon, R. 1976. Studying Public Policy. *Canadian Journal of Political Science* 9(4):548-80.

Simon, H. A. 1976. *Administrative Behaviour.* 3rd ed. New York: Free Press.

Smart, D. 1974. Origins of the Secondary Schools Libaries Scheme. In Jecks, D. A. , ed. *Influences in Australian Education.* Perth: Carroll's.

Smart, D. 1975. Federal Aid to Australian Schools: Origins and Aspects of the Implementation of the Commonwealth Science Laboratories and Libraries Schemes. Unpublished Ph.D. thesis, ANU, Canberra.

Smart D. 1978. *Federal Aid to Australian Schools*. St Lucia: University of Queensland Press.

Smiley, D. V. 1976. *Canada in Question: Federalism in the Seventies*. 2nd ed. Toronto: McGraw-Hill Ryerson.

Smith, B. 1976. *Policy Making in British Government: An Exercise of Power and Rationality*. London: Martin Robertson.

Smith, R. F. I. 1974. Victorian Labor Since Intervention. *Labor History* 27:41-60.

Smith, R. F. I. 1974a. Farmers and the Australian Wheat Board — Emergence of a Farmer Majority. *Farm Policy* 14(2):49-54 (part 1) and 14(3):87-93 (part 2).

Smith, R. F. I. 1976. Intergovernmental Aspects of Wheat Stabilisation: The Evolution of the 1948 Scheme. In Burns, R. M. et al. *Political and Administrative Federalism*. Canberra: Centre for Research on Federal Financial Relations.

Smith, R. F. I. 1976a. Australian Cabinet Structure and Procedures, *RCAGA, Appendix* 4, 190-211.

Smith, R. F. I. 1977. Ministerial Advisers: The Experience of the Whitlam Government. *Australian Journal of Public Administration* 36(2):133-58.

Smith, R. F. I. 1977a. Australian Cabinet Structure and Procedures: The Labor Government 1972-1975. *Politics* 12(1):23-37.

Smith, R. F. I. 1977b. Public Policy and Political Choice: A Review Article. *Australian Journal of Public Administration* 36(3):258-73.

Smith, R. F. I. and Weller, P. 1975. The Bureaucracy: Royal Commission — a Chance for Change? *Contemporary Australian Management* 1:22-26.

Smith, R. F. I. and Weller, P. 1976. *Public Servants, Interest Groups and Policy Making*. Canberra: Department of Political Science, RSSS, ANU.

Smith, R. F. I. and Weller, P. 1977. Learning to Govern: The Australian Labor Party and the Institutions of Government. *Journal of Commonwealth and Comparative Studies* 15(1):39-54.

Smith, R. F. I. and Weller, P., eds. 1978. *Public Service Inquiries in Australia*. St Lucia: University of Queensland Press.

Social Welfare Commission. 1976. *An Idea Before Its Time*. Canberra (mimeo).

Solomon, D. 1977. Australian Foreign Policy Under the Whitlam Government. Unpublished seminar paper, December 1977 quoted with permission. Department of International Relations, RSPacS ANU, Canberra.

Solomon, D. 1978. *Inside the Australian Parliament*. Sydney: Allen and Unwin.

Spann, R. N. 1973. *Public Administration in Australia*. Revised ed. Sydney: NSW Government Printer.

Treasury. 1974. Submission No. 385 to RCAGA.

Troy, P. N. 1978. *A Fair Price: The Land Commission Program 1972-1977*. Sydney: Hale and Iremonger.

Tullock, G. 1965. *The Politics of Bureaucracy.* Washington, D. C. : Public Affairs Press.

Vernon Report. 1965. *Report of the Committee of Economic Enquiry,* 2 vols. Canberra: Government Printer.

Vickers, G. 1965. *The Art of Judgment: A Study of Policy Making.* London: Chapman and Hall.

Visbord, E. M. W. 1976. Economic Policy Formulation in the US and Australia. RIPA — ACT Group *Newsletter* 3(2):4-13.

Viviani, N. and Wilenski, P. 1977. The Australian Development Assistance Agency: A Post-Mortem Report. Draft paper for Development Studies Centre, ANU, Canberra seminar, May 1977, quoted with permission.

Walker, J. 1975. Labor in Government: Terrigal 1975. *Politics* 10(2):178-87.

Watt, A. 1968. The Australian Diplomatic Service 1935-65. In Greenwood, G. and Harper, N. , eds. *Australia in World Affairs 1961-1965.* Melbourne: Cheshire.

Watt, A. 1972. *Australian Diplomat.* Sydney: Angus & Robertson.

Weller, P. 1974. Caucus Control of Cabinet: Myth or Reality? *Public Administration* (Sydney) 33(4):300-306.

Weller, P. , ed. 1975. *Caucus Minutes: The Minutes of the Meetings of the Federal Parliamentary Labor Party 1901-1949* 1. Melbourne: Melbourne University Press.

Weller, P. 1976. The Power and Influence of Party Meetings. In Mayer, H. and Nelson, H. , eds. *Australian Politics: A Fourth Reader.* Melbourne: Cheshire.

Weller, P. 1977. Splitting the Treasury: Old Habits in New Structures? *Australian Quarterly* 49(1):29-39.

Weller, P. 1977a. Public Servants and the Briefing of Party Committees. *Australian Journal of Public Administration* 36(2):186-96.

Weller, P. 1977b. The Treasury and the Politics of Advice. *Public Policy Paper No. 9.* Hobart: Department of Political Science, University of Tasmania.

Weller, P. 1978. Forward Estimates and the Allocation of Resources. In Smith R. F. I. and Weller, P. , eds. *Public Service Inquiries in Australia.* St Lucia: University of Queensland Press.

Weller, P. and Cutt, J. 1976. *Treasury Control in Australia: A Study in Bureaucratic Politics.* Sydney: Ian Novak.

Weller, P. and Smith, R. F. I. 1975. The Impossibility of Party Government. In Scott, R. and Richardson, J. , eds. *The First Thousand Days of Labor* 1. Canberra: CCAE.

Weller, P. and Smith, R. F. I. 1976. The Bureaucracy: Plus ça change . . . *Politics* 11(1):53-57.

Weller, P. and Smith, R. F. I. 1976a. Setting National Priorities: The Role of the Australian Government in Public Policy. In Mathews, R. , ed. *Making Federalism Work: Towards a More Efficient, Equitable and Responsive Federal System.* Canberra: Centre for Research on Federal Financial Relations.

Weller, P. and Smith, R. F. I. 1977. Inside the Inquiry: Problems of Organising a Public Service Review. In Hazlehurst, C. and Nethercote, J. R. , eds. *Reforming Australian Government: The Coombs Report and Beyond.* Canberra: ANU Press.

Wettenhall, R. L. 1975. *Bushfire Disaster: An Australian Community in Crisis.* Sydney: Angus & Robertson.

Wheeler, F. H. 1967. Some Observations on the Commonwealth Public Service Board as a Coordinating Agency. *Public Administration* (Sydney) 26(1):7-20.

Whitlam, E. G. 1973. Speech in House of Representatives, 24 May 1973. *CPD,* H of R, 84, 2644.

Wildavsky, A. 1973. If Planning Is Everything, Maybe It's Nothing. *Policy Sciences* 4, 127-53.

Wildavsky, A. 1975. On Incrementalism or, Yes, Virginia, There Is No Magic Size for an Increment. Working paper No.36, Graduate School of Public Policy. Berkeley: University of California.

Wilensky, H. L. 1967. *Organizational Intelligence: Knowledge and Policy in Government and Industry.* New York: Basic Books.

Wilson, H. 1976. *The Governance of Britain.* London. Weidenfeld and Nicolson.

Wilson, J. Q. 1973. *Political Organizations.* New York: Basic Books

Wilson, R. 1976. L. F. Giblin: A Man for All Seasons. *Search* 7(6):307-15.

Wiltshire K. 1976. Staff Ceilings. Consultant's Report to RCAGA, *Appendix* 1, 113-145.

Wright, M. 1977. Public Expenditure in Britain: The Crisis of Control. *Public Administration* 55(2):143-72.

Index

reorganizations of, 120; reunited by McMahon, 115; role of, 104, 112, 117, 122–24; second "secretary to cabinet", 121; split of, 47, 66, 113, 118; tensions within, 113, 119, 124. *See also* coordinating agencies
prime ministerial government, 52–53, 99–101, 123, 282–83
Prime Minister's Office, (Canada), 55, 110, 115
Priorities Review Staff, 82, 96, 116, 117, 119, 120, 123, 238–40, 243, 249–50
Privy Council Office (Canada), 56, 110
problem definition, 232, 236, 249–50
problem identification, 186–87
procedural problems, impact on individuals, 200–201
process studies, 8, 10
Productivity, Department of, 99
Public Accounts Committee, 236
public policy: adversarial process, 44; ambiguity of, 6, 16–18, 196–97; ambiguous theories of, 9; and garbage can model, 280; and incrementalism, 160, 178, 280; as continuous process, 251; as hortatory studies, 285; as learning process, 20; as puzzling, 20; as a rational process, 22, 277, 278; as sequential process, 277, 280; as struggle for influence, 41–42; changes of, 160; coalitions in, 13, 16; complexity and muddle of, 21, 22, 28, 278, 284, 285; conflict over, 241; context of, 10; coordination, 46; definition of problems, 281; development of, 54, 160; distribution of influence, 6; expectations of, 279; failures of, 5; formation of, 9; general theories of, 10, 18; influence of actors, 23; influences on, 23; integration of, 106; lessons from 285; levels of, 23; limitations of, 10; maintenance of, 9, 21, 47, 201–2; meaning of, 7, 21–23, 279; need for realism, 285; outcomes of, 279; overview of, 284; pluralist pro-

cesses of, 22, 23; politics and administration dichotomy, 28, 185; processes of, 21; restrictions on, 161; role of ideas in, 10–12, 16; role of individuals, 10, 13, 22; role of institutions, 10, 15, 16; study of, 1, 6; use of institutions, 10, 15, 16; study of, 1, 6; use of analytical techniques, 10, 17, 47, 280; use of options, 280; uses of, 278, 281
Public servants. *See* bureaucrats
public service: and elections, 166; centre-periphery, 45; cohesion of, 44; of mandarinate, 152; growth of, 44, 106; role of second division, 44
Public Service Act, 141, 150, 156, 234, 240
Public Service Board, 103, 219; abolition of staff ceilings, 149; access to cabinet submissions, 93; and change, 151–53, 155; and forward staffing estimates, 151, 154, 157; and machinery of government, 153; and RCAGA, 244, 248, 282; and RCAGA members, 246; appointment of permanent heads, 154; as coordinating agency, 104, 140, 155; assistance to RCAGA, 239–40; attacks on, 145, 147; attitude to RCAGA, 235–38; attitude to coordination, 153; changes to, 105, 154; claim to independence, 150; classification of staff, 107, 154; comparison with Treasury, 141; conflict among central agencies, 156; control of numbers, 141–44, 148, 151, 153, 284; criticized by Labor government, 146; dangers of staff ceilings, 105; defender of public service, 155; development of second division, 152; expansion of influence, 105, 141, 143; formal powers, 141; functions of, 140, 151; interpreting government decisions, 143; involvement in policy, 140; powers of, 105, 107, 234, 283; problems of new agencies, 146; RCAGA's terms of reference, 240–41; recruitment, 142;